Advance praise for
Wisdom, Knowledge, and Faith

"This is a timely collection of thoughtful essays by Episcopal theologians that should spark a robust and creative conversation on theological formation in The Episcopal Church. The essays in this volume are not detached academic exercises; rather, they are grounded in pastoral realities and in the moral and social challenges faced by local communities and their people. The rich diversity of personal narratives and theological themes explored in this volume is striking. What results is a theological vision that is as diverse as the number of contributors yet deeply rooted in Anglican spirituality. This collection itself reflects the characteristic nature of Anglican theological tradition lived out by these theologians in the contemporary time. This is a must read for bishops, church leaders and really anyone who is concerned with theological formation in The Episcopal Church."

—The Rt. Rev. Allen K. Shin,
Bishop Suffragan of the Episcopal Diocese of New York
and Chair of the House of Bishops Committee on Theology

"In gathering this gem of an essay collection, Rob MacSwain and Kelli Joyce offer a wonderful gift to The Episcopal Church. *Wisdom, Knowledge, and Faith* weaves together many strands of profound theological reflection from scholar-practitioners who separately and collectively herald a promising new chapter in the development of an Episcopal theological identity. Where this volume's contributions begin to lay such a foundation, more should surely follow! Take and read."

—The Rev. Dr. Kirsten Guidero,
Ecumenical and Interreligious Officer of The Episcopal Church

"I've frequently lamented the state of theology in The Episcopal Church, but this volume was a balm to my soul and an occasion to lift up my head in hopeful gratitude. The winsome, personal essays gathered here showcase the broad diversity and creative fidelity of Episcopal theologians and their approaches to the task. Each of these theologians—from well-established senior scholars to graduate students still cutting their teeth—writes with a sense that theology is a discipline that personally and existentially implicates its practitioners in God's gift of Godself in Jesus Christ and the Holy Spirit. May their tribe increase."

—Dr. Eugene R. Schlesinger,
Santa Clara University and author of
Ruptured Bodies: A Theology of the Church Divided

"As Anglicanism rapidly reorganizes—both ecclesiastically and theologically—the authors present catalytic essays that helpfully frame theological reflection as a practice of wisdom, knowledge, and faith. These themes are negotiated through critical and creative reflections on tradition, community, social location, liturgy, identity, and vocation. This compendium gathers many of the leading lights of theology within The Episcopal Church. I cannot imagine a more important contribution for leaders and emerging leaders in the Episcopal Church to read, mark, and learn from as we make our way."

—The Rev. Dr. William J. Danaher Jr., Rector,
Christ Church Cranbrook, Michigan

"Drawing together seasoned voices as well as exciting younger scholars, this book offers both hope and challenge to Episcopalians—hope in the quality, faithfulness, and distinctiveness of contemporary theology done by Episcopalians, and challenge to The Episcopal Church's neglect of this fundamental discourse of the faith. It is essential reading for understanding theology today in The Episcopal Church."

—The Rev. Dr. Ross Kane,
Associate Professor of Theology, Ethics,
and Culture at Virginia Theological Seminary
and host of the *Love Your Neighbor* podcast

WISDOM, KNOWLEDGE, AND FAITH

New Essays on the Future of Theology
and The Episcopal Church

Edited by
ROBERT MacSWAIN and
KELLI JOYCE

Foreword by Sean Rowe,
28th Presiding Bishop of The Episcopal Church

Seabury Books
NEW YORK

Copyright © 2026 Robert MacSwain and Kelli Joyce

All rights reserved. No part of this book may be reproduced, stored in a retrieval system, or transmitted in any form or by any means, electronic or mechanical, including photocopying, recording, or otherwise, without the written permission of the publisher.

Unless otherwise noted, scripture quotations are from The Revised Standard Version Bible (RSV) and The New Revised Standard Version Bible, which are copyright © 1989 National Council of the Churches of Christ in the United States of America. Used by permission. All rights reserved worldwide.

Scripture quotations taken from the Holy Bible, New Living Translation are copyright © 1996, 2004, 2015 by Tyndale House Foundation. Used by permission of Tyndale House Publishers, Inc. All rights reserved.

Cover image: Johannes Vermeer, *Christ in the House of Martha and Mary* (circa 1655), National Gallery of Scotland, Edinburgh.

Seabury Books
19 East 34th Street
New York, NY 10016
www.churchpublishing.org

Seabury Books is an imprint of Church Publishing Incorporated

Cover design by David Baldeosingh Rotstein
Typeset by Nord Compo

ISBN 978-1-64065-825-7 (paperback)
ISBN 978-1-64065-826-4 (hardback)
ISBN 978-1-64065-827-1 (eBook)

Library of Congress Control Number: 2025915396

This volume is dedicated in memory
of Mark Allen McIntosh (1960–2021)

O God, by your Holy Spirit you give to some the word of wisdom,
to others the word of knowledge, and to others the word of faith:
We praise your name for the gifts of grace
manifested in your servant Mark,
and we pray that your Church may never be destitute of such gifts;
through Jesus Christ our Lord, who with you and the Holy Spirit
lives and reigns, one God, for ever and ever. *Amen.*

A Collect of a Theologian and Teacher
The Book of Common Prayer (1979): 248–49

Table of Contents

Contributors ix

Foreword xv
Sean Rowe

Introduction xvii
Robert MacSwain

The Anglican Way in My Work 1
  Kathryn Tanner

**Accounting for the Movement:
  The Vocation of the Theologian** 17
  Anthony D. Baker

Reflections on God's Presence 35
  Thomas Holtzen

My Theological Formation 53
  Katherine Sonderegger

Theology, Damage, Affordance 69
  Maxine King

**"He Must Increase, and I Must Decrease":
  Jesus Christ as the Center of Proclamation** 83
  Kara N. Slade

**The Promise and Perils of Theological Imagination
  in The Episcopal Church** 99
  Scott MacDougall

**Douglas Adams, Chuck D, and the Making
  of a Theologian** 117
  Jason A. Fout

An Anglican Theology of Hope for a Common Future 133
  Joy Ann McDougall

Toward An Embodied and Transformative Theology 153
  Olufemi Gonsalves

**Theologizing and Organizing Together:
Constructing Liberative Anglican Ecclesiologies** 171
Francisco J. García Jr.

**The Water of Life: Baptismal Faith,
Theological Plumbing, and Encounter
with the Living God** 187
Kelli Joyce

Becoming (Still) a Theologian 205
James W. Farwell

The Future of the *Via Media* in The Episcopal Church 223
Sameer Yadav

Afterword 241
Matthew Ichihashi Potts

Index 247

Contributors

Anthony D. Baker is the Clinton S. Quin Professor of Systematic Theology at the Seminary of the Southwest. He holds graduate degrees from Olivet Nazarene University (M.A.) and the University of Virginia (Ph.D.). His publications include *Diagonal Advance: Perfection in Christian Theology* (SCM, 2011), *Shakespeare, Theology, and the Unstaged God* (Routledge, 2020), and *Leaving Emmaus: A New Departure in Christian Theology* (Baylor, 2021).

James W. Farwell is the H. Boone Porter Professor of Liturgics at the General Theological Seminary, and Professor of Theology and Liturgy at Virginia Theological Seminary. He holds graduate degrees from the General Theological Seminary (M.Div.) and Emory University (Ph.D.). An Episcopal priest canonically resident in the Diocese of Atlanta, his publications include *This Is the Night: Suffering, Salvation, and the Liturgies of Holy Week* (T&T Clark, 2005), *The Liturgy Explained* (Morehouse, 2013), *Ritual Excellence* (Seabury, 2023), and *The T&T Clark Handbook of Sacraments and Sacramentality* (co-edited with Martha Moore-Keish, Bloomsbury, 2023).

Jason A. Fout is Chief of Staff, Chief Operating Officer, and Associate Professor of Theology and Mission at Bexley Seabury. He holds graduate degrees from Seabury-Western Theological Seminary (M.Div., M.T.S.) and the University of Cambridge (Ph.D.). An Episcopal priest canonically resident in the Diocese of Southern Ohio, his publications include *Fully Alive: The Glory of God and the Human Creature in Karl Barth, Hans Urs von Balthasar, and Theological*

Exegesis of Scripture (T&T Clark, 2015), and *Learning from London: Church Growth in Unlikely Places* (Forward Movement, 2019).

Francisco J. García Jr. is an Episcopal priest, organizer, and theological educator. He holds graduate degrees from UCLA (M.A.), Claremont School of Theology (M.Div.), and Vanderbilt University (Ph.D.). He's a cofounder and cochair of Sacred Resistance, an immigrant rights, solidarity, and accompaniment ministry in the Episcopal Diocese of Los Angeles. His work centers around collaborative community, labor, congregational, and interfaith organizing that integrates racial, economic, and environmental/eco-justice efforts, and his research focuses on social movement-oriented ecclesiologies outside of formal church structures through an exploration of faith practices among Latine-immigrant workers organizing in their workplaces and communities.

Olufemi Gonsalves is a vocalist, pianist, and songwriter who teaches music and creative writing. A 2025–26 Madeleva Fellow at the Center for the Study of Spirituality at Saint Mary's College, Notre Dame, Indiana, she holds graduate degrees from Fuller Theological Seminary (M.A., M.Div.) where she is also a current Ph.D. student. Her research focuses on the intersection of theology, mental health, and the arts, and her calling as a public theologian is to engage in dialog and policymaking concerning perceptions and beliefs on trauma and mental illness.

Thomas Holtzen is Professor of Historical and Systematic Theology at Nashotah House. He holds graduate degrees from Gordon-Conwell Theological Seminary (M.A.) and Marquette University (Ph.D.). An Episcopal priest canonically resident in the Diocese of Wisconsin, his publications include *Newman and Justification:*

Newman's Via Media *"Doctrine of the Justifying Presence"* (Oxford, 2024).

Kelli Joyce holds graduate degrees from Yale Divinity School (M.Div.) and the University of Durham (M.A.) and is a candidate for the Ph.D. in theological studies at Vanderbilt University. Her research focuses on the development, reception, and rhetorical uses of the baptismal theology of the 1979 Book of Common Prayer. In addition to her current research and ministry in the Diocese of Tennessee, she has also served as a parish priest in the Diocese of Arizona, as a member of General Convention's Task Force on Communion Across Difference, and as an instructor for Bexley Seabury Seminary and the Seminary of the Southwest.

Maxine King holds a graduate degree from Virginia Theological Seminary (M.Div.) and is a current Ph.D. student at Princeton Theological Seminary. Her publications include "Toward a Theology of Trans Opacity: Trans Studies' Critique of Queer Theory in Conversation with Karl Barth's Doctrine of Revelation," *Anglican Theological Review* 106 (2024): 430–43, the winner of the journal's Charles Hefling Essay Prize for 2024.

Scott MacDougall serves as the Director of Theological Resources for The Episcopal Church. Prior to that, he taught theology at the Church Divinity School of the Pacific for nearly a decade. He holds graduate degrees from the General Theological Seminary (M.A.) and Fordham University (Ph.D.). His publications include *More Than Communion: Imagining an Eschatological Ecclesiology* (T&T Clark, 2015) and *The Shape of Anglican Theology: Faith Seeking Wisdom* (Brill, 2022).

Robert MacSwain is Associate Professor of Theology at the University of the South. He holds graduate degrees from Princeton Theological Seminary (M.Div.), the University of Edinburgh (M.Th.), and the University of St. Andrews (Ph.D.), as well as a postgraduate diploma in Anglican Studies from Virginia Theological Seminary. A priest of the Oratory of the Good Shepherd, his publications include *Solved by Sacrifice: Austin Farrer, Fideism, and the Evidence of Faith* (Peeters, 2013), *Essays Anglican and Analytic: Explorations in Critical Catholicism* (Eerdmans, 2025), and *Saints as Divine Evidence: The Hagiological Argument for the Existence of God* (Cambridge, 2025).

Joy Ann McDougall is Associate Professor of Systematic Theology at Candler School of Theology, Emory University. She holds graduate degrees from Yale Divinity School (M.A.R.) and the University of Chicago (Ph.D.). Her publications include *Pilgrimage of Love: Moltmann on the Trinity and Christian Life* (Oxford, 2005) and the forthcoming *Rising with Mary: A Feminist Re-imagining of Sin and Grace*.

Matthew Ichihashi Potts is Pusey Minister in the Memorial Church and Plummer Professor of Christian Morals in the faculty of divinity, Harvard University. He holds graduate degrees from Harvard's Divinity School (M.Div.) and Graduate Program in Religion (Ph.D.). An Episcopal priest canonically resident in the Diocese of Massachusetts, his publications include *Cormac McCarthy and the Signs of Sacrament: Literature, Theology, and the Moral of Stories* (Bloomsbury, 2015) and *Forgiveness: An Alternative Account* (Yale, 2022).

The Most Rev. Sean Rowe is the 28th Presiding Bishop and Primate of The Episcopal Church. He holds graduate degrees from Virginia

Theological Seminary (M.Div.) and Gannon University (Ph.D.). He previously served as the Bishop of Northwestern Pennsylvania.

Kara N. Slade is the Associate Rector of Trinity Church, Princeton, and Canon Theologian of the Diocese of New Jersey. She holds graduate degrees from Duke University (M.S. and Ph.D. in mechanical engineering and materials science; M.Div. and Ph.D. in Christian theology and ethics). Her publications include *The Fullness of Time: Jesus Christ, Science, and Modernity* (Cascade, 2021).

Katherine Sonderegger is Distinguished Professor of Systematic Theology at Virginia Theological Seminary. She holds graduate degrees from Yale Divinity School (M.Div., S.T.M.) and Brown University (Ph.D.). An Episcopal priest canonically resident in the Diocese of Virginia, her publications include *That Jesus Christ Was Born a Jew: Karl Barth's "Doctrine of Israel"* (Penn State, 1992) and an ongoing multivolume series in systematic theology published by Fortress Press.

Kathryn Tanner is the Frederick Marquand Professor of Systematic Theology at Yale Divinity School. She holds graduate degrees from Yale University (M.A., M.Phil., Ph.D.). Her publications include *God and Creation in Christian Theology: Tyranny or Empowerment?* (Blackwell, 1988), *Theories of Culture: A New Agenda for Theology* (Fortress, 1997), *Jesus, Humanity and the Trinity: A Brief Systematic Theology* (Fortress, 2001), *Christ the Key* (Cambridge, 2010), and *Christianity and the New Spirit of Capitalism* (Yale, 2019), which is based on her Gifford Lectures delivered at the University of Edinburgh.

Sameer Yadav is Associate Professor of Religion at Baylor University. He holds graduate degrees from Yale Divinity School (S.T.M.) and Duke University (Th.D.). His publications include *The Problem of Perception and the Experience of God: Toward a Theological Empiricism* (T&T Clark, 2015), a forthcoming monograph with Brock Bahler titled *God and Race* (Cambridge University Press), and the forthcoming *How to Do Theological Things with Biblical Words* (Baker Academic).

Foreword

If you are looking for a crash course in the urgent need for the theological wisdom of The Episcopal Church, I recommend being elected Presiding Bishop during a time of institutional upheaval and global turmoil. At every turn, our church is being called upon to make a theologically robust, winsome case for a vision of Christianity that counters our culture's dominant narrative. Without the scholarship on display in this volume, making our witness would be even more daunting than it already is.

The stakes are high. In today's world, we have a front-row seat to what Scott MacDougall, in his essay, calls "the death-dealing power" of theology. Political proclamations are often laced with racism and dominance borne of Christian nationalism, and we regularly hear Christian discourse framed with the terror of Armageddon or prosperity gospel greed. What passes for Christianity in our contemporary public discourse too often regards our faith as a tool of dominion rather than a promise of liberation.

As you will read in these pages, our church does not lack the raw material to make a different case. Here, you will find a heartening display of the best theological thinking in today's Episcopal Church, across the breadth of what Rob MacSwain, in his introduction, identifies as "traditional, post-Barthian, and contextual" schools of thought. At a time when our church's need to form theological thinkers is greater than ever, the autobiographical nature of these essays also demonstrates the many and varied ways in which our parishes and institutions can foster scholars who will help shape our future.

For us to form theologians, however, is not enough. To promulgate their wisdom, we must build our institutional capacity both for theological education that prepares people for ordination and for formation that sparks robust theological imagination in the people we serve. Our preaching, teaching, and institutional communications must be both theologically grounded and accessible, and we must also undergird our governance structures, leadership development practices, and budgets with theological wisdom that strengthens our resolve to participate in God's mission, no matter where it might lead us.

It is fitting that a volume pointing us toward an unknown missional future is inspired by the life and work of Mark McIntosh, one of our church's greatest theological thinkers in recent decades. Together with Bishop Frank Griswold, Mark transformed my life by tethering Anglican theology to the classical mystical tradition. His scholarly and spiritual vision provides us with the wisdom we need to understand that God's call to us is constantly changing, and we must be a church that can respond faithfully.

I give thanks for Mark's life and legacy, and for the authors who have amplified it here.

The Most Rev. Sean W. Rowe
Presiding Bishop of The Episcopal Church

Feast of Benedict of Nursia
July 11, 2025

Introduction

Robert MacSwain

Quite literally, everything we do in The Episcopal Church is theological. This includes the way we interpret the Bible and talk about God and Jesus, what we sing, say, enact, and even wear in worship, and how we understand the two great sacraments of Baptism and Eucharist, as well as the five other sacramental rites. It also encompasses the three orders of bishops, priests, and deacons being open to all people, regardless of gender, along with our moral beliefs and social commitments. Additionally, it reflects our openness to learning from the natural sciences and other disciplines such as philosophy and history, as well as the essential role of lay people in church governance and Christian ministry. Our theology is, in fact, what makes us Episcopalians rather than Baptists, Methodists, Presbyterians, Pentecostals, Roman Catholics, or any other form of Christianity. Without our distinctive theology, The Episcopal Church would simply cease to exist as an alternative among the many different American Christian denominations. Moreover, our distinctive theology is drawn from the venerable Anglican tradition, which began in the Church of England and has now spread around the globe as the Anglican Communion—the third-largest distinct grouping of Christian churches—of which we are a founding member. Our theology thus connects us to millions of other Anglicans in over 165 countries, speaking over 2,000 languages and representing over 500 different cultures.[1] It is a theological heritage

---

1. See "The Anglican Communion," https://www.archbishopofcanterbury.org/about/anglican-communion.

of great spiritual depth, intellectual sophistication, literary richness, aesthetic appeal, cultural diversity, social engagement, and ecumenical scope.[2]

And yet, over the past few decades, it seems that many Episcopalians (clergy as well as laity) have either lost interest in or otherwise become disconnected from their own theological tradition. Or, perhaps more accurately, they seem to have either lost interest in or otherwise become disconnected from theology *as such*. Unfortunately, this means that they are increasingly uninformed both *by* and *about* the theological convictions that historically created and currently sustain The Episcopal Church.[3] There are many reasons for this regrettable situation, and it must be admitted that the discipline of theology is itself partly to blame. Theology has become a highly technical and specialized academic subject, producing erudite monographs and journal articles that are practically unreadable to those without a doctoral degree. Episcopal theologians belong simultaneously to the Church and to the academy and must somehow try to address both of these audiences, but it is a difficult balancing act. Anti-intellectualism is a formidable force in American culture to which Christians have long

---

2. For some helpful introductions, see Mark Chapman, *Anglican Theology* (London: T&T Clark, 2012), which is historical in nature; Ralph McMichael, ed., *The Vocation of Anglican Theology* (London: SCM Press, 2014), which is arranged by doctrine; Scott MacDougall, *The Shape of Anglican Theology: Faith Seeking Wisdom* (Leiden/Boston: Brill, 2022), which is focused on method; and Stephen Burns, Bryan Cones, and James Tengatenga, ed., *Twentieth Century Anglican Theologians: From Evelyn Underhill to Esther Mombo* (Chichester: Wiley-Blackwell, 2021), which deals with individual figures of that specific century.

3. While I am here focusing on the past few decades, this is actually a problem of long standing and is possibly even endemic to Episcopal/Anglican theology: for more historic perspectives, see David L. Holmes, *A Brief History of the Episcopal Church* (Harrisburg, PA: Trinity Press International, 1993), 159–63; and the chapters by Gardiner H. Shattuck Jr. and Charles Hefling in *A New Conversation: Essays on the Future of Theology and the Episcopal Church*, ed. Robert Boak Slocum (New York: Church Publishing, 1999), 36–47 and 48–59, respectively.

been susceptible, and widespread suspicion of claims to expertise has only been growing in recent years. Many congregations are increasingly focused on survival in the face of shrinking membership and declining finances, and practical concerns seem more pressing than abstract concepts. For various reasons, there is now a commendable and growing interest in spirituality, justice, and ecology, along with the related issues of class, race, gender, sexuality, and colonialism. However, for many contemporary Christians, ancient doctrines such as the Trinity, Incarnation, and Atonement often appear less urgent or helpful to engage with.

Nevertheless, this book emerges from its contributors' shared and profound conviction that a deeper knowledge of theology is necessary for the health and continued existence of The Episcopal Church. Volumes like this, which seek to convince Episcopalians of theology's importance and value, have indeed appeared at regular intervals over the past seventy-five years—sometimes written by a single author or two, sometimes compiling essays by different scholars; sometimes published with a degree of official status, sometimes entirely independently. While not a formal sequel, this volume can be considered a timely follow-up to a substantial book edited twenty-five years ago by Robert Boak Slocum, with chapters by almost thirty distinguished contributors, both academic theologians and senior leaders: *A New Conversation: Essays on the Future of Theology and the Episcopal Church*.[4] Much has changed since then, so a fresh effort is required now.

---

4. Cited in the previous note. For some of the earlier volumes alluded to here, see James A. Pike and W. Norman Pittenger, *The Faith of the Church*, Volume 3 in The Church's Teaching, with the editorial collaboration of Arthur C. Lichtenberger, and with the assistance of the Authors' Committee of the Department of Christian Education of The Protestant Episcopal Church (Greenwich, CT: The Seabury Press, 1951); Richard A. Norris, *Understanding the Faith of the Church*, Volume 4 in The Church's Teaching Series, with the assistance of a group of editorial advisors under

While contributing to the same crucial task, this volume stands out from its various predecessors by seeking to introduce The Episcopal Church not just to its *theology* but to some of its current *theologians*—those individuals who have devoted themselves to study, teaching, and writing on behalf of the Church they wish to serve. We want readers to come away with a better understanding of where our theology "comes from," as well as the diverse backgrounds, educations, and personalities of those who practice it. Some of the theologians featured in this book are established scholars, while others are just getting started. Some teach or have taught at Episcopal seminaries or other academic institutions; some are based in a parish, chaplaincy, or nonprofit organization. Although all are Episcopalians, they represent very different understandings of the theological enterprise, as well as a cross-section (although obviously not comprehensive) of the Church's racial, ethnic, gender, and sexual identities. And, as noted above, the book is intentionally inter-generational (including between the two editors). Holding the strong belief that personal narrative is both inherently interesting and conceptually valuable, each chapter incorporates some element of autobiography. From Augustine's *Confessions* to contemporary "narrative theology," Christians have pondered how their individual stories intersect both with God's story and the story of God's people. Some contributors have shared more and others less of this personal information, and their differing degrees of self-disclosure are sometimes motivated

---

the direction of the Church's Teaching Series Committee (New York: The Seabury Press, 1979); Arthur A. Vogel, ed., *Theology in Anglicanism*, The Anglican Study Series (Wilton, CT: Morehouse Barlow, 1984); Ephraim Radner and George R. Sumner, ed., *Reclaiming Faith: Essays on Orthodoxy in the Episcopal Church and the Baltimore Declaration* (Grand Rapids: Eerdmans, 1993); Mark McIntosh, *Mysteries of Faith*, Volume 8 in The New Church's Teaching Series (Cambridge, MA: Cowley, 2000); and Jesse Zink, *A Faith for the Future*, Volume 3 in the Church's Teachings for a Changing World (New York: Morehouse, 2016).

by specific theological reasons.[5] All of the primary contributors have been asked to answer the same questions and yet have been given complete freedom to write their chapter in whatever way they wanted:

1. How did you become a theologian?
2. What is your understanding of the theological enterprise? What themes and topics are central to your work as a theologian?
3. What is your vision for the future of theology in The Episcopal Church?

I will return to these thematic questions in a moment, but a significant factor in this book's inspiration was the recent and tragically premature death of one of The Episcopal Church's most gifted theologians, Mark A. McIntosh. A graduate of Yale, Oxford, the General Theological Seminary, and the University of Chicago, Mark began his academic career at Loyola University Chicago; was appointed as the Van Mildert Canon Professor of Divinity at Durham University and Durham Cathedral; and then returned to Loyola as the inaugural holder of their new Chair in Christian Spirituality. Ordained to the priesthood in 1986, in addition to serving in various parishes, Mark was the Canon Theologian to Presiding Bishop Frank Griswold and was appointed to the Anglican-Roman Catholic International Commission (ARCIC). He contributed a chapter to *A New Conversation* and wrote the volume on doctrine in The New Church's Teaching Series, as well as authoring several deeply

---

5. A good example of this genre by a prominent contemporary figure is Stanley Hauerwas, *Hannah's Child: A Theologian's Memoir* (Grand Rapids: Eerdmans, 2010). And for a recent collection of short theological autobiographies from members of various Christian denominations, see Derek R. Nelson, Joshua Moritz, and Ted Peters, ed., *Theologians in Their Own Words* (Minneapolis: Fortress Press, 2013). Nelson's introduction provides a helpful orientation to this contested enterprise. One of our contributors, Kathryn Tanner, is also included in this earlier volume.

learned and devout monographs exploring the intimate connection between spiritual and systematic theology.[6] Sadly, Mark developed amyotrophic lateral sclerosis (ALS) in 2017 and died on October 13, 2021, at the age of 61. His death was a significant loss not only to his family and friends but also to The Episcopal Church and the academy. This volume was conceived as neither a formal Festschrift nor a posthumous tribute to Mark, but it is dedicated to his memory and seeks to both honor and perpetuate his generative commitment to the highest standards of academic theology performed in faithful service to the Church.[7]

* * *

Returning to the questions presented to each of the primary contributors, I will answer them briefly myself in order to make my own modest contribution before reflecting on what the following chapters might reveal about the future of theology and The Episcopal Church:

---

6. In addition to his *Mysteries of Faith*, cited in note 4, see Mark A. McIntosh, *Christology from Within: Spirituality and the Incarnation in Hans Urs von Balthasar* (Notre Dame: University of Notre Dame Press, 1996); *Mystical Theology: The Integrity of Spirituality and Theology* (Malden, MA: Blackwell Publishing, 1998); *Discernment and Truth: The Spirituality and Theology of Knowledge* (New York: Crossroad Publishing, 2004); *Divine Teaching: An Introduction to Christian Theology* (Oxford: Blackwell, 2008); and *The Divine Ideas Tradition in Christian Mystical Theology* (Oxford: Oxford University Press, 2021). At an advanced stage of ALS, he also co-authored two volumes with Frank T. Griswold, *Seeds of Faith: Theology and Spirituality at the Heart of Christian Belief* and *Harvest of Hope: A Contemplative Approach to Holy Scripture*, both published by Eerdmans in 2022.

7. For series of moving tributes to Mark, see *Anglican Theological Review* 105, Issue 1 (2023), especially the valuable review article by Jacob W. Torbeck, "Sharing Divine Ideas: The Theological Trajectory of Mark A. McIntosh," 41–57, and Frank T. Griswold's remarkable homily from the Memorial Eucharist for Mark Allen McIntosh: November 20, 2021, St. Luke's Episcopal Church, Evanston, IL, 66–70. Bishop Griswold died on March 5, 2023, at the age of 85.

(1) I became a theologian because I had to figure out what I believed, given the many conflicting and occasionally problematic versions of Christianity that I encountered growing up. My father's family were Episcopalians with Scottish and Anglo-Welsh roots, and my mother's family were Roman Catholics from Italy. Although I was baptized as an infant at Our Lady of Mount Carmel Catholic Church in Newport News, Virginia, neither of my parents attended church during my earliest years. At around age six, my best friend's mother invited me to worship with them, which at the time happened to be at the Episcopal Church of the Epiphany at 1530 Lafayette Boulevard in Norfolk, Virginia. This led to a self-conscious decision to accept Christ, a decision with momentous implications for my extended family and future career path.

However, for various reasons, the rest of my childhood in Virginia and North Carolina was spent wandering through an odd mixture of Christian congregations and theological influences: charismatic and Calvinist, evangelical and Episcopal, denominational and non-denominational. Because of this confusing mélange, despite being confirmed by Bishop Sid Sanders in the Diocese of East Carolina in 1987, the very next year I incongruously enrolled at Jerry Falwell's Liberty University in Lynchburg, Virginia, an institution which was then small, struggling, and trying (unsuccessfully) to transition from its fundamentalist origins to a broader evangelical identity. This decision obviously made sense to my eighteen-year-old self. However, by the time I graduated from Liberty in 1992, I was ready to move on both theologically and politically from conservative right-wing Christianity, whether evangelical or charismatic, although I was not sure what a viable alternative might look like. I therefore went to Princeton Theological Seminary with the idea of earning a Master of Divinity *en route* to a Ph.D. in philosophy.

During my first year in Princeton, I was rather unexpectedly drawn back to The Episcopal Church, specifically to the parish of All Saints' under the pastoral care of the Rev. Dr. Orley Swartzentruber, and receiving spiritual direction from the Rev. Dr. Victor Preller—an associate priest there who was also Professor of Religion at Princeton University and a Priest of the Oratory of the Good Shepherd.[8] Compared to the low-church Southern Episcopalianism that I had previously experienced, this more Anglo-Catholic form of liturgy, theology, and spirituality in the Mid-Atlantic opened up a whole new world for me. Other important influences at this time were Diogenes Allen, professor of philosophy at Princeton Seminary; Stanley Hauerwas, professor of theological ethics at Duke Divinity School (whom I had met just before moving to Princeton); and Eleonore Stump, professor of philosophy at Saint Louis University (whom I had encountered while still a student at Liberty). They all helped me find my way forward.

Returning to The Episcopal Church raised the question of ordination to the priesthood, which I grappled with for the next six years. An exchange program between Princeton Seminary and the University of Edinburgh led to a year in Scotland, where I had the good fortune to study with the irenic Dominican philosopher Fergus Kerr. After a brief stint teaching religion at an Episcopal boarding school in New England, I completed a year of Anglican studies at Virginia

---

8. For tributes to the pastoral influence of Swartzentruber, see the chapters by William P. Alston and Marilyn McCord Adams in *God and the Philosophers: The Reconciliation of Faith and Reason*, ed. Thomas V. Morris (New York: Oxford University Press, 1994), 19–30 and 137–61, respectively. This is a book of spiritual autobiographies by Christian philosophers, and McCord Adams also contributed to *Theologians in Their Own Words* (cited in note 5). For a collection of essays compiled as a posthumous tribute to Preller, see Jeffrey Stout and Robert MacSwain, ed., *Grammar and Grace: Reformulations of Aquinas and Wittgenstein* (London: SCM Press, 2004).

Theological Seminary and then another year as a research assistant to Archbishop George Carey at Lambeth Palace. Ordained to the diaconate by Archbishop Carey in Canterbury Cathedral, I returned to the United States and the Diocese of East Carolina for my curacy at St. Mary's Church in Kinston, where I was ordained to the priesthood by Bishop Clifton Daniel (Hauerwas preached).[9] Three years later, I was back in the UK for a Ph.D. at the University of Durham, writing a dissertation on the Oxford theologian, philosopher, and biblical scholar Austin Farrer (1904–68), expertly supervised by the Rev. Canon Professor David Brown and enhanced by inspiring conversations with Professor Ann Loades.[10] Brown moved to St. Andrews in 2007, and so I moved with him, graduating with my doctorate in 2010. The year before, I began teaching theology and Christian ethics at the School of Theology at the University of the South in Sewanee, Tennessee, and aside from some sabbatical research leaves I have been doing so ever since.

I share this long series of institutions and influences to provide some sense of what I have struggled with as I sought to find a version of Christianity that made sense to me both rationally and morally, and that fed me both spiritually and aesthetically. It was not a simple or straightforward path, but it forced me to become both a theologian and an Anglican. This leads to the second set of questions.

---

9. See his "Sacrificing Priests: A Sermon on the Occasion of Rob MacSwain's Ordination—February 2, 2002—St. Mary's Church, Kinston, North Carolina," in Stanley Hauerwas, *Disrupting Time: Sermons, Prayers, and Sundries* (Eugene, OR: Cascade Books, 2004), 137–41.

10. In *Twentieth Century Anglican Theologians*, ed. Burns, Cones, and Tengatenga, cited in note 2 above, I wrote the chapter on Farrer (54–64), Stephen Burns wrote the chapter on Loades (157–66), and Christopher R. Brewer wrote the chapter on Brown (185–94). Brown was McIntosh's immediate predecessor as Van Mildert Canon Professor at Durham, one of the great chairs of Anglican theology, with previous occupants including Michael Ramsey (1904–88), Stephen Sykes (1939–2014), and Daniel W. Hardy (1930–2007).

(2) I view the theological enterprise primarily according to the ancient motto of St. Anselm of Canterbury: *fides quaerens intellectum* ("faith seeking understanding"). I think the first task of the theologian is to humbly receive the Christian tradition in all its complexity and then try to understand and explain it as best as possible. I am deeply drawn to William J. Abraham's description of Christian doctrine (or what he calls "canonical theism") as "that rich vision of God, creation, and redemption developed over time in the scriptures, articulated in the Nicene Creed, celebrated in the liturgy of the church, enacted in the lives of the saints, handed over and received in the sacraments, depicted in iconography, articulated by canonical teachers, mulled over in the Fathers, and treasured, preserved, and guarded by the episcopate. The full exposition of this, together with its unity and diversity, is properly the task of systematic theology."[11] I believe that this theological task includes criticism and even revision of the tradition when necessary, but, in my view, these activities are secondary to interpretation, understanding, and explanation.

Although I teach Christian doctrine at Sewanee, my main research interests are in philosophical theology or the philosophy of religion. That is, I teach my students the great doctrines of God, creation, Christology, soteriology, ecclesiology, sacramentology, and eschatology, but unlike many of the contributors to this volume I have rarely published on these essential topics or performed theology systematically or constructively (at least, so far). Instead, I have focused on basic and preliminary questions such as the rationality of religious belief, the interpretation of Scripture, the idea of divine revelation, and human holiness or sainthood. I am also particularly interested in the nature of Anglican theology. This is why I wrote my

---

11. William J. Abraham, *Crossing the Threshold of Divine Revelation* (Grand Rapids: Eerdmans, 2006), 43–44.

doctoral dissertation on Farrer—widely regarded as one of the greatest Anglican minds of the twentieth century.[12]

(3) My vision for the future of theology in The Episcopal Church is that, first, the Church finally realizes that theology is both inevitable and essential rather than avoidable and unnecessary. That is, we simply cannot do without theology, so the only question is whether we will perform our theology well or poorly, conscientiously or cluelessly. Not only that, but bad theology is oppressive and harmful, as many who have been wounded by it can sadly attest. (Indeed, people often come to The Episcopal Church seeking refuge from bad theology, which should compel us to pay closer attention to our own.)

Second, my vision is also that, given the necessity and importance of theology, The Episcopal Church will finally begin to pay more careful attention to the various institutional settings in which its theology takes place. We are currently blessed with a number of theological seminaries, diocesan schools for ministry, and study programs, but compared to many other American denominations The Episcopal Church has been remarkably insouciant in maintaining such institutions and has indeed invested almost nothing in the vital enterprise of theological education, as well as in higher education more generally.

Third, my vision is that Episcopalians finally return with renewed interest and curiosity to the distinctive but neglected tradition of

---

12. My three authored books to date are *Solved by Sacrifice: Austin Farrer, Fideism, and the Evidence of Faith* (Leuven: Peeters, 2013), *Essays Anglican and Analytic: Explorations in Critical Catholicism* (Grand Rapids: Eerdmans, 2025), and *Saints as Divine Evidence: The Hagiological Argument for the Existence of God* (Cambridge: Cambridge University Press, 2025). I have also edited or co-edited a number of volumes dealing with related issues, including two on Farrer: Ann Loades and Robert MacSwain, ed., *The Truth-Seeking Heart: Austin Farrer and His Writings* (Norwich: Canterbury Press, 2006), and Robert MacSwain, ed., *Scripture, Metaphysics, and Poetry: Austin Farrer's* The Glass of Vision *with Critical Commentary* (Farnham: Ashgate, 2013; republished by Routledge in 2016).

Anglican theology. As I have written elsewhere, "attention is currently focused on the sustainability of the Anglican Communion as an *institution* (or set of institutions). But institutional futures cannot be separated from conceptual ones. Unless and until those charged with the task of teaching theology in Anglican churches have their intellectual imagination *re-engaged* with their own tradition, questions of institutional sustainability are moot."[13]

* * *

Turning then to the contents of this volume, in providing their own answers to these thematic questions, it seems that the contributors have fallen naturally into three broad groupings, and in so doing, they have helpfully shown that there are three main types of theology currently being practiced in The Episcopal Church, which I will here call (1) "Traditional," (2) "Post-Barthian," and (3) "Contextual."[14]

---

13. Robert MacSwain, "Above, Beside, Within: The Anglican Theology of Austin Farrer," originally published in *Journal of Anglican Studies* 4 (2006): 33–57, now reprinted in my *Essays Anglican and Analytic*, 35–62, citing from 38. In addition to the works cited in note 2 above, for a brief survey of some leading figures in Anglican theology, see John Booty, "Standard Divines," in *The Study of Anglicanism*, ed. Stephen Sykes, John Booty, and Jonathan Knight, rev. ed. (London: SPCK; Minneapolis: Fortress Press, 1998), 176–87. They include Richard Hooker, Lancelot Andrewes, Jeremy Taylor, Joseph Butler, John Henry Newman, Edward Bouverie Pusey, F. D. Maurice, Charles Gore, and William Temple. I mention some more recent figures and allude to racial, feminist, and postcolonial concerns about this historic tradition further below.

14. Interestingly, somewhat similar threefold typologies are provided by Rowan Williams in his essay collection, *On Christian Theology*, and by Owen C. Thomas and Ellen K. Wondra in their textbook, *Introduction to Theology*. Williams divides theological modes into what he calls the celebratory, the communicative, and the critical. He says that all three are necessary and that "to try and arrange these in some kind of hierarchy, to regard one as the true paradigm or the goal to which the others aspire, is a serious misunderstanding of the way in which theology works"—a thought to which I will return below. See his *On Christian Theology*

(1) By "traditional," I mean those contemporary Episcopal theologians whose work draws primarily on classical Christian sources from the patristic, medieval, and Reformation eras, along with specifically Anglican authors, typically from the sixteenth and seventeenth centuries. Such theologians believe that figures such as Origen, Augustine, Gregory of Nyssa, Maximus the Confessor, Anselm, Thomas Aquinas, Julian of Norwich, Martin Luther, John Calvin, Teresa of Ávila, Richard Hooker, and Jeremy Taylor should still inform our doctrinal reflection today. They are often interested in the relationship between doctrine and spirituality, as well as in theology that is performed (in a characteristically Anglican manner) through liturgy, sermons, poetry, and other forms of literature. In addition to several contributors to this volume, recent examples of this approach in The Episcopal Church can be found in the work of Mark A. McIntosh, discussed above, and Ellen T. Charry.[15]

(2) By "post-Barthian," I mean those contemporary Episcopal theologians who have first accepted the necessity of going through the "liberal" Enlightenment critique of classical theology, particularly as it was conceived and expressed in nineteenth-century Germany, but who have then embraced Karl Barth's influential "critique of the critique" and reformulation of Christian doctrine on the other side of it. Such theology might thus be described more generically as *post-modern* or *post-liberal*, but calling it *post-Barthian* is more specific and

---

(Oxford: Blackwell, 2000), xii–xvi, citing from the final page. Likewise, Thomas and Wondra say that theology has three main approaches associated with three distinct contexts, namely the academy, the church, and amidst struggles for freedom and liberation. See their *Introduction to Christian Theology*, 3rd ed. (Harrisburg, PA: Morehouse, 2002), 1, and 1–5 for more detail.

15. See her two major books, *By the Renewing of Your Minds: The Pastoral Function of Christian Doctrine* (New York: Oxford University Press, 1997) and *God and the Art of Happiness* (Grand Rapids: Eerdmans, 2010), along with her edited volume, *Inquiring after God: Classic and Contemporary Readings* (Oxford: Blackwell, 2000).

accurate. As Daniel W. Hardy writes on behalf of this perspective, Barth's impact

> has been so extensive as to be virtually coterminous with the history of theology during and since his lifetime [1886–1968]. Since his work was both so decisive in its method and so comprehensive in its scope, we continue to meet it both in those whose approaches coincide with his, in those who argue—against him—for other ways, and also in those who extend the topics with which he was concerned within and outside his frame of reference. So much did he reconstitute and consolidate the state of Christian theology for the twentieth century that he is always a point of departure for others.[16]

In Episcopal circles shaped by post-Barthian theology, Barth has displaced the previously dominant Paul Tillich (1886–1965), divine revelation trumps human experience, and process theology has given way to more transcendent understandings of God. In addition to several contributors to this volume, perhaps the primary example of this approach in The Episcopal Church is the late Hans W. Frei (1922–88), whose teaching and writing continue to bear fruit.[17]

---

16. Daniel W. Hardy, "Karl Barth," in David F. Ford with Rachel Muers, *The Modern Theologians: An Introduction to Christian Theology Since 1918* (Oxford: Blackwell, 2005), 39. See also the editors' provocative claim in the preface that the "German-language tradition of academic theology" as it developed in the nineteenth and twentieth centuries is arguably "the best single tradition through which to be introduced to what it means to Christian theology in intelligent engagement with modern disciplines, societies, churches, and traumatic events" (ix).

17. See Hans W. Frei, *The Eclipse of Biblical Narrative: A Study in Eighteenth and Nineteenth Century Hermeneutics* (New Haven: Yale University Press, 1974); *The Identity of Jesus Christ: The Hermeneutical Bases of Dogmatic Theology* (Philadelphia: Fortress Press, 1975); *Types of Christian Theology*, ed. George Hunsinger and

(3) By "contextual," I mean those contemporary Episcopal theologians who self-consciously begin their work by reflecting on their particular social and cultural setting and the implications of their personal racial, ethnic, gender, sexual, and/or class identity. These theologians belong to the broader school of liberation theology, now increasingly informed by postcolonial concerns, and thus focus on the moral and political consequences of Christian convictions, often leading to direct activism seeking justice on behalf of their respective communities. Such theologians self-identify as Black, feminist, womanist, queer, Latinx, Asian, disabled, and so on, and they often find that the Christian tradition in general, and the Anglican tradition in particular, needs substantial critique and revision in order to be truly life-giving. In his contribution to this volume, Francisco García prefers the label "constructive theology" over "contextual theology" on the excellent grounds that all theology is contextual, even if some theologians fail to recognize that crucial fact! However, for this very reason, I think it is arguably still helpful to retain the term "contextual theology" to describe those theologians whose personal context is—by contrast with the other two approaches—not just actually but *intentionally* and *methodologically* central to their work. In addition to several contributors to this volume, recent examples of this approach in The Episcopal Church are Carter Heyward, Kelly Brown Douglas, Kwok Pui-lan, and Patrick S. Cheng.[18]

William C. Placher (New Haven: Yale University Press, 1993); *Theology and Narrative: Selected Essays*, ed. George Hunsinger and William C. Placher (New York: Oxford University Press, 1993); and the important Festschrift edited by Garrett Green, *Scriptural Authority and Narrative Interpretation* (Philadelphia: Fortress Press, 1987). Among the contributors to this volume, Katherine Sonderegger, Kathryn Tanner, and Joy Ann McDougall studied with Frei at Yale, as did Mark McIntosh.

18. For just some representative publications from their extended bodies of work, see Carter Heyward, *Touching our Strength: The Erotic as Power and the Love of God* (San Francisco: Harper & Row, 1989); Kelly Brown Douglas, *Stand Your Ground:*

Of course, not all theologians fit neatly into just one of these three types, and indeed it is rare to find pure laboratory samples out in the wild. And it is also true that the vaunted *via media* character of Anglican theology means that even those primarily committed to a particular method often strive intentionally to incorporate other voices in their work, seeking a deeper integration or more comprehensive fusion of theological traditions than may be typical of representatives of other forms of theology. Several contributors to this volume highlight this tendency or reflect on its significance in various ways, whether historically or constructively.[19] However, all that being said, I do think that current Episcopal theologians at least tend to identify primarily with one of these three approaches, even if aspects of the others are still present in their work, or even if they also draw on additional resources such as post-Vatican II Catholicism.[20] I will let readers decide for themselves how to classify the various contributors. Still, from my own answers to the assigned questions, it is clear that my main sympathy is with the "traditional" approach, although I think that the other two are necessary as well. Indeed, I am convinced that we need all three types. They each express a different kind of integrity: (1) engages with our patristic and Anglican roots, (2) engages with ongoing developments in modern/postmodern thought, and (3) engages with the full range of human experience that belongs to the Body of Christ. As stated above in dialog with García, I agree

---

Black Bodies and the Justice of God (Maryknoll, NY: Orbis, 2015); Kwok Pui-lan, *The Anglican Tradition from a Postcolonial Perspective* (New York: Seabury Books, 2023); and Patrick S. Cheng, *From Sin to Amazing Grace: Discovering the Queer Christ* (New York: Seabury Books, 2012).

19. I am grateful to an anonymous reader for pushing for greater acknowledgement of this point.

20. Indeed, for many post-Barthians, the primary alternatives to wrestle with are Roman Catholics such as Henri de Lubac (1896–1991), Karl Rahner (1904–84), and Hans Urs von Balthasar (1905–88) rather than any liberal Protestant theologians.

that all theology is "contextual." That is, all theology comes from a specific location. Some theologies are explicitly structured around the conceptual resources and pressing needs of a particular community. Other theologies try to speak more universally, address more than one audience, and even strive to describe the truth as such. Both the particular and the universal are characteristic of human thought. If so, we simultaneously need to be aware of our own context and yet also seek to transcend it. This is my own view, however, and after this introduction, my editorial role is to get out of the way and facilitate other voices![21]

So far, I have focused almost exclusively on theology in The Episcopal Church. In conclusion, it is important to mention that—in addition to ecumenical conversation partners in other Christian traditions such as Roman Catholicism, Eastern Orthodoxy, Lutheranism, and so forth—Episcopal theologians have always been in close communication with theologians in other Anglican provinces, especially the Church of England. Many of the contributors to this volume have been deeply influenced by the work of recent British scholars such as Rowan Williams, David Ford, Sarah Coakley, John Webster, Oliver O'Donovan, Ann Loades, John Milbank, Graham Ward, Catherine Pickstock, and David Brown. This is partly because of

---

21. Thus, it is quite apparent that my own social context is primarily white, Southeastern, and middle-class, and my intellectual influences are significantly Eurocentric, partly due to my British and Italian background and partly due to seven years of living, working, and studying in the United Kingdom. To pretend that my context is any less determinative for my theology than García's context is for his would be a blatant case of self-deception. For example, my "struggles" are more individual, abstract, and epistemological (as I seek to understand my faith) and his are more communal, practical, and ethical (as he seeks justice for his community). While both of our theologies may be valid responses to our respective contexts, I must allow myself to be challenged by García and others—that is, I must ask how my context may shield me from essential insights into the Christian faith and its moral/political imperatives.

these theologians' generative writings, but also because Episcopalians have often crossed the Atlantic to study at universities such as Oxford, Cambridge, Durham, and King's College London. This is itself partly because The Episcopal Church, for all of its vaunted resources, conspicuously lacks a strong academic culture of research universities at which scholars can gather, create communities of intellectual inquiry, and both teach and be formed at the doctoral level. However, as mentioned above, theology does not flourish simply because of the brilliance of individual thinkers but requires substantial institutional and communal support. And yet, as also said above, institutional futures cannot be separated from conceptual ones. To a very great extent, therefore, the future of theology and The Episcopal Church depends on the Church's values and priorities in the years ahead.[22]

Further Reading Recommendations

Brown, David. *Divine Generosity and Human Creativity: Theology through Symbol, Painting, and Architecture.* Edited by Christopher R. Brewer and Robert MacSwain. London: Routledge, 2017.

Burns, Stephen and James Tengatenga, eds. *Anglican Theology: Postcolonial Perspectives.* London: SCM Press, 2024.

Coakley, Sarah. *The New Asceticism: Sexuality, Gender and the Quest for God.* London: Bloomsbury, 2015.

Slocum, Robert Boak, ed. *A New Conversation: Essays on the Future of Theology and the Episcopal Church.* New York: Church Publishing, 1999.

---

22. In addition to two anonymous readers, I am grateful to Kelli Joyce for helpful comments on an earlier version of this introduction, and for co-editing this volume with me.

The Anglican Way in My Work

Kathryn Tanner

I came to the study of theology via an undergraduate major in philosophy at Yale. My later doctoral work at the same institution didn't initially distinguish, in fact, between the two—my combined area of study was philosophy of religion and theology. However, I ended up concentrating on theology for several reasons. One was the fundamental decency of the scholar who became my mentor at Yale—Hans Frei (1922–88). To be truthful, I didn't have a great deal in common with him intellectually; his sensibilities were historical and literary whereas mine were analytical and primarily philosophical. Nevertheless, he was extremely supportive of my work, despite all my differences from him, and, more to the point, I very much respected him as a person.[1]

The second reason had to do with the narrow and rather desiccated character of philosophy at the time. It didn't seem to be about much of anything besides talk about talk about talk. It had, as I like to term it, a kind of "the cat is on the mat" quality. That is, after extensive, painstaking analysis of the meaning and reference of the words "the," "cat," "is," and so on, one concluded that "the cat is on the mat" is true if and only if the cat is on the mat. Such a conclusion,

---

1. To get a sense of his character, watch his contribution to the Fortunoff Video Archive for Holocaust Testimonials, Hans Frei, at https://editions.fortunoff.library.yale.edu/essay/hvt-0170.

however convincing, might well strike one as trivial and hardly worth all the effort.

What theology had going for it, on the contrary, was an expansive range of subject matters of potentially much greater human importance. Even if no one else at the university cared to listen, theology had the license, as an academic discipline, to talk about God and everything else in relation to God—which simply means everything. Since God is related to the whole world, by virtue, for example, of being its creator, nothing fell outside the purview of theology. Anything and everything was fair game from a theological perspective, employing whatever disciplinary methods seemed appropriate for the matters at hand. In my scholarly career, I have, accordingly, spent as much time talking about economics, politics, and social issues as I have discussing strictly theological matters like sin and salvation.

Finally, what one said about all these things potentially mattered to people outside the academy; non-academics, church people in particular, had reason to care about them. Theologians were able to talk about matters of vital importance to most people from a perspective that Christians, in particular, had a stake in. These matters concerned the fundamental shape of one's relations to other people and the world, as Christians understood them. Given Christian commitments, in particular, how should one live one's life in all its complex economic, social, and political dimensions? As a scholar familiar with the long historical record of Christian thought and action, I could help Christians understand this to address the current challenges facing not just them but everyone—for instance, an upsurge in economic inequality or anti-democratic threats of violence against political opponents, and so on. How should Christians position themselves on these matters in light of beliefs about sin and salvation, for example?

The fundamental theological task, as I understood it, was to figure out what Christianity was all about, given the diversity of Christian witness to Jesus Christ over the course of centuries, and, on that basis, to determine what Christianity should stand for in the world—the allegiances of an economic, social, and political sort that such an understanding of Christianity would warrant.[2] The primary theological task was, in other words, to show how the great variety of things that Christians commonly believe hang together in a sufficiently coherent fashion to direct Christian action in a concerted way. Despite the diversity of all these beliefs and the diversity of Christian interpretations of each one of them, one should try to make sense of these beliefs together, to help clarify the courses of action in everyday life that are defensible on Christian grounds. Should one, as a Christian, for example, support—or not—equal human rights to material wellbeing, given beliefs about the nature and extent of God's love for humanity and the centrality of those beliefs for the rest of one's faith? Such issues could, of course, be raised piecemeal, but a coherent understanding of what Christianity is all about can help make one's life a consistent whole, with some overall integrity of purpose.

The task of creating a coherent whole out of the vastly different things that Christians have believed is obviously simplified if one limits oneself to a particular corner of Christendom. However, that is not typical of what is often termed the Anglican Way. While there are many luminaries of Anglican theology worthy of sustained reflection and even loyalty—Richard Hooker, Charles Gore, William Temple, among them—the Anglican Way does not require a theologian to continue in the line of thought of any one theologian or theological movement, in the way, for example, a Lutheran theologian needs to

---

2. For more on this understanding of the theological task, see Kathryn Tanner, "Introduction," *Jesus, Humanity, and the Trinity: A Brief Systematic Theology* (Minneapolis: Fortress, 2001).

show themselves to be a follower of Luther—by, say, discussing how Luther is properly understood and still relevant today. Particularly in virtue of its often Catholic-leaning form of Protestantism, the Anglican Way frees the theologian *from* such particular theological commitments, at least as any sort of initial default position. It also frees the theologian *for* a much more expansive range of theological dialog partners—modern, premodern, Catholic, Protestant, Eastern Orthodox, and so on. One can shape one's thought in whatever way one thinks best, so as to more adequately reflect the historical diversity of Christian witness, according to one's own considered judgment about what is properly Christian, intellectually credible, and of lasting importance.

Mark McIntosh, in whose memory this book is dedicated, was such a theologian, working in accordance with this understanding of the Anglican Way. While making creative contributions to theological topics he deemed of primary importance—notably, topics in Christology, Christian mysticism, and spirituality—he did so by threading together insights across a broad spectrum of theologians, among them Hans Urs von Balthasar, Maximus the Confessor, and Bonaventure. With different theological emphases and drawing on different theological figures, I have tried to do much the same thing in my own work and, accordingly, believe this to be the right course for theology in our church to take in the future.

In order to make what I'm suggesting more concrete, let me spend the rest of this essay reviewing how my own theology weaves together strands from Protestantism, Catholicism, and Eastern Orthodoxy, by way of a perhaps typically Anglican focus on incarnation. The core of it all, the hinge holding it all together, is the way I make central to the whole Christian story of creation, fall, and redemption the idea that God gives us God's own life through Christ. From the very beginning, God's intent in creating the world was to give us not just the good of created life—our existence and human capacities to be put to good use—but the good of God's own life, an end that is achieved, at the same time as obstacles to it in the form of sin are overcome, through God's unity with the humanity of Christ and our union with him thereby.

The most general theological principles underlying this entire account of God's relation to the world are Thomistic. Although I argue in my first book that these principles can be found in a vast array of theologians, spanning differences in denominational affiliation, metaphysical inclination, and historical context, the principles are perhaps most evident in the theology of Thomas Aquinas, one of the significant figures, of course, in Catholic theology; Aquinas indeed was my own entryway into them.[3] The fundamental idea behind such principles is to make divine transcendence—God's difference from the world—the foundation for an understanding of God's active relation to the world that is all-encompassing and direct in every case. God is transcendent, not to be identified with the world or anything in it, in that God is not a kind of thing, not in a genus. For that reason, God does not relate to creatures in the way a creature would, as one force or principle among others within the same plane of acting and counteracting influences, but across the whole of it in every respect that can be considered good.

Take the relationship that God has with the world as its creator. Without having especially close associations with any particular sort of created thing—say, with those things distinguished from others by qualities of intelligence and order—God can create the whole of created existence, inclusive of all the differences that set one sort of creature apart from another. In short, because God is not a kind of

---

3. For a fuller treatment of these principles, see Kathryn Tanner, *God and Creation in Christian Theology: Tyranny or Empowerment?* (Oxford and London: Blackwell, 1988).

thing, God can create all kinds of things, and not just those purportedly like God in virtue of their exceptional created qualities.

Without being nearer or farther, so to speak, from any one sort of creature rather than another, God can, moreover, bring about the whole of what exists, from the bottom up, in the same immediate way in every case. Although creatures have relations with one another within that whole, those relations are not the necessary mediators of God's own influence on them. Whatever their relations with other things, God's influence on them remains direct. As a result, no one creature is more the creature of God than another by virtue of the way creatures are ordered to one another. While nothing about this general account of God's relation to the world rules out the existence of hierarchies within the world, what is on top of such a created hierarchy is no closer to God than what is on the bottom, and therefore the top cannot be the required means or pathway by which God relates to the bottom.

To get a better sense of how God relates to everything in the same direct way at once, picture the horizontal plane of the whole world, in all its dimensions and whatever its internal arrangement, held up in existence at every point by the vertical plane of God's creative agency. And notice that, following this picture, God's creation of the world is not temporally indexed to a first moment in time. Creation means, instead, that everything exists, for however long it exists, in a relation of dependence upon the creative action of God, who holds it up in existence and maintains it across the whole complex, changing course of its vibrant internal composition.

The created world that God sustains, through this same creative agency, includes, as it turns out, our own agency. Agency is one of the gifts that a beneficent God extends to us as our creator. God creates us, then, across the course of our own active agency, from start to finish, and in this sense, God works *with* us, neither supplementing our agency nor substituting for it in the way another ordinary created agent would. Rather than working outside of us to redirect our actions through either coercion or persuasion, God, as our creator, gives rise to us in our own self-initiated activity to alter ourselves and the world, including every facet of that activity that can be considered good. This is the usual account of double agency, or primary and secondary causality, that Thomas is famous for advocating.

The non-competitive character of the way divine and human agency are brought together here—because one gives rise to the other—can be extended, moreover, to the account of Christ.[4] Although Aquinas himself doesn't develop the idea—it is more typical of early Eastern theology—the idea of non-competitive double agency helps make sense of the unity of humanity and divinity in Christ to begin with, without suggesting any tradeoff between incompatible, irreconcilably different things. God is simply not an ordinary kind of thing that can come into conflict in that way with another kind of thing, the human, as if the relationship between divinity and humanity in Christ were something like the competing creaturely influences of hot and cold. Instead, the divinity of Christ gives rise to the humanity made one with God in Christ, a humanity that has no existence, indeed, apart from that relationship of unity with God that brings it about. This unique relation of utter dependence of Christ's humanity on his divinity is fundamentally why there is no tradeoff between them.

The same non-competitive double agency also helps make sense of the interplay of divinity and humanity over the course of Christ's life and death. Rather than competing with his humanity, pushing it out or supplanting it, the divinity of Christ, through union with

---

4. For more on this account of incarnation, see Chapter 1, *Jesus, Humanity, and the Trinity*.

Christ's humanity, perfects that humanity, sanctifying it as the supreme manifestation of human life in divine form. By performing otherwise ordinary human acts, such as dying on a cross, Christ saves us from sin, heals us, and elevates us to a life beyond death, as only God can do for us. In this way, the human and the divine work together in Christ's life for the same saving effects, in conformity with the general way that, according to Aquinas, God as creator brings about the very human acts and effects that achieve God's own ends. This is the theanthropic character of Christ's work that an Eastern theologian like John of Damascus stresses.

Unusually, I combine this account of double agency with an almost hyper-Protestant view of sin, both before and after Christ's coming. With Thomas, I affirm that double agency holds with respect to whatever it is about our acts that is good; double agency does not apply in the same way to the sinful character of our acts, since a good God's creative agency cannot be creating us in those very respects. In short, God does not will our sinfulness in the same way God wills the goodness of our actions.

But the world in which we live, from a Protestant point of view, is thoroughly marred by pervasive sin; there is not much good to speak of, then, to which double agency might apply in an unqualified way. Double agency does not hold in the way it ideally should, in other words, since the world itself is so far from ideal. Contrary to what double agency might lead one to expect, human beings, of their own accord—that is, in following their own motives and intentions—are never doing exactly what God wants them to do. Their sin, in other words, blocks the direct realization of God's will for them as it would otherwise follow from God's own creative agency with respect to them. For example, God wills them to be creatures of love, and instead they are driven by selfish disregard for the well-being of others, even by hatred for them.

Of course, God can still fulfil God's own good intentions for the world by way of flawed human instruments; what humans intend for evil, God can intend for good and thereby overrule. This might mean redirecting the consequences of sinful actions, after the fact, so that what we intend to happen doesn't. But it might also mean God's overriding of the sinful character of such acts at once, in the way, for example, a doctor's intentions to heal can take precedence over a subordinate's intentions to harm in and through the very same painful surgical procedure. In any case, given an account of double agency, God must still be working with sinful agents—their activity would otherwise amount to nothing at all. But what God wants and what we want remain severely misaligned. Even when the effects of our agency conform to God's, we do what we do for the wrong reasons, in much the way that the crucifixion, which is the product of sinful human action, nevertheless has a saving character by way of divine power.

Moreover, because human beings are made for a close relationship with God—indeed, for the very closest of relationships as that which is found in Christ—sin wrecks everything and is thereby magnified. It's not just that sin interrupts the intimacy of one's relationship with God; once *that* is disrupted, everything else is too. Sin prevents us from having the sort of close relationship with God that is a precondition for the excellent operation of our ordinary human faculties.

In my understanding of human persons, they are not created to have self-sufficient operations that simply actualize their own created capacities; instead, they require the gift of divine powers—the Holy Spirit—to operate well, even as the human creatures they are, knowing, willing, and desiring well in their everyday affairs. For this reason, by disrupting the gift of God's presence to us as an active influence on our lives, sin prevents us from exercising even basic human functions as one should; one cannot know or will or desire well in matters of even ordinary life. One's faculties are, in this way, corrupt and incapacitated from top to bottom. Utter depravity, as Calvin would have it, is the norm, in short, apart from Christ. This is true in a quite radical and uncompromising fashion, in that even the external appearance of rectitude and wisdom in ordinary affairs is lost by way of the warping of one's relationship to God through sin.

I affirm, furthermore—with Luther more than Calvin—that the struggle against sin continues with surprising virulence in Christian lives. Everything is different, at once and absolutely, by virtue of what God has accomplished for us in Christ; we are now new creatures, forgiven and favored by God through the gift of Christ and the Holy Spirit to us, forming a kind of new motor sufficient for leading transformed lives. In meeting people whose lives have already been shaped by sin, what Christ has accomplished for us nevertheless takes time to show itself fully in our lives; sin remains in us as an ultimately vanquished but not yet fully overcome enemy. In quantitative terms, regarding the degree and extent of manifest sin, there may indeed be little to show for what is qualitatively different about us in virtue of Christ's accomplishments for us; we may not be obviously better than we were before or better than many non-Christians. Such a conclusion is partly based on empirical observation of Christian behavior, but the primary theological lesson to be drawn from the recognition of continuing Christian fault is to refocus attention, in good Lutheran fashion, on what Christ has done for us, which is final and sufficient, and to turn attention away from comparative judgments of relative human sanctity. It is, of course, important that we make every effort to lead holier lives—Christ and the Holy Spirit have become ours for just that purpose. However, the degree and extent of that transformation relative to others are really of little moment and easily tempt one into unseemly forms of boasting and self-congratulation that downplay the importance of what Christ has already done, for all intents and purposes, without us.

Despite my emphasis on the seriousness of sin, my treatment of Christ's saving work does not put sin front and center. Instead, in a more Eastern theological fashion, Christ's elevation of the human beyond the limitations of finitude is the focus. From the very beginning of God's relationship with the world, God has intended to give us the gifts of God's own life to the greatest degree possible, as that might be achieved by establishing the closest possible relationship with us in Christ. Through Christ, we participate in God and thereby come to enjoy what only God would otherwise enjoy—eternal life. Death (as both something natural and the consequence of sin) is, in that way, overcome, along with all the other features of finitude that go along with it—loss, corruption, disappointment, conflict, decomposition, disintegration, and so on.[5]

The means of accomplishing all that also provides a remedy for sin—destroying its dominance in human life. The primary intent of God from the beginning was to give us God's own life through Christ; sin is simply overcome on the way to that primary end. A kind of blip—awful though it may be—in the course of God's own efforts to fulfil God's primary intentions for the world, sin will be overcome through the very mechanism God designed from the beginning: the gift to us of eternal life through Christ.

When the elevation of the human to participation in God's own life—or deification—is the primary matter for discussion, it is the incarnation that comes to the fore, not just the fact of it, but the way it underlies everything else that Jesus does and suffers in order to save us over the course of his life and death. Incarnation means that the humanity of Christ has been brought into unity with the divine in him

---

5. I am following Athanasius here in my understanding of the relationship between death and sin. Death is a natural feature of created existence, but apart from sin, the fact of it would have been stayed by the gift of grace to human beings at their creation. The loss of grace through sin therefore leads to a world of actual death.

so as to communicate thereby what is divine—eternal life—to that humanity (and through him to us). The mechanism of that transfer, or "happy exchange," as Luther would call it, is the uniting of the one to the other that God in Christ brings about—in other words, the way, to use more traditional language, God assumes the human to itself, making it God's own in the one person of Christ.

For all its mystery, the idea of transfer here, by way of unity, is rather common-sensical. To use an old patristic analogy, consider the way the properties of fire are transferred to iron, which is otherwise nothing like it, through contact with a lit torch to which, let's say, it has been firmly and irrevocably affixed. Without ever being more than iron in and of itself—were the flame to be removed, it would return to its cold, hard self—the iron now enjoys what is other than itself—light and heat—enjoying them as its own only by way of attachment to what it is not: a flame.

In the process of being elevated beyond itself, the iron's own impurities (those elements that might impede its becoming red-hot) are also purged by the fire, burned out of it. Following this analogy, think of our sins as impurities preventing the reception of divine life, which union with God is in the process of eradicating. Because Christ's humanity is joined from the first with God—because that humanity has no existence apart from unity with God—the unimpeded power of a purely good God in Christ's human life makes sin simply impossible for him. The divine life which blankets his humanity also addresses the effects of human sin on him, so as to heal and resurrect him from the sin he suffers. When Christ makes contact with us by way of the humanity he shares with us, our sins are also thereby in the process of being burned up or wiped out, in a fight or struggle against the sin already active in us. Our own unity with God, by way of Christ's, assures our victory over sin, however dim the prospects may be when considered simply in light of our continued failings.

In short, the problem of sin and the limits of finitude—for example, death and conflict—are both overcome through the same mechanism of incarnation. By being taken up into unity with the divine, the suffering and death that Jesus undergoes are defeated—he is resurrected to eternal life—and sin is overthrown.

If sin were the focus rather than deification, the incarnation might not figure so centrally in the understanding of Christ's saving work. One might, instead, highlight his obedience to God in the mission upon which he was sent, or the way his death paid the penalty for sin or appeased the wrath of God that would otherwise have been directed at us. Moral and legal categories, in sum, might easily provide the frame for understanding Christ's saving work. Making incarnation itself the primary mechanism of Christ's saving work avoids those categories or radically re-interprets them. Thus, what primarily happens on the cross is Christ's suffering and death brought into unity with the divine in him and, in that way, defeated. Everything that Christ does and undergoes over the course of his life is brought into unity with the divine with saving effects, and his death is no different. He dies *for* us, then, not in a juridical sense of substitution—an innocent man paying the penalty for the guilty (which could easily seem morally and legally objectionable)—but in the sense of benefiting us by overcoming death through undergoing it himself in ways that will become ours through him.

Notice how these seemingly disparate elements—from Catholic, Protestant, and Eastern theologies—hold together. The center is the Eastern idea of deification, the idea that God has created us to begin with in order for us to enjoy the highest good of God's own life through participation in God. Deification solves the problem, so to speak, of finitude; it remedies the conflicts and losses that are endemic to created life per se. Though created life is good despite all its inherent problems, God wants to give us more—Godself through unity with God.

Although sin is not the preoccupation here in the way it would be if God's primary goal for us were simply moral probity, it nonetheless leads to extreme worries about the effects of sin on human life. Rather than downplaying the seriousness of sin relative to the deficiencies of finitude, my account shows how magnified worries about sin and a stress on deification go together. If human beings were created at the start to live their lives in God—it being their original created condition—the loss of that state is likely to be completely disabling. Hyper-Protestant worries about sin follow in this way from an account of deification as our original state. God gives us the requisite grace from the start, though in a way that we can forfeit by sinning. The gift that God intends us to have is so great that the loss of it through sin becomes an equally profound calamity.

An account of incarnation is also central to all this, since Christ represents the goal of human life—the enjoyment of life in God—and the means by which we gain it in an irrevocable way, despite our sin. From the very beginning, we were to be like Christ through him, that is, those who, in unity with God, have the gift of God's own life for their own. Through Christ, we are to become like Christ in a way we cannot forfeit, whatever the extent of the sin that still remains in us. By virtue of the humanity he shares with us and the Holy Spirit he spreads abroad in the depths of our hearts, Christ makes us his own, even as the sinners we are, with a power to renovate our lives both now and after death. In this way, the saving effects of incarnation bring to perhaps surprising fruition the general Thomistic idea that fulsome gifts from God are ours by way of dependence upon God, the greater that dependence—in its intimacy and extent—the better.

Finally, this way of synthesizing different theological strands of the Christian tradition has a clear practical force; it provides direction for

Christian life. First of all—and perhaps most obviously—it suggests the need to respect the equal dignity of all created things. Whatever their differences and relative ranking for different purposes, everything is created in the same direct way by God and is to be valued as such, from at least a baseline of equality. God's loving concern as creator is not a matter of degree but holds in the same way for everything; we are therefore to respect that fact in our treatment of them, so as to promote their well-being and flourishing.[6]

Perhaps less obviously, there are principles that God abides by across God's relations with the world as its creator and redeemer, which have an ethical import.[7] The principle of unconditional giving, for example, is found in different forms across God's relations with the world. God gives to the world unconditionally in creating it, in the sense that there is nothing in the world to condition God's creation of it. Nothing precedes God's creation of the world to make it more or less likely to happen or to help establish what it is that God creates. God, instead, out of sheer beneficence, creates the world from the ground up in a thoroughly comprehensive way. God remains, moreover, the creator of the world—its sustainer—whatever we do; God exercises unconditional mercy toward us in maintaining us in existence despite our sins. And, of course, God's grace in Christ is unconditional, or without prior requirements, in that Christ saves us while we are still sinners, without our having done anything of ourselves to deserve it. The same principle of unconditional giving could be carried over in some appropriate new way into our own lives—for example, by working for the well-being of others without setting conditions that have to be met by them beforehand.

---

6. For more on this, see Kathryn Tanner, Chapter 5, *Politics of God: Christian Theologies and Social Justice* (Minneapolis: Fortress, 1994; 30th Anniversary Edition, 2022).

7. For more on these principles, including the principle of unconditional giving, see Kathryn Tanner, Chapter 2, *Economy of Grace* (Minneapolis: Fortress, 2005).

What I've provided here is simply an example of my own efforts to make sense of what Christianity is all about and, on that basis, to propose some ideas about what Christianity should stand for in the world. If the historical record is any indication, Christianity can mean many different things to different people, for both good and ill. Because nothing has been finally settled, every Christian has to assume responsibility for making sense of Christianity for themselves as a way of living. As followers of an unusually broad Anglican way, we are uniquely positioned to do so, I believe, in ways that both reflect contemporary challenges and speak to the whole church.

Further Reading Recommendations

MacDougall, Scott. *The Shape of Anglican Theology: Faith Seeking Wisdom.* Leiden: Brill, 2022.

McIntosh, Mark. *Mysteries of Faith.* Cambridge, MA: Cowley, 2000.

Tanner, Kathryn. *Jesus, Humanity and the Trinity: A Brief Systematic Theology.* Minneapolis: Fortress, 2001.

Williams, Rowan. *On Christian Theology.* Oxford: Wiley-Blackwell, 1999.

Accounting for the Movement: The Vocation of the Theologian

Anthony D. Baker

What Is Theology?

Christian theology is, first of all, a study of motion. When Augustine describes his youthful explorations of Manicheism, he explains how he eventually turned aside from this doctrine not because he was able to outthink its rhetors, but rather because he had lost "hope of making any progress" in it.[1] There was simply no trajectory for moral and contemplative growth within the rigid dualism of that intellectual system. The parable of the Prodigal provides the *figura* for the *Confessions*: his life is the story of a journey from and to his home with the Father. Even before he was conscious of the one calling him home, he says, "I began to rise up, in order to return to you."[2]

Of course, faith and theology are not the only ways of remaining in motion. Life itself is movement. A human life moves in all the ways that animal life does—toward food, shelter, companionship, and procreation. Humans also define themselves by a kind of meta-motion, a movement of all this motion toward meaningfulness. To

---

1. Augustine, *The Confessions* V. 10,18. All references are from *Confessions*, trans. Maria Boulding (Hyde Park, NY: New City Press, 2012).
2. Augustine, *Conf.* III. 4,7.

live a human life is to have hopes, to live with regrets, and to seek to shape ourselves and our lives in ways that bring us joy. To stall out in this internal journey, to cease making progress toward meaning and joy, is to lose track of our own existence. It is even, perhaps, to fall into depression or into an aggressive and unscrupulous pursuit of our own self-made meaningfulness. Augustine recognized this latter potential for a vicious movement, noting within it a deeper sense that one is no longer progressing toward anything true. So even while stalling out with the Manichees, he "was walking a dark and slippery path, searching for you outside myself and failing to find the God of my own heart."[3] There are thus many ways of moving through life that diminish us, but only a movement toward our creator expands and increases our being.[4]

For this reason, Christian faith is not a faith in what simply keeps us in motion, but in what keeps us in motion toward our true end, the God who is both beyond us and ever more deeply within us.[5] As Augustine worked his way through the major doctrinal mysteries posed by faith in Christ's resurrection, this question of rightly directed movement remained central. The story of God becoming human is, at its core for him, an invitation toward the paradoxical motion of the God-human: "But we by pressing on imitate him who abides motionless; we follow him who stands still, and by walking in him we move toward him, because for us he became a road or way in time by his humility, while being for us an eternal abode by his divinity."[6]

---

3. Augustine, *Conf.* VI. 1,1.

4. See Marie-Anne Vannier, "Aversion and Conversion," in *The Cambridge Companion to Augustine's "Confessions,"* ed. Tarmo Toom (Cambridge: Cambridge University Press, 2020), 63–74.

5. *Conf.* III. 6,11.

6. *De Trinitate* VII. All Augustine references are from *The Trinity*, trans. Edmund Hill (Brooklyn: New City Press, 1991).

The incarnate God is a way that opens for commerce between eternity and time.

Eventually, even his image of God as "him who abides motionless" undergoes a revision. To see creation as filled with vestiges of the triune God suggests that there is something akin to movement in God. Thus, he comes to describe the triune God as the pattern for all human charity: God is something like lovers approaching one another.[7] Or again, as he gives more attention to God's unity than his "two lovers" model allows, he suggests that the soul's capacity for remembering, understanding, and willing has an analog in God.[8] The creator, that is to say, is something like a desire that reaches to recall and understand a memory: a single *substantia* who exists in the passage among these three nodes.

Crucially, though, we are *imago dei* not simply as external imitations, as if the divine pattern were transferred to us as to a new piece of cloth. That is too static an image of our sharing in God's nature. Since God is the pattern of all patterns, not an extrinsic other to anything that is, the only way into the pattern is also the pathway into God. To move toward God is to move into God, and so the real source of the soul's existence as a divine image is the simple fact that always, within the depths of any remembering, understanding, and loving, the soul is "able to remember and understand and love him by whom it was made."[9] In this sense, then, to move into God's presence is to move into God's motion; the deified person is the one who changes so as to remember with divine memory, to know with God's understanding, and to desire with God's *caritas*.

If we understand this motion to be about our growing awareness of God's coming near to us and our response of progressing toward

---

7. *De trin.* VIII.
8. *De trin.* XIV.
9. *De trin.* XIV.15.

and ultimately into God, then prayer is its most essential form. To be a theologian is, in the broadest sense, to move in contemplation toward God. This is why Evagrius tells us that the one who prays is a theologian, and the theologian is the one who prays.[10]

But in a more focused sense, the theologian is the one who attends to the movement itself, which structures all Christian life and prayer. How might I give an account in language of the way in which God approaches us, and the way by which we, so often stuck inside our own limited visions and horizons, approach God? This account-giving is the primary work of the specialized discipline of constructive (sometimes called "systematic," "doctrinal," or "dogmatic") theology.

To define theology in this way is already to make it obvious, I hope, how the discipline serves the church. A church, whether Episcopal, Independent Baptist, or Syrian Orthodox, is a community that exists as, and only as, a participation in God's life-giving movement. When human creatures gather to worship the risen Christ through Word and Table, we are doing the hard work of bringing all the motion that has constituted and is constituting our lives along with us as we make our way toward God. In worship, we make the bold and hope-filled claim that all that has formed us as the people we are can journey with us toward God's altar.

Again, in a broad sense, all that happens in a life of faith can be characterized as theology. More narrowly, theology is the work of disciplining our language—as we pray, preach, sing hymns, counsel a friend, mourn at a funeral, or laugh at a wedding—to ensure that we are bearing witness as faithfully as possible to the God who comes near us and to the Spirit-filled motion of a Godward human life.

---

10. Evagrius Ponticus, *Chapters on Prayer* 61. In Evagrius Ponticus, *The Praktikos and Chapters On Prayer*, trans. John Eudes Bamberger, OCSO (Collegeville, MN: Cistercian Publications, 2022).

Like Augustine, the Greek Church developed a vision of Christian faith with divine motion at its center. The term *perichoresis*, sometimes translated (not that helpfully) as "circumincession," and meaning motion, circulation, dance, or interpenetration, is a fascinating study in its own right. Though never one of the primary vocabulary terms debated at the councils, it endures across the centuries in light of its compelling imagery. The fourth century uses the term primarily as a way of maintaining the unity and duality of Christ: he is a single *hypostasis* in which divinity and humanity interpenetrate. The eroticism we have already seen in Augustine, and familiar to the later mystics, manifests itself here as fundamental Christology: Christ is a union so powerful and irrevocable that it is like two bodies connecting not just externally but deeply within one another.

Since the arguments for the unity and duality of Christ are always the reverse of arguments about the vocation of human life itself—"He, indeed, assumed humanity that we might become God"[11]—the motion of *perichoresis* is a fitting way to describe divinization. The intimacy of the union of Christ's humanity with the divine Logos, that is to say, is an intimacy also offered to us: "I said, you are gods" (John 10:34, RSV). This is no more the extinction of our humanity, though, than Christ's divinity was the dissolution of his. Like sexual union, our hoped-for union with God only manifests in light of the duality, and the duality is at its most pronounced in the act of unification. Thus, the dance of *perichoresis* is a testimony about the being of Christ as well as a testament to the great Christian hope. In Christ, we find that creatures are ultimately nothing more nor less than a set of innumerable and unique ways of pressing on toward the eternal God.

---

11. Athanasius, *On the Incarnation* 54, from the edition at CCEL: https://ccel.org/ccel/athanasius/incarnation/incarnation.ix.html.

That is how Gregory of Nyssa put it, anyhow, borrowing language from Paul's letter to the Philippians.[12]

It was several centuries later that John of Damascus made use of the term to speak of the movement interior to the Godhead. Intentionally echoing the Christological language of the Council of Chalcedon, three hundred years prior, John wrote that the Father, Son, and Holy Ghost "are united, as we said, so as not to be confused, but to adhere closely together, and they have their circumincession one in the other without any blending or mingling and without change or division in substance."[13] The God whose unity cannot be described without or beyond the distinctiveness of persons is a God of intrinsic motion. God is something like a parent who moves in love toward a child. And yet, God is also a child who stretches in love back toward the parent. Further, God is the one for whom that exchanged love is so singular and alive that it can only be described as a consubstantial third.

In this way, the witness of the Christian faith could be characterized as a *perichoresis* of *perichoreses*: an intimate coordination of convergent movements. We creatures are invited to move in our laden finitude toward the movement that is the dance of humanity and divinity in Christ; this movement does not come to a standstill in the divine nature, but enters the eternal dance that is the Triune God. Our everlasting Sabbath's rest, Maximus the Confessor says, is to move only with the loving motion of the triune God.[14]

---

12. Gregory, *Life of Moses* 225. In Gregory of Nyssa, *The Life of Moses*, trans. Abraham J. Malherbe and Everett Ferguson (Mahwah, New Jersey: Paulist Press, 1978).

13. John of Damascus, *On the Orthodox Faith* I.8, in Saint John of Damascus, *Writings*, trans. Frederic H. Chase (Washington, DC: Catholic University of America Press, 1958).

14. Maximus, *Ambiguum* 7.1076C, in Maximus the Confessor, *On Difficulties in the Church Fathers: The Ambigua*, trans. Nicholas Constas (Cambridge, MA: Harvard University Press, 2014).

Theology, to repeat, is the discipline of disciplining our faith language, so as to ensure that we are speaking as well as we know how to speak of these perichoretic *perichoreses*. The ancient and medieval councils, at their best, passed along to the churches the Creeds and their interpretations as guides to this way of speaking. (At their worst, such as at the iconoclastic council of 754, they passed along ways of speaking that were later deemed blockades to this Godward movement.) As such, they offer something like a grammar of the animated life of the Christian church. Speak carefully of Christ and the Spirit, these Creeds warn, lest you wind up offering a doctrine in which the disciple of Jesus can make no progress. Or worse, one in which she can only progress away from the bountiful life of her creator.

Theology, then, is the grammar of the grand adventure of a life lived toward and ultimately within the God who has, from eternity, been alive with loving movement.

My Life in Theology

My first adventures with this study in divine motion were in my youth, in a Christian world centered on the Holiness churches—mostly the Church of the Nazarene, but also my grandparents' Wesleyan Church—of Indiana. From the pulpits on Sunday mornings and nights, Wednesday nights, and every night of the week during spring and fall revivals, I heard sermons preached about reverence for God's holiness and the importance of a commitment to sanctified living. As I entered my teenage years, not surprisingly, I began to entertain doubts and questions about both the character of that God and the human morality implied by that character.

My parents are committed students of the Bible, and my father, in particular, is eclectic and somewhat voracious in his selection of other readings. From my earliest days, I saw enchanting titles on the family bookshelf, such as Edith Schaeffer's *The Tapestry*, C. S. Lewis's *The Great Divorce* ("How can divorce be great?" I wondered), and Paul Tillich's *The Eternal Now*, sandwiched between the *Baseball Encyclopedia*, the complete works of Dickens, and the poetry of Alexander Pope. A key moment in my theological formation came one Sunday after hearing a sermon that made use of one of our pastor's favorite sayings: the reminder of our calling to follow "God's clearly revealed will." That evening, over our habitually simple Sunday supper (the midday meal being the feast), Dad made an observation that meant more to my teenage angst than I imagine he intended: "I don't think God's will has ever been all that clearly revealed to me." That confession became my permission to ask questions and acknowledge complexity, even if the Christian mentors around me were nervous about where this searching might lead. I had not yet read Augustine, but I was sensing in my body what the ancient saint observed in language: while I could make no progress toward the God of that sermonic adage, my father's honest reflection revealed a God who was beckoning me from the shadows.

My quest for this mysterious God led me to break away from a path toward ordained ministry at the Nazarene university I attended. By that time, I was too steeped in Karl Barth, Søren Kierkegaard, and the classical and postmodern philosophers to feel I had a moment for practical questions about church administration or pastoral care. My theology professor fed me books at just about the speed at which I could digest them, and let me know that I had a gift for patient and thoughtful interpretation of challenging texts.

Perhaps the most important detour in my pathway into theology came during a study abroad program in my junior year, in Nizhni Novgorod, Russia. I ended up there somewhat by chance—or, more accurately, because of my late-adolescent habit of procrastination. Two friends and I had devised a plan to add a Spanish major to our primary courses of study by spending a fall semester in a university-sponsored program in Costa Rica. My friends secured their places, but by the time I got around to calling the program, it was already full. "We do have space in our Russian Studies Program," the organizer told me. "OK," I said, and I recall saying it with barely concealed gloominess, "I'll go there."

So off I went, alone, to post-Soviet Russia. The program director was a lovely and brilliant Mennonite named Harley, and the students were all, in one way or another, young adults trying to work out the existential intersection where faith meets the strange beauty of human culture. Along with studies of the language, close readings of Tolstoy, and explorations of the splendid and threatened ecology of Lake Baikal, we read and discussed a good bit of theology and church history. We learned about the Old Believers, studied the icon of the Virgin of Vladimir, explored Orthodox monasteries, and interviewed priests and monks. On one such outing, an unsponsored excursion that a couple of my classmates and I took, I came within a hair's breadth of being re-baptized by a group of the faithful under the orders of an itinerant prophet who happened to look—and sound, as I imagine him—like Rasputin. As it happened, the parish priest intervened, operating from a sounder ecclesiology and anthropology, and the young American was sent back to the university just as Protestant and singly baptized as when he had arrived.

During my time there, I also met some evangelical Protestant missionaries who spoke with charisma about their vision to bring salvation to a godless Russia. I began to feel a contrast between the faith they were offering and the faith I had been coming to terms with in those Orthodox churches. I told Harley what I was puzzling over, and he said it sounded as though I had just landed on my topic for the required research paper, due in December. So, I wrote my first theology paper, entirely with pen and paper. My thesis was that the word "salvation" meant something different to those Russian Orthodox believers than it did to the American missionaries. I cannot imagine that my essay was very good, but I came home with a strange feeling that I had discovered a way of combining language, curiosity, and love for God that I would never get over.

To be honest, I didn't like the Orthodox way at first. I rejected the solemnity with which they chanted their prayers and scoffed at the awe and reverence displayed by the old and young as they kissed the icons. But as I matured with those memories, I came to see that the God of Dad's unclear revelation was the God of ancient liturgical mystery. Looking back, I can see that I was discovering a faith that was a good bit wilder than the domesticated holiness of my youth. I began to see that there were Christians, some contemporary, some a thousand and a half years old, who were more committed to moving Godward than I had ever been.

I walked alone through many old churches that fall. Several were in ruins, while others had been repurposed as storage units for grain, tractors, or construction materials. Sometimes I would enter during the Divine Service and see the worshipers huddled over in one corner or side chapel around a makeshift iconostasis and altar. Once, I wandered through a roofless brick church out in the countryside, where the entire nave was filled with several feet of dirt. I discovered that a cave had been dug out under one end, and candles and icons had been brought in. Another time, I watched a man who could barely walk fall to his knees in the street in genuflection in front of his village church, before struggling back to his feet and limping off with his cane.

This was a faith, I was gathering, with a capacity to endure, to stay in motion despite all efforts to bring it to a standstill.

By the time I was in a graduate program in theology at the University of Virginia, it was clear that I was migrating away from the Church of the Nazarene toward the world of ancient liturgy. This was a common pattern among holiness and evangelical youth of my generation, and several of us found one another and gave each other much-needed encouragement as we discerned whether to stay and, if not, where to go. I attended Roman Catholic Mass a few times, joined Orthodox worship when I could, and eventually found my way into an Episcopal Church. Sister Ellen at St. Paul's Church in Indianapolis, the city where I lived while writing my dissertation, was a member of some Episcopal order that I've forgotten. She was a great help to me in shaping my intellectual journey into a journey of faith. After hearing her teach one Sunday on prayer, I walked up to her with a Book of Common Prayer in my hands and said something like, "Help?" We met together, and I began discovering that the words of Episcopalians were ones in which I, too, could move Godward.

The rector soon asked me to be theologian-in-residence, which meant that I had the challenge of sorting out which aspects of what I was reading and writing were helpful to a group of laypeople seeking to deepen their faith. I imagine I swung at more pitches than I hit back in those early days. But I felt a growing sense within me that theology is a language that lives in churches, a language that inherits the disciplined wisdom of ancient councils, and one that is utterly useless if it cannot offer a praying people a way to move in Christ toward the triune God.

By the time I arrived at the Seminary of the Southwest in Austin as a newly minted Ph.D. and assistant professor of systematic theology, I had begun a life pursuing that God of the shadowy corners with the aid of—among others—Augustine, the Greek Fathers, and a rather orthodoxy-bending group of Russian Orthodox theologians.

I also brought with me my childhood and adolescent passage through those Holiness churches. When I was confirmed at St. David of Wales in Austin, Texas, I wrote a letter to one of my ancestors. A (then) living aunt, skilled in genealogy, had found photos and stories of the woman in that branch of the family who, in the middle of the nineteenth century, had first left the Church of England to become a dissenter and evangelist. So I wrote a letter to "Grandma Lightly." I explained to her that I didn't see my movement back to Canterbury as undoing hers, but rather as a way of taking along all the formation that the Holiness tradition had given me and carrying it back to the Church that had birthed it. I suggested we consider ourselves as bookending a familial detour, one that was formative for the faith of our family and might, in some small part, return as a gift both to the Holiness churches and to the Anglican tradition.

My Work in Theology

The question that constantly motivates me to read more deeply and write more honestly is one that springs from my father's confession on that long-ago Sunday evening. Who is this God who never appears except as mediated by the less-than-clear revelations of bodies and language?

My most recent book, *Leaving Emmaus*, asks this question in a broad and summarizing way, imagining the moment of Christ's sudden absence from the table in Luke 24 to be the moment when theology begins.[15] The disciples must leave home—literally, but also figuratively, by letting go of their isolated convictions—so that they can begin to work together to craft and discipline a language that

---

15. Anthony D. Baker, *Leaving Emmaus: A New Departure in Christian Theology* (Waco: Baylor University Press, 2021).

bears faithful witness to the resurrected Christ. I designed this book as a single-volume systematic theology, or what is sometimes called a minor dogmatics.

As I work with the question of God's hidden revelations, I am especially drawn to formulations of holiness, no doubt an inheritance from my Christian upbringing. My first book asked a fairly simple question and found a rather complex answer: Can participation in the divine nature be the goal of human life without destroying or dissolving human nature?[16] The answer that I found, as I worked through key texts from scripture to literature to postmodern philosophers, was that God's nature can be our perfection only if God is not the sort of being who confronts us as an "other," but is instead the deep and transcendent truth of all natures that exist. So the little perfections we find in our finite life become diagonal lines that stretch toward God's infinitely perfect being. I hope to return to this project eventually and expand it into a fuller, multi-volume account of deification, or Christian holiness.

Nested within this central focus of my writing are other foci that provide windows onto the question of God's ambiguous and mediated revelations. A project on Shakespeare was born when I learned that Elizabethan and Jacobean theater outlawed any direct references to doctrine. What if Shakespeare's plotted explorations of grace, wickedness, and human transformation, I wondered, are in fact ways of practicing theology when God is ordered off stage? Further, could it be that the discipline of keeping God off stage makes for better theology than much of the more direct God-talk in the pamphlets and sermons of his day? The fun for me, in what eventually became *Shakespeare, Theology, and the Unstaged God*, was the

---

16. Anthony D. Baker, *Diagonal Advance: Perfection in Christian Theology* (Eugene, OR: Cascade, 2011). Published by SCM in the UK.

ever-present paradoxical "rhyme" at the center of his dramaturgy (at least as I interpreted it) and my theological work: the God whose will and being are never clearly revealed is the God of the deepest, most compelling revelations.[17]

Another pursuit nested in that larger project is a fascination with biology, especially shaped around a search for God in the fragility and resilience of living things. Could the long experimental history of evolution be a kind of *perichoresis*—a stretching out, that is, toward the wild and excessive life of God? If so, what ways of interacting with the world of non-human life increase our collective capacity to move toward God? What modes of interaction have the opposite effect? I find myself consistently circling a thesis here that continues to come as a surprise: if God is hidden in living things, we gain or lose the capacity to know and love God as we gain or lose the capacity to know and love the lives with which we share God's world.

Theology and The Episcopal Church

Two decades of teaching theology at the Seminary of the Southwest and at Saint Julian of Norwich Episcopal Church, where I now serve as theologian-in-residence, have revealed to me a church that is both rich in and in dire need of good theology.

Our movement toward God is rarely aided, I suspect, by the lunging movements that comprise the global culture wars. My first year in the seminary classroom was also the year of The Windsor Report, the Anglican Communion's study of ecclesiology and human sexuality in light of the consecration of the first openly gay bishop in the Communion. I saw students with deep affection for one another,

---

17. Anthony D. Baker, *Shakespeare, Theology, and the Unstaged God* (London: Routledge, 2019).

yet with little idea of how to converse across their differing convictions. In the years since, as the United States and other nations have seen divides deepening between rich and poor, right and left, urban centers and peripheral towns, these conversations have not gotten any easier. In classrooms and churches, I have observed divisions between those who disdain the Creeds as the documents of old, dead (somehow) white men, and those who hold to the Nicene verbiage in a manner similar to how my old evangelical friends held to the formulaic proclamations of a decision for Christ. In none of that, I find, is there room for much theology. Nor do I find there any promise of progress.

This is not to say that complex questions of ethics and politics fall beyond the pale of theology. To the contrary, questions that people of faith ask about difficult topics like the configurations of races and genders, immigration, wealth, and the sometimes competitive goods of care for women and care for unborn children ought to rely on theology for their discernment. The trouble comes when convictions about those difficult topics become the magnetic pull on our language, prior to any of the theological account-giving I referenced above. Thus, many communities of faith have dealt with the growing cultural divisions by branding themselves for one side over the other. That, I believe, is a strategy to walk down Augustine's ultimately abandoned dark and slippery path. It suggests that theology is a kind of group conviction, a shared way of thinking and speaking that allows those thinkers and speakers to feel as though they belong. Theology is that, but it is not yet theology if that is all it is. If theology were a disciplinary name for the courageous utterance of self-assured convictions, I would be ill-suited for this vocation.

As I attempt to teach and practice it, theology is the communal language that emerges across time and space as Christians take the risk of offering to one another, for mutual disciplining, their words about the always murkily revealed God. Have I spoken of the Incarnate God in a way that interferes with our prayers to rest in God's eternal dance? Help me—classmate, mentor, parishioner, Gregory of Nyssa, Teresa of Ávila—to find better words. I cannot do this without a cloud of witnesses, living and dead, who are prepared to take this risk with me.

This is the dire need of The Episcopal Church for good theology: within and around our churches exist people who are pulled and pushed in various directions. Can we rediscover a disciplined language that will give them the best possible opportunity to find themselves approached by God in Christ and moved by the Spirit into what the Apostle Peter calls a *koinonia*—fellowship, participation, another "dance" sort of word—with the divine nature (2 Peter 1:4)?

But our church is also rich with resources for theological adventuring. We have a prayer book filled with carefully structured language, designed to habitualize this desired movement in our churches, families, and private prayers. It also offers us disciplines like the observation of a holy Lent, with its call to self-examination, invoking in us a deep questioning as to what sort of path we find ourselves moving down.

Further, as may be obvious from all I have said above, one of the most welcoming aspects of Episcopal theology for me is its lack of proprietary sectarianism. Our church, seminary, and private libraries can fill up with books by Anglicans and Catholics, Orthodox and Pentecostals. We learn from philosophers, conservationists, poets, and playwrights.

The only way to wander out of bounds, in this expansive tradition, is to move ourselves and others away from the perichoretic God revealed in the perichoretic Christ to be our perichoretic end. This is the ancient faith of Augustine and so many others, and it consists most simply in the hope and trust that every creaturely movement comes to its fullest and most expansive flourishing as it finds its way into its creator. The church's theologians are tasked with nothing more or less than reminding us to keep taking the risk of speaking well of that journey.

Further Reading Recommendations

Coakley, Sarah. *God, Sexuality and the Self: An Essay "On the Trinity."* Cambridge: Cambridge University Press, 2013.

Mascall, E. L. *Existence and Analogy: A Sequel to* He Who Is. Foreword by Rowan Williams. Brooklyn: Angelico Press, 2023. Originally published in 1949.

Rogers, Eugene F., Jr. *Elements of Christian Thought: A Basic Course in Christianese.* Minneapolis: Fortress Press, 2021.

Sonderegger, Katherine. *Systematic Theology, Volume 2. The Doctrine of the Holy Trinity: Processions and Persons.* Minneapolis: Fortress Press, 2020.

Reflections on God's Presence

Thomas Holtzen

How Did You Become a Theologian?

Growing up on a farm in rural Nebraska, I had a deep sense of God's presence all around me. Most of my early life was spent outdoors, from sunup to sundown. I saw God's presence in the sunrise when the sky was aflame with orange, in the damp must of the earth being turned for spring planting, in the green ribbons of growing crops, in the sweet, dry brome grass of summer pastures, in the rivers of golden grain that poured forth during harvest, in the ewes giving birth to January lambs, and in the sky aflame with red, orange, and pink hues as the sun set over fields of sand-colored corn stalks in winter. To me, these daily revelations in nature were witnesses of God. I was too young to explain it; I only knew that I longed to respond.

One day, when I was a young boy and my mother was working in the kitchen, I told her, "I want to be a minister." She promptly told me, "Put that idea out of your head." My mother was very religious, one of the godliest people I have ever known, but she was also very practical. My father, a farmer, was chairman of the board of the Methodist Church to which we belonged. He oversaw the building of the new Methodist Church in our small hometown, which was full of good, salt-of-the-earth people. We were a religious family, if that can be measured by never missing a Sunday at church. But their son, a minister? Farmers measured the value of things by their productivity, like the number of lambs, piglets, or calves the livestock produced, the number of eggs the chickens laid, or the yield of crops. Unlike farmers, ministers were college-educated, not very practical people, and it was hard to say what, if any, yield they had. My aspirations were impractical. At the time, I accepted their impracticality and put them aside. My future was already decided: I was going to be a farmer.

Yet God has a strange way of intervening when we least expect it. During Christmas break of my freshman year at the University of Nebraska-Lincoln (UNL), my father died in a farm accident. As we dealt with the aftershocks, my brothers and I took over farming the home place. Every weekend, I drove home from college to the farm. Managing the farm work as well as my classes was difficult enough. But worse, my agricultural economics classes were not satisfying. After discussing the situation with a good friend, he suggested that I take classes at the university next semester that I might enjoy. In the library one day, as I was pondering my future, I found an old book lying on a table. It was about the history of Christianity, and I picked it up, started reading, and was immediately enthralled. I had to learn more, so the next semester, I took my friend's advice and enrolled in religion classes. Eventually, I changed my major and graduated with a pre-seminary degree. Upon graduating from college, I spent two more years farming before leaving to attend Gordon-Conwell Theological Seminary in South Hamilton, Massachusetts, an interdenominational evangelical school close to the ocean, which I had never seen before. At Gordon-Conwell, after taking a class on Karl Barth, I first knew I wanted to study theology seriously. It was also there that I first began attending The Episcopal Church.

I found a home in The Episcopal Church. I was deeply attracted to the liturgy and sacraments; many of the hymns were the same beloved ones I had sung as a child. It also provided common ground for my wife, who had been raised Eastern Orthodox, and me. Eventually, we moved to Milwaukee so that I could pursue a Ph.D. in Systematic Theology at Marquette University (a Jesuit institution), and soon after our arrival, I was confirmed in The Episcopal Church. Upon graduation, while also teaching at Marquette, I was offered a part-time job teaching Systematic Theology at Nashotah House, where I completed classes in Anglican Studies in preparation for ordination to the Episcopal priesthood. The following year, I was ordained and began to serve at St. Paul's Episcopal Church in Ashippun, Wisconsin. It was the only rural Episcopal church in the Diocese of Milwaukee and the one where Lewis A. Kemper, son of the great missionary bishop Jackson Kemper, had served for twenty-five years in the late nineteenth century. Eventually, I was offered a full-time position at Nashotah House.

At Nashotah House, I teach and study theology in the kind of rural setting I have always loved. For over twenty years, I have taught theology while pastoring the same small rural congregation, a pattern of ministry shared by many Nashotah House professors before me. Over the years, I have found that serving as priest-in-charge of a congregation keeps my theology deeply grounded. Above all, the reality of parish ministry has convinced me that academic theology must always serve the life of the Church if it is to be anything more than a mental exercise.

What Is Your Understanding of the Theological Enterprise?

Whether we experience the beauty of God in nature or know him through the holy scriptures, God has chosen to make himself known to us. Theology studies the knowledge of God that arises from divine revelation in both these forms. In the *Summa Theologiae*, Thomas Aquinas called this knowledge of God sacred doctrine (*sacra doctrina*), although today, it is often more broadly termed "theology" or the study of God.[1] Through divine revelation, God is known in two ways: through creation and scripture. The knowledge of God in creation is available to reason, but the knowledge of God that comes from scripture must be believed by faith. Thus, faith takes us deeper into the knowledge of God than reason because only scripture gives us a saving knowledge of God, for, as Aquinas said, "it was necessary for the salvation of humans that certain truths which exceed human reason should be made known to them by divine revelation."[2]

Although we can know that God *exists* through his general revelation in nature, we only know *what God has done for our salvation* through his special revelation in scripture. For example, when the Lord passed before Moses on Mount Sinai, he proclaimed his name as "The Lord, the Lord, a God merciful and gracious, slow to anger, and abounding in steadfast love and faithfulness, keeping steadfast love for thousands, forgiving iniquity and transgression and sin, but who will by no means clear the guilty" (Ex 34:6–7, RSV). There is, perhaps, no better description of who God is than this. God is merciful and gracious, so he forgives the sins of the repentant and brings righteousness to the world through his people who walk in his ways. Another scriptural example can be seen in the Morning Prayer canticle, the Song of Zechariah (*Benedictus Dominus Deus*), when it declares that "the knowledge of salvation" for God's people is found "in the forgiveness of their sins" (Lk 1:77, RSV). Both passages

---

1. Thomas Aquinas, *Summa Theologica*, trans. Fathers of the English Dominican Province (Westminster, MD: Christian Classics, 1981), 1a.1.2.

2. Aquinas, *Summa Theologica*, 1a.1.1; translation altered.

proclaim the steadfast love of God in the forgiveness of human sin. This is the heart of God. The primary task of Christian theology, then, is to teach God's people the knowledge of salvation by the forgiveness of sins in Jesus Christ our Lord.

We can know God through divine revelation because, in it, he reveals his nature to us. To put the point more precisely, as Karl Barth said of God in his *Church Dogmatics*, "He reveals Himself *through Himself*."[3] While this may appear to be a tautological statement, it is not. In response to Enlightenment skepticism and the attempt to ground belief in God in human reason, Barth was making an important point about how we know God; namely, the veracity of our knowledge of God is grounded in God's act of revelation that creates the gift of faith, not in our mental capacity to prove that God exists. Faith is needed to know God because it extends beyond the natural limits of what reason can prove. Barth used modern language to articulate an ancient principle about how we know God. The early Church Father Irenaeus summed this up when he said, "The Lord taught us that no one can know God unless God teaches him; that is, without God, God cannot be known."[4] We come to know God as he gives himself to be known, and since God reveals himself to us as Father, Son, and Holy Spirit, we know God is a Trinity of divine Persons.

We chiefly come to know God in the incarnation when the eternal Word of God assumes human flesh. As Irenaeus explains, "The Father, therefore, has revealed himself to all by making his Word visible to all; and, in turn, the Word, since he may be seen by all,

---

3. Karl Barth, *Church Dogmatics*, gen. ed. G. W. Bromiley and T. F. Torrance, 4 vols. in 13 (Edinburgh: T & T Clark, 1956–75), 1:296.

4. Irenaeus, *Irenaeus of Lyons: Against the Heresies*, Books 4 and 5, trans. Dominic Unger, introduced with further revisions by Scott D. Moringiello, Ancient Christian Writers (Westminster, MD: Newman Press, 2024), 24 (4.6.4).

has shown the Father and the Son to all."[5] Here, Irenaeus echoes St. John's Gospel: "And the Word became flesh and dwelt among us, full of grace and truth; we have beheld his glory, glory as of the only Son from the Father" (Jn 1:14, RSV). By knowing Jesus, we know God in human flesh. This truth was formally defined in the Nicene-Constantinopolitan Creed, which taught that Jesus Christ is "consubstantial with the Father" (*homoousion to patri*).[6] Jesus and the Father are one God, so to know Jesus is to know God, for "in him the whole fulness of deity dwells bodily" (Col 2:9, RSV).

Consequently, the content of theology is shaped by the history of God's revelation to his people. This history is recorded in scripture when God reveals himself in the world's creation, at the fall of humankind into sin, through the redemption of humanity in Jesus Christ, and in the promise of our bodily resurrection to glory, as Jesus' bodily resurrection confirms. This pattern of redemption is called "salvation history" (*Heilsgeschichte*), and it forms the meta-narrative of theology. For example, the discipline of Systematic Theology naturally follows the *loci* of creation, fall, redemption, and glorification in articulating the faith. This is a well-established pattern of theological thinking; it is found in the Nicene-Constantinopolitan Creed, Irenaeus's *Apostolic Preaching*, Justin Martyr's *First Apology*, Augustine's *Enchiridion*, John Calvin's *Institutes of Christian Religion*, Karl Barth's *Church Dogmatics*, and many other works of theology.

The incarnation serves as the apex of the arc of salvation history because it ties creation with redemption, as Jesus Christ is the instrument of both. Jesus is the eternal Word through which God speaks his creation into existence and the eternal Word made flesh for our

---

5. Iranaeus, *Against the Heresies*, 24 (4.6.5).

6. *Decrees of the Ecumenical Councils*, ed. N. P. Tanner, 2 vols. (Washington, DC: Georgetown University Press, 1990), 1:24.

salvation. As St. Athanasius says repeatedly, the instrument of our creation becomes the instrument of our "re-creation."[7] We regain our lost knowledge of God through the incarnation, since in the incarnation, we know God in human flesh.[8] The incarnation is revelatory since Jesus is revealed as "God with us" (Mt 1:23, RSV). At the same time, the incarnation is transformative since the eternal Word assumes flesh to redeem and heal human nature from sin and death through that assumed humanity. Scripture says that it is from Christ's "fulness" that we receive "grace upon grace" (Jn 1:16, RSV). Grace flows from Christ's humanity to ours. St. Augustine explained this truth when he said Christ's humanity acts like a "fountain of grace" (*fons gratiae*), since each "human being becomes a Christian from the beginning of his faith by the same grace by which that man became Christ from his beginning. Each person is reborn by the Spirit by whom he was born. The same Spirit produced in us the forgiveness of sins who brought it about that he had no sin."[9] The incarnation of Jesus Christ by the Holy Spirit allows the grace of the Holy Spirit to flow from Christ's humanity to ours so that our human nature may be recreated and made whole. As Irenaeus put it, salvation comes to the soul through "the two hands of God," Christ and the Holy Spirit.[10]

Given the incarnation of Christ by the Holy Spirit, it is not hard to see how theological teachings or "doctrines" describe God's being and action in the world. Take, for example, the doctrines of the Trinity

---

7. Athanasius, *On the Incarnation: Greek Original and English Translation*, trans. John Behr, preface by C. S. Lewis (Crestwood, New York: St. Vladimir's Seminary Press, 2011), 65 (7), 79 (14), 81 (14).

8. Athanasius, *On the Incarnation*, 83 (15).

9. Augustine, *The Predestination of the Saints*, in *Answer to the Pelagians IV*, ed. John E. Rotelle O.S.A., trans. Roland J. Teske S.J., Works of Saint Augustine, I/26 (Hyde Park, NY: New City Press, 1999), 124 (15.31). BA 24:554–55.

10. Irenaeus, *Against the Heresies*, 58 (4.20.1), 131 (5.1.3), 138 (5.6.1).

and baptism. In *On the Apostolic Preaching*, Irenaeus explains that the three articles of the faith are the divine Persons of the Trinity themselves. The "first article" is "God the Father, uncreated" who is "Creator of all"; the "second article" is "the Word of God, the Son of God, Christ Jesus our Lord," who "became a man amongst men … in order to abolish death, to demonstrate life, and to effect communion between God and man"; while the "third article" is the "Holy Spirit, through whom the prophets prophesied and the patriarchs learnt the things of God" and "who, in the last times, was poured out in a new fashion upon the human race renewing man, throughout the world to God."[11]

Similarly, the doctrine of baptism describes God's triune action in salvation. Irenaeus goes on to say that "the baptism of our regeneration takes place through these three articles, granting us regeneration unto God the Father through His Son by the Holy Spirit; for those who bear the Spirit of God are led to the Word, that is to the Son, while the Son presents them to the Father, and the Father furnishes incorruptibility."[12] In other words, the doctrine of baptism describes the manner of our incorporation into God's triune life: in the Spirit through the Son to the Father. Hilary of Poitiers also speaks of baptism as incorporation into the triune life when he calls it "the creed of my regeneration when I was baptized in the Father, Son, and the Holy Spirit."[13] The substance of the doctrine of baptism, the sacrament of faith, is our incorporation into God's triune life. Baptism is far more than a liturgical rite of passage, since it regenerates the soul by God's inhabitation, which grants the gift of eternal life and causes renewal. Here we can see that for early Church Fathers like Irenaeus

---

11. Irenaeus, *On the Apostolic Preaching*, Popular Patristics Series (Crestwood, NY: Saint Vladimir's Seminary Press, 1997), 43–44 (6).

12. Irenaeus, *Apostolic Preaching*, 44 (7).

13. Hilary of Poitiers, *The Trinity*, Fathers of the Church, trans. Stephen McKenna (Washington, DC: Catholic University of America, 1954), 543 (12.57).

and Hilary, grace is nothing less than the presence of God indwelling the human soul. This insight is at the heart of my understanding of the enterprise of theology.

What Themes and Topics Are Central to Your Work as a Theologian?

Perhaps not surprisingly, given my personal history, grace as God's presence has been a central theme throughout my theological work. The idea of grace as God's presence first caught my attention when I was writing an early article on the therapeutic nature of grace in St. Augustine's theology.[14] For Augustine, grace is God's presence in the soul. He grounds this teaching in the idea that the Spirit is the bond of love between the Father and the Son in the Trinity. Because "God is love" (1 Jn 4:8, 16, RSV), "God is Spirit" (Jn 4:24, RSV), and "God has given us of his Spirit" (1 Jn 4:13, RSV), the Holy Spirit is distinctively the gift of God's love given to the soul (Rom 5:5, RSV).[15] Augustine often calls the Holy Spirit the "gift of God" (*donum Dei*), since the Spirit is the gift of God's love to the soul that causes humans to love God in return.[16] As Augustine summarizes, "So the love which is from God and is God is distinctively the Holy Spirit; through him the charity of God is poured out in our hearts, and through it the

---

14. Thomas L. Holtzen, "The Therapeutic Nature of Grace in St. Augustine's *De Gratia et Libero Arbitrio*," *Augustinian Studies* 31, no. 1 (2000): 93–115.

15. Augustine, *The Trinity*, 2nd ed., ed. John Rotelle O.P., trans. Edmund Hill O.P., Works of Saint Augustine, I/5 (Hyde Park, New York: New City Press, 1991/2015), 543 (15.17.31).

16. For example, Augustine, *The Trinity*, 543 (15.18.32); Augustine, *The Enchiridion of Faith, Hope, and Charity*, in *On Christian Belief*, ed. Boniface Ramsey, trans. Bruce Harbert, Works of Saint Augustine, I/8 (Hyde Park, NY: New City Press, 2005), 299, 340 (12.40, 31.117).

whole triad dwells in us."[17] This is similar to what the sixteenth-century Anglican *Homilies* teach when they call the Holy Spirit "the very bond of our conjunction with Christ."[18]

The theme of grace as God's presence is also found in my work on John Henry Newman's *via media* theology of justification through God's "justifying Presence."[19] Before his conversion to Roman Catholicism in 1845, Newman rejected Roman Catholic and Protestant theologies of justification in favor of a "doctrine of the justifying Presence." He understood that justification had to be defined by what was happening in salvation, not by any predetermined theory. Hence, he saw that both Roman Catholic and Protestant theologies of justification were partly right and partly wrong. Scholasticism had correctly understood that justification consisted of a gift given to the soul. But instead of treating justification as constituted by that gift, scholasticism held that justification occurred through the intermediary of created grace and not by God's presence itself. In other words, justification happened by the Holy Spirit creating a grace in the soul to move it back to God. Against this, Newman asserted that the gift of God's presence itself justified. Similarly, he thought that Protestants, particularly English evangelicals, had rightly understood that Christ's righteousness justified the soul. But they spoke of justification as separate from the indwelling of the Holy Spirit, who brought Christ to the soul for justification. This made justification

---

17. Augustine, *The Trinity*, 544 (15.18.32).

18. John Griffiths, ed., *The Homilies: Appointed to Be Read in Churches*, rev. ed. (Herefordshire, England: Brynmill/Preservation Press, 2006), 322.

19. T. L. Holtzen, *Newman and Justification: Newman's Via Media 'Doctrine of the Justifying Presence'* (Oxford: Clarendon Press, 2024). See also T. L. Holtzen, "Newman's Interpretation of Luther: A Reappraisal," *Theological Studies* 78, no. 1 (2017): 121–46; T. L. Holtzen, "Newman's *Via Media* Theology of Justification," *Newman Studies Journal* 4, no. 2 (2007): 64–74.

merely forensic, or something that happened externally and outside the Christian believer.

Contrary to these Roman Catholic and Protestant views, Newman held that Christ dwelt in the soul by the Holy Spirit, so a person was counted righteous by Christ's indwelling presence and made righteous by the sanctifying Spirit. Justification was neither by inherent righteousness, as Roman Catholics taught, nor by imputed righteousness, as Protestants taught, but only by the imparted righteousness of Christ inhabiting the soul through the Holy Spirit. For Newman, God's indwelling presence alone explained the mystery of salvation. He understood profoundly that justification was defined by God's presence, so it could not be separated from sanctification, nor even from glorification, because all of these were caused by God inhabiting the souls of believers.

While Newman's theology of justification takes on the hue of deification, like the soteriology of the Eastern Fathers, in reality, he was following St. Augustine's teaching that the Holy Spirit is the love of God given to the soul. In articulating this teaching, he relied on Richard Hooker's theology of justification, in which the gift of "the Spirit of Christ" in adoption precedes the actual justification of the soul.[20] In baptism, one receives the gift of the Spirit, is united to Christ, and is justified, while at the same moment, the process of sanctification begins. Like Hooker, then, Newman also held that God's presence in the soul effectively converts the soul, gives the gift of participation in God, and causes one to walk in holiness before God.

The other major theme in my thinking has been the uniqueness of Anglican theology. In a paper on sacramental causality in Richard

---

20. Richard Hooker, *Of the Laws of Ecclesiastical Polity: A Critical Edition with Modern Spelling*, ed. Arthur Stephen McGrade, 3 vols. (Oxford: Oxford University Press, 2013), 163 (5.5610–11).

Hooker's eucharistic theology, I argued that Hooker followed neither the Roman Catholic teaching of transubstantiation nor the Lutheran teaching of consubstantiation, nor yet the Calvinist teaching of virtualism, but rather that he understood Christ's presence in the Eucharist in terms of moral causality.[21] This places Hooker in continuity with late medieval teaching on eucharistic causality. Hooker thought that the sacraments act as moral instruments that are duties to be performed if we are to receive God's grace. There is an objective presence of Christ in the sacraments. But to receive this sacramental grace of Christ's presence, the Christian must partake of the sacraments. The sacraments thus act as moral instruments, without which we do not receive God's grace. In this, Hooker closely follows the teaching found in the Anglican Catechism that there are two sacraments "generally necessary to salvation," baptism and the Eucharist.[22]

In an essay on the history of the Anglican *via media*, I have argued for the uniqueness of Anglican theology.[23] Using the classical notion of a *via media* as a moderation between two extremes, my essay explores how notable English divines from the seventeenth to the nineteenth centuries variously understood the Anglican *via media* as moderation in reform. Our current understanding comes largely from John Henry Newman, who famously attempted to construct "the doctrine of the Anglican *via media*" between Protestantism and Roman Catholicism. After his conversion to Roman Catholicism,

---

21. T. L. Holtzen, "Sacramental Causality in Hooker's Eucharistic Theology," *Journal of Theological Studies* 62, no. 2 (October 2011): 607–48.

22. *The Book of Common Prayer and Administration of the Sacraments and Other Rites and Ceremonies of the Church*, reprint, 1662 (Oxford: Oxford University Press, 1969), 355.

23. T. L. Holtzen, "The Anglican *Via Media*: The Idea of Moderation in Reform," *Journal of Anglican Studies* 17, no. 1 (May 2019): 48–73.

however, he claimed that his endeavor had ended in failure. Newman's assessment of failure notwithstanding, the doctrine of the Anglican *via media* has had something of a chronic vigor in the life of the Anglican Church. Whether his idea of the Anglican Church as a *via media* between Roman Catholicism and Protestantism will be further received within the wider Anglican Communion remains in question.

Finally, in a chapter in a book on Lutheran ecclesiology, I have argued for the distinctiveness of Anglican ecclesiology when compared to that of Lutheranism.[24] The two churches share both unity and diversity. On the one hand, both define the Church as Word and Sacrament. Article 19 of the Anglican Thirty-Nine Articles, which teaches that the Church is where "the pure word of God is preached and the sacraments faithfully administered," was adapted from Article 5 of the *Augsburg Confession*. On the other hand, in contrast to some forms of Lutheranism, modern Anglicanism holds that apostolic succession is essential to the Church. As I set forth in my essay, in the Anglican view, apostolic succession belongs to the essence (*esse*) of the Church and is not something that exists only for its well-being (*bene esse*). This teaching became generally accepted in Anglicanism when the Chicago-Lambeth Quadrilateral articulated that apostolic succession was one of the four criteria essential for intercommunion with other churches. The teaching of apostolic succession bore fruit in the ecumenical agreement "Called to Common Mission" between the Evangelical Lutheran Church in America (ELCA) and The Episcopal Church (TEC), which established full communion between the two churches.

---

24. T. L. Holtzen, "Unity and Diversity in Anglican and Lutheran Ecclesiology," in *Church as Fullness in All Things*, ed. Jonathan Mumme, Richard J. Serina, and Mark W. Birkholz (Lanham, MD: Lexington/Fortress, 2019), 189–204.

What Is Your Vision for the Future of Theology in The Episcopal Church?

My hope for the future of theology in The Episcopal Church is that the church will speak winsomely about grace as the remedy for the ruptured relationships between God and humans, among humans, and with creation. Only God's grace can heal these broken relationships. In this regard, the church's sphere of influence is naturally limited. While it remains a voice for social conscience and change, its primary job is the cure of souls because all broken relationships originate in damaged souls. The church's remedies are Word and Sacrament. These means of grace bring salvation to the soul because they mediate God's life-giving presence. Only the church can offer our fractured world salvation through the forgiveness of sins in Jesus Christ our Lord. It comes from no other place. The church possesses the gift of God's saving grace, which it can, in turn, give to our broken world. Grace alone accomplishes this healing ministry because only it can order our relationship to God, others, and creation. I believe that inspiring and guiding people to live this reality of grace in every aspect of their lives is the primary task of The Episcopal Church, or any church. It is where all our relationships should begin and end.

Both as a theologian and a priest actively serving a congregation, I have reflected often on how grace orders our relationship with God. As I understand it, grace makes us wholly new at the resurrection by healing the corruption of sin we experience in soul and body. While we are in this life, it is through God's grace that our sins are forgiven, we are enabled to keep God's commandments, and we have the gift of the Holy Spirit as the "guarantee" (*arrabon*) of our future resurrection (2 Cor 1:22, 5:5; Eph 1:14). Grace means we do not have to struggle for salvation on our own. We have the comfort of grace at every step. As St. Paul puts it, "Though our outer nature is wasting away, our inner nature is being renewed every day" (2 Cor 4:16, RSV). In our diminished human nature, we cannot yet fully bear the image of Christ, but grace holds the promise of human wholeness. As St. Paul again reminds us, "Just as we have borne the image of the man of dust, we shall also bear the image of the man of heaven" (1 Cor 15:49, RSV). And as Ignatius said in his *Epistle to the Romans*, it is only at death that "I will be a human."[25] Then we will be fully recreated into the image and likeness of Christ. Then we will be fully human because we will be free from all sin. Until then, as St. Paul said, we are in a state of struggle until Christ is formed in us (Gal 4:19). By walking through life according to the Spirit of grace and not gratifying the desires of the flesh, we are recreated into the image and likeness of God in Christ through the sanctification of the Holy Spirit (Gal 5:16).

Grace equally orders our relationship with others. Through grace, we see the image of God (*imago Dei*) in others, just as it is in ourselves. We recognize that others need God's love and that they need to be loved just as God has loved us. This means sharing the good news of God's love for us in Jesus Christ. As we have seen, the knowledge of salvation consists in knowing our sins are forgiven (Lk 1:77). If we take this seriously, it means that the good news of Jesus Christ is for everyone. Further, it means that Jesus wants to save us from the kinds of sinful ways that bring death (Rom 6:23). As he said, "The thief comes only to steal and kill and destroy; I came that they may have life, and have it abundantly" (Jn 10:10, RSV). The grace of forgiveness is a first step toward abundant life. Grace gives us the ability to love those who do not love us. For this is what God did in Jesus: "We love, because he first loved us" (1 Jn 4:19, RSV). As Jesus pointed out

---

25. Ignatius, "Romans," in *The Apostolic Fathers*, ed. and trans. Bart D. Ehrman, 2 vols., Loeb Classical Library (Cambridge, MA: Harvard University Press, 2003), 1:279 (6.2).

to his disciples, we have no reward if we only love those who love us (Mt 5:46). Ours is the job of loving the unlovable. That is what God has done for us. He loved us in our unlovely state. So, through grace, we learn to love as we have been loved.

Lastly, grace orders our relation to creation, since creation does not exist independently of God's grace. The fact that creation is sustained by God's grace means that humans do not exist in a state of pure nature; we are not merely biological beings who exist completely independently of God. Rather, we, too, are God's creation ordered by grace. Recognizing that grace orders creation keeps us from two errors that, in different ways, cause human estrangement from creation. On the one hand, estrangement from creation occurs when humans understand themselves to stand over and against a purely material creation as its overlords, which leads to the misuse of creation by treating it as though it exists apart from humans and solely for their use. This way of thinking denies our common integrity with creation and fails to see that creation's goodness is ordered by grace to our creaturely goodness. On the other hand, estrangement from creation also occurs within the individual when personal wants and desires are ordered to the self rather than by grace to God's glory. When this happens, human goods become separated from their God-given purpose of creaturely goodness. In both cases, human stewardship of creation is essential in overcoming estrangement from creation. Stewardship cares for a creation that, east of Eden, is fallen and needs tending. There is a deep truth to Tennyson's poem *In Memoriam* in the well-known line: "Nature, red in tooth and claw." What *is* in nature is not always what *should be*. Creation needs a steward, as any farmer will tell you. The stewardship of creation in accordance with grace helps to mitigate creation's fallenness by ordering creation to God and thus allowing God's created goodness to flourish.

Further Reading Recommendations

Athanasius. *On the Incarnation: Greek Original and English Translation.* Preface by C. S. Lewis. Trans. John Behr. Crestwood, New York: St. Vladimir's Seminary Press, 2011.

Augustine. *The Enchiridion of Faith, Hope, and Charity.* In *On Christian Belief.* Ed. Boniface Ramsey. Trans. Bruce Harbert. Hyde Park, New York: New City Press, 2005.

Irenaeus. *On the Apostolic Preaching.* Ed. and trans. John Behr. Crestwood, NY: Saint Vladimir's Seminary Press, 1997.

Wilken, Robert Louis. *The Spirit of Early Christian Thought: Seeking the Face of God.* New Haven: Yale University Press, 2003.

My Theological Formation

Katherine Sonderegger

In the midst of his massive *Doctrine of Reconciliation*, Karl Barth pays quiet tribute to Abel Burkhardt, the Swiss author of a children's book of Bible stories, hymn texts, and songs. Like many of Barth's asides, this unassuming recollection from a theologian's childhood carries surprising weight. In a few crisp and moving memories, Barth paints in vivid colors the terrain he will cover in his larger, more abstract account of Biblical authority in the age of higher criticism. The *Church Dogmatics* will enact the insights gained from that childhood experience of a Christ who announced Himself—a present Lord, demanding, fascinating, compelling, bringing us, as by our mother's hand, to the manger, warmed by animals' breath, to the hillside covered with bread, and to a hill outside a city wall where death and life would meet. This Christ did not need to be made present; rather, He simply lived and made us, by His victory and gracious call, present to Himself. All very simple and tuneful, as Barth says, but his future lies chrysalis-like in the pages of a children's Gospel book.

I, too, have a book that lies at the ground floor of my theological calling. I make the analogy here, I hasten to say, not to Barth and his superb *Church Dogmatics*, but rather to the children's book, and its place in a theological *Bildung*. The post-war years that shaped me saw a number of children's books that artfully sewed together fictional and historical characters: Esther Forbes's *Johnny Tremain*, a foil for the

Revolutionary War generation; *The Helen Keller Story* by Catherine Owens Peare, a lightly fictionalized recounting of Keller's re-birth; and Scott O'Dell's *Island of the Blue Dolphins*, a haunting re-telling of a young indigenous girl's survival on a deserted island, recorded in nineteenth-century American annals: all absorbing reading for me in my early years. But the book that laid the deepest foundation for me was a Sunday School reader by the Pittsburgh Theological Seminary historian Elwyn Smith: *Men Called Him Master*. Like the other children's books of my era, *Men Called Him Master* combined historical—that is, Biblical—figures with fictional characters, and rendered concrete the theological conviction that Immanuel is God with us, in our world, under our sun.

The realism of the narratives, their confident blending of Palestinian life—its fishing villages and sea-faring ways; its roiling relation to the Roman occupation; its Synagogues and festivals and halakha; the slaves, the gentiles, the broiling sun, the tang of trawling nets and freshly cut fields and noon-day meals—all with the Presence of the Son of Man and His authority: these captivated me. They enacted, without theoretical fanfare or heavy lifting, a Realism that gave faith and history a happy marriage. Later in his career, the Barth scholar Hans Frei, with his customary baroque idiom, warned us of a danger he called "epistemological monophysitism": an inability to see the real in anything but one source, a Biblical or doctrinal one. Frei made a plea for the place of secular history—an independent and reliable source of knowledge of the real—in theological judgment; Van Harvey's *The Historian and the Believer* remained a key text for him to life's end. As a kind of early inoculation, I suppose, my childhood reading showed me that history and fiction lie side by side, as did secular and Scriptural history. Neither incommensurate nor dialectical, not sentimental or mystical: these books were simply my world, the human past, with me integrated, by the power of image and tale, into its broad plains. Of course, I did not think then about the minefields of epistemological monophysitism! (And just how are we to confront monism properly and coherently, anyway?) But as I reflect on my own up-bringing, and the roots of my own theological formation, I see before my eyes that small book with its modest brown cover and simple illustration, unassuming, confident, unapologetic, and I recognize there the gifts it has given me, more ample, surely, than Elwyn Smith could have known when he assembled his historical re-telling of the Gospels.

Men Called Him Master gave me a second gift as well. The title says it all: this is a re-telling of Jesus as Lord. The early chapters of the book relate encounters with a Rabbi who does not impose His authority but rather simply carries it. He is recognized at once as One with mastery, not like the Scribes. Of course, this is a Biblical motif, hardly an importation of Smith's! But it is a striking feature of these early chapters—striking certainly to me—that the leading characteristic of Jesus Christ is His simple command. He does not assert; He does not defend or argue or lay claim; rather, Jesus of Nazareth here simply possesses a Lordship which presents itself as fact. "Lord" is who He is, and everyone knows it. I might say that Smith considers the identity of Jesus to be Master but that is rather too high-flown an apparatus for the simple power of Smith's re-telling. The Teacher who emerges from *Men Called Him Master* is not a wonder-worker or instructor who gains acclaim or authority as He moves through Galilee. We are not left wondering here, Who does He say He is; Who do others claim Him to be; Could He truly be what they claim? Of course, these are Biblical questions as well, and not to be rudely dismissed! But the Jesus portrayed in this children's book does not question or pose them; He *enacts* authority. Effortlessly, magnetically, He moves among the Jews and gentiles of His day as Lord, and no one denies His Presence or His royalty. *Men Called Him Master* certainly recounts opposition and betrayal; but nothing of indifference. To be in this One's Presence is to be overtaken. It is no miracle of trust or courage that the Sons of Zebedee left all to follow; it is rather a law of nature, the Lord's Nature.

Elwyn Smith published the book in 1948; I encountered it a decade or so later. These were the years of Barth's ascendancy in American theological circles. Certainly the figures of "Neo-Orthodoxy" were prominent in my Presbyterian upbringing: Paul Tillich, Reinhold Niebuhr, Rudolf Bultmann. But the genius of Barth underlay it all. The realism of the Biblical exegesis, the confidence of the proclamation, the worldliness of the religious temper, and above all, the Lordship of the Son of Man: these were the *Leitmotive* of my religious education. And as proper musical themes they were not isolated or explicitly named but rather *sounded*. Everything rang with these tones. Throughout *Church Dogmatics IV*, Barth rings the changes of Christ's Lordship. Indeed, *Kyrios Christos* might be taken as the root metaphor, the germ, for Barth's Christology as a whole, and, under the idiom of Revelation, for his Trinitarian Doctrine of God. At Pittsburgh Seminary, Elwyn Smith surely entered this mainstream of Barth studies. But Smith's work was not didactic. It simply carried out, without explicit mention, what the history of encounter with such a One would be like. I found that compelling as a child; I still do.

Men Called Him Master arrived at a happy time for my theological formation, as my family had settled into my hometown in a house next door to the Fines, a Jewish couple who maintained a kosher home. Joseph Fine was a city commissioner and later mayor in my small town. As neighbors, patient and kind to an inquiring child, the Fines introduced me to observant Jewish life. Striking in Smith's Gospel sketches are the detailed and vibrant portraits of first-century Palestinian Judaism—the liturgy, the commandments, the dress, the devotion. A life-world was opened to me, and I saw in the gracious exchange over a neighborhood fence that this world continued—altered and expanded and differentiated, to be sure, but a living Judaism that was not disbelief or repudiation or fossilized, but rather the embodied obedience and worship of a faith that gave me my Master. I salute my Sunday School teachers, my Christian Education director, my pastors, and preachers: I received the faith once delivered from them, and my encounter with the unquestioned moral and intellectual seriousness of the Christian faith stems directly from their teaching and example. As I cast my mind's eye back, I see an outpost of the old Christendom—not dominant, not proud or expansive, but simply present, a cultural fact, rather tattered and threadbare by then, but one that joined the spiritual and the earthy and the daily calendar to one another——a total world, a total way of life. But this large-scale cosmology, determinative as it was, pales before the individual and the particular. A child's casual conversation with Joseph Fine, his astonishing generosity to a nervous and awkward child, was a God-sent teacher. Such deep roots shape a life and support its growth silently, steadily, to be nurtured and fed, utterly underground.

But this essay is not actually a memoir. A full accounting of my theological training would have to include much more than this slight retelling—my long schooling and my teachers; my long-time attraction to The Episcopal Church (a girlhood spent for some years at an Episcopal boarding school); my spiritual wrestling and instruction; my politics; my struggles to find a dogmatic voice; my deep indebtedness to Barth and reluctant opposition to him; my priesthood. It would take another pair of eyes, I think, to weigh all these elements and see what lasts and what has been worn away by riper years and, perhaps, clearer judgment. I want here instead to simply reflect on how these two childhood events impressed upon me the fundamentals of the theological task.

I cannot shake the conviction that doctrine is properly written not outside of, or in a hermetic sense, within, but rather, under Tradition. It is hard to express a conviction that lies as deep as this. It is easy to articulate a conceptual fidelity to the dogmatic and creedal statements of the Church and even the indefectibility of a still fallible Church. And easy too, though perhaps more conceptually fraught, to capture the sense of Christian doctrine as a *Denkwelt* one inhabits rather than studies. But it is far harder, I find, to articulate the Way of Life that a theologian enacts as she lives beneath the Tradition of the faith. It is a kind of virtue, a *habitus*, and though it accepts the Conciliar Tradition as given, it demands more. It is an *attitude*, an approach, a confidence that I found expressed, indirectly and without second-order notice, in Elwyn Smith's book: unapologetic, unironic, simple. This is hard to capture, I think, because it appears to endorse, thoughtlessly and uncritically, everything the Ecumenical Councils have taught, and glibly or perhaps arrogantly waves away the long struggle to gain leverage on a total civilization that was Christendom. Has such an endorsement failed to achieve a differentiated view of the Christian past, an honesty before the tribunal of conscience and of truth—a haunting phrase of Rahner's, who knew something of Church suspicion and dominance? Certainly, I recognize and confess the weakness, folly, and error of the Church! No one who endorses the kind of feminist and class analysis that I do could hold the Church and its teachings blameless. And the long, utterly implacable and enduring anti-Judaism and antisemitism of the Christian faith can only be the legacy and call of life-long repentance for theologians. My confidence in the Church's indefectibility, that is, is neither conservative nor traditionalist. I am eager to advance the progressive agenda of much of The Episcopal Church. Yet none of this touches my conviction about the place of the theologian, under the Tradition of the Church. Can only a happy inconsistency allow such belief? No doubt there is that;

but not simply that, for the revolution of God is etched into that Tradition, a radicality that undoes the order of things.

To speak of this treasure, Christian theology best makes use of plain speech. Of course, this is self-involving! But it is so much more than this complex of the objective and subjective movements in the theologian's task. It is Realism; yes. I recognize and admire many systematic presentations of the faith that do not endorse Realism, of either a metaphysical or epistemic sort, but I cannot see that such conceptual Irrealism permits the confidence, submission, loyalty, and simplicity that theology demands. Perhaps because of my Reformed upbringing, confession in a straightforward voice strikes me as the proper posture of the Christian theologian. But Catholicity demands an adherence to a Conciliar past, and to the Doctors of the Church. Plain speech simply avows: this is the Church's teaching; here is my presentation, exploration, and defense of that doctrine. Certainly, this is Anselmian: *fides quaerens intellectum*. But it is more. Christian theology properly faces outward. It hears and receives the teachings of the *seculum*, but not as though it is tongue-tied or shame-faced before it. Properly, Christian theology does not attempt to show that it, too, holds to worldly or academic conviction and, in turn, offers *apologia* on those grounds. It does not find secular wisdom more interesting, more compelling, more legitimate, or more sophisticated than Christian teaching; it does not need or seek other grounds than its own Scripture and its exposition—the "revealed principles and the science of the blessed," as Thomas Aquinas expresses this. Academic theology can, of course, inhabit such plain speech: the Schoolmen demonstrated this with blinding clarity. But the university can entice the theologian to produce credentials that obscure the plain confession of the faith, giving it the air of a diplomat without portfolio, traveling far afield. My own attempt to write systematic theology for and within the Church strives to receive the faith as delivered to me, to explore its limitless complexity, to admire its coherence and ineffability, to articulate its Scriptural ground, that fathomless well, to appreciate and to love it. My resistance to the otherwise admirable German seminar system of the footnote, and my reversion to the older fashion of a capitalized vocabulary, is not intended to be archaizing—though I grant, it certainly seems so. Rather, it is designed to signal a confession that inhabits the mark of Catholicity, and does not consider the modern the great rupture with all that precedes it. Perhaps this attempt at plain speech, in the end, is simply the modern expression of St. Augustine's proclamation that *caritas* is the restless heart of Christian confession.

My childhood experience awakened in me not only a curiosity about Jews and Judaism but also a loyal passion for them. This is not the two-covenant theology of Paul van Buren, as I understand him, nor, I hope, an unquestioned philosemitism. It is rather an abiding wonder, as Buber would style this, before the Covenant People and the enduring mystery of their Election. I don't think this entails a systematic focus on an *Israellehre* or Christian-Jewish encounter. It would welcome it, certainly, but not entail it. It seems to me that Christians should approach with caution the notion of "theology after Auschwitz." Jews are not simply the object of vile hatred and persecution, nor should Judaism be reduced to the record of its attempted destruction. Christians, too, should be wary of passing judgment on Judaism, as if it were a world, a fidelity, a commandment, and a task that Christians have a right to assess. Certainly, a proper Christian theology reads in Judaica; it knows about the controversies and disputes within its House, but it does not claim it has standing to promote or rebuke or elaborate on intra-Jewish debate. Instead, Christians confess that Judaism is the Mystery that erupts into the world when the Holy God scorches the earth with the Breath of His Mouth, and a People is born. Scripture records that eruption, with searing honesty and proper pride. Certainly, Jews and Judaism exist beyond and apart from Scripture's witness! The New Testament is decidedly not the era of Late Judaism, as our nineteenth-century modernists in the Church once termed it. But Holy Scripture is the well-spring of Judaism; the well-spring of the Church. For that reason, I believe, Christians are called to harken especially to Israel's Scriptures and to acknowledge them as *Magistra* of the Church.

But how is this to be done? Christians should be wary of an easy answer. As old as Justin Martyr is the conviction that Christians, not Jews, own the title to Israel's Scriptures; that claim by Christians is properly repudiated. To claim ownership is a Biblical supersessionism whose arrogance is matched only by that of Covenant supersessionism, recapitulated in the Christian teachings of contempt. However, the alternative to such supersessionisms is not ready to hand. One tempting, and frequent, move in our era is to simply renounce a holding in Israel's Scriptures altogether. In an odd amalgam of Marcionism and benevolence, Christians in the modern era have eagerly handed over these Books to Jews, foresworn the title, "Old Testament," and declared them, variously, the Hebrew Bible, the First Covenant, or the Jewish Scriptures, the Tanakh. It is not transparent how the unity of the Christian canon is preserved by such maneuvers; that may not even be the goal. If it is, it seems that Schleiermacher's solution—the Old Testament is a Jewish book of background for the New—is the only avenue for these theologians to stitch them back together. But is this such a benefit? A dubious honor it is, after all, for a People to serve as mere backdrop to another's splash in the spotlight. But how else is the contest over interpretation to be soothed? I have spoken here of hermeneutical dilemmas, but in truth, it is far more costly than this bitter dispute.

For Christians to claim to supersede Jews as the Lord's Covenant People is the most brutal form of Christian anti-Judaism. Putting the unity of the Canon aside, we might dare to examine directly how the

Church reads the Bible as a judgment on Judaism. We must ask: How are we to understand the wrenching cry of the Apostle Paul about his People; the menace of "the Jews" in the Gospel of John; the litany of woes by St. Stephen; the construction of the Gospels as a story of betrayal, or self-justification, or legalism, or refusal to love? Do they all forge a newly established Church at the very great cost of portraying Judaism as the People who rejected God, the People rejected by Him in turn? I can only say: *me genoito*; God forbid! But the question must still be posed: How is the Passion of our Lord to be properly understood? The patterns much beloved in Christian exegesis, of prophecy and fulfillment, of foreshadowing and type, of preparation and recollection, all turn on the Passion of Christ, and this, Christians have said, is the terrifying unity that welds the Covenants together, or worse, replaces one with the other. We stand at the heart of the Mystery of Christ, born a Jew, born under the Law, David's Son and Lord, and I don't pretend that the proper position for Christians to take on these matters is plain to the eye. There may be, on this side of the consummation of all things, no complete and condign solution. But we cannot honor Israel's Scriptures as *Magistra*, cannot begin our proper work of Christian repentance, without offering an interim proposal.

For my part, I think there is no partial remedy to this spiritual crisis, no first step to this resolution, without understanding ourselves—we Christians—as ingredients in the Eternal Covenant with Israel, from the days of our first disobedience to the summons out of Ur of the Chaldees, to the thunder at Sinai, cleaving the earth, and the records of the sad tales of the death of kings, to the birth of the Savior, and His death and rising on the third day. All of it, Israel's story; all of it, the Christian story. We stand in wonder and terror at Sinai, I say; and we sit in the seat of the scornful; we deny, betray, and scourge our Lord; we mock Him as we pass by under His cruciform shadow. This is the *justificato impii*, to receive pardon and welcome by the God we betray. Now, this is the Christian story; it is even, I believe, the story of Israel. But it is not the story of Judaism. Just this, I think, is the force of Calvin's decision to speak of the Assembly of Israel as Church, and to teach that Israel possessed the Sacraments, though under shadow and type. Certainly, this is an imperfect solution, perhaps a culpable one. It threatens to divide Judaism from Israel, hardly a benefit. And it must rely on a kind of "benign supersessionism," as Jacob Neusner would have it, or in more anodyne terms, a "Branch theory" of Israel in which two Traditions emerge from one, complex, and living past. But I believe this is the most promising, least damaging route.

The Christian story must be held distinct from the Jewish one: Judaism is the Tradition, observance, and teaching that emerges from Jerusalem and Jabneh, and from the Tannaim. It builds its Tradition through study and commentary on the Talmud, itself a commentary on Scripture; it emerges from the medieval West in various schools and parties, and presents to the world today a living Covenant People, within the State of Israel and in diaspora, faithful to Torah and loyal to the Name. Judaism crosses and intersects with Christianity, time and again, but it is not a simple denial of Christian tenets: it is not a parallel but an inverted Church. Robert Jenson has likened this relation to a literary theory of a novel's ending—one thinks of Frank Kermode here—in which a single story reaches completion in two distinct manners, and the entire architecture of the narrative, its arché and development and climax, are altered and overcast by the ending it anticipates. The whole assumes the character of the ending, such that the Christian story becomes the chasm of the Cross and the Spiritual radiance of the Empty Tomb. Judaism becomes the wonder of Election and Covenant, the enthronement of the Lord on the praises of Israel, the rupture and purgation of the Prophets, the Mystery and Commandment of life before the Eternal. As a

Christian, I am captured in the one story, and a God-fearer in the other, an insider and outsider at once in the ancient narrative of a Holy God with His frail creatures. As a theologian, I stand under these Sacred Books, and they instruct me in the ways I should go. All Christian theology, I believe, should allow Israel's Scriptures to speak in this way, with authority and with direction.

To do so, I believe, will lead Christians to affirm with a stronger voice the unicity of God. Of late, Christians have foregrounded the Dogma of the Holy Trinity as if it were an alternative or, worse, an opposition to the One God—to Monotheism. A marked attention paid to the distinction of the Divine Persons, even Their unique Wills, drives a wedge, I say, between Trinitarian belief and Divine Unicity and Simplicity. The attempts to forge Triunity from unity of Will or from an appropriated Attribute such as Love do not strike me as a strong candidate for unicity, nor a candidate for endorsement by Lateran IV. But these are problems endemic to Trinitarian theology, and no more patent of easy solution than that of the Canon. The loss of particular focus on Divine Oneness can also throw an odd shadow on the Doctrine of God as an intellectual structure. A perennial temptation for Christian theology, I believe, is to set out its Doctrine of God as if it were a compilation of all the distinctives of the Christian religion. An identity marker, this Christian God speaks out of and to the Church in such a way that its Nature and Being are unintelligible to those beyond the Baptismal font. Rather than honoring the Lord who is Wholly Other—its aim, I believe—this Doctrine of God teaches the strange lesson that Christians hold to a kind of local Deity, one known only by citizens of the realm. That is not to advocate for an Ideal or logical Deity, unanchored to Scripture or Tradition! Rather, it is to say that Israel in the *Shema* teaches the Unicity of God, the transcendence of God beyond image, likeness, and form, and it is to this Sovereign Mystery that we are to return worship and praise. That the One God of Israel is the Lord of the whole earth is fundamental to Christian Doctrine, I say, and underwrites our kinship (not identity) with all those who honor a Unitary God and His supreme Aseity. The Dogma of the Holy Trinity, I believe, should be understood as an instance of this Unicity, a form of Monotheism. Just so would Christian theology show its proper harkening to Holy Scripture and the Lord who taught the *Shema* as ground for the Great Commandment.

I have gladly taken on work of this kind as a theologian of The Episcopal Church. It is a fallible Church, I know, but also, I believe, an indefectible one: It will not teach fatal error nor lead the little ones to stumble so as to fall. The Episcopal Church takes its part in the Anglican Communion, and it is this heritage that I believe will be deeply nurturing for theology in the future. The English Reformation, as is well known, is a complex and not a simple thing. Anglican identity—that perennial topic—cannot receive a single definition and, as a worldwide Communion, resists almost every attempt to do so. But I say, "almost." I do think there is a commonality, rooted in history, in accident and happenstance, but in Providence, too, about a place of innovation within the Church Catholic that is a gift to the entire Christian world. Anglicanism takes its place within a broader Conciliarism, and its Ecclesiology is autocephalic—at least for the time being. Rather than ordering the Church or the Communion to a single Primate, Anglicanism has recognized member Churches with their own Primate or President – hence, "autocephalic" or "self-headed." But Anglicanism has developed a theology distinct from both Continental Conciliarism and Orthodox autocephaly in Church order. Our own form of "autonomous Churches in Communion" has emerged from the particularities of the English Reformation.

If we look at the Tudor debates, we catch a glimpse of this new doctrinal pattern: a secure foundation in Holy Scripture; an appeal to the "sounder Fathers"; an attraction to the "undivided Church," taken to be the Christian collegium before the fatal divide of the Greek and Latin Churches; a healthy respect for argument and coherence; a loyalty to the Ecumenical Councils, with primacy given to Nicaea and Chalcedon; and a conviction that local adaptation of rite and ritual does not harm unity, which remains in "essentials." (Just how to define *adiaphora* remains contested, of course, as it did in the Reformation era.) Certainly, Richard Hooker typifies these traits, but I believe they are widely shared among defenders of the Church of England, its polemicists, and its dogmaticians. As the whole world knows, we are in the midst of a Church-dividing argument over homosexuality, and the acridity of this debate, along with the silence, unease, and weariness that attend it, test the vitality and generativity of the Anglican pattern. But Christian doctrine written under its canopy remains vibrant, elastic, strong. The place of innovation within Christian Tradition is a cause worthy of theology's task. The fact of doctrinal change appears undeniable; just this motivated Newman's great theory of development. Yet finding and articulating the logical space in which Catholic teaching grows and adapts and changes is a far more daunting conceptual feat than a simple nod to development. This logic, I believe, is one of Anglicanism's charisms for Christian theology. But not the only! There is also constancy, uniformity, and endurance: Anglicanism has elevated Tradition as it emerged in Late Antiquity, and it is to that generative era that Anglican theologians have turned, time and again. Kathryn Tanner and Sarah Coakley are two systematicians who demonstrate the remarkable vitality of Patristic theology for contemporary doctrine. Yet to turn to the Doctors of the undivided Church is to acknowledge an authority that is *chosen*, a self-binding obedience and loyalty to the past which carries its own doctrinal perils. Can one "stand under" a Tradition that has been placed overhead by one's own hand? How does it bind when one's heart and mind long to head in other directions? This is the dilemma of authority in the age of modernism, and we have not settled these matters doctrinally; perhaps we do not have the range of vision to do so. But I think a kind of Kantian account of duty lies at the base of Anglican accounts of authority—and this is a wonderfully fertile ground to work in. Theology in The Episcopal Church will thrive in the matrix of the Anglican pattern, I believe. The next generation of systematicians inhabits graduate programs and parishes at this hour, and I am eager to read their work, to be guided and challenged and deepened by it. The Lord God will not be without His witnesses. He alone will stir up the voice of the prophet and teacher, alone call to His Presence the intellects that will serve His cause, in argument and in prayer. I believe the Anglican legacy in theology will continue to innovate and conserve the past: freedom and constraint will be the twin reins of its progress Homeward. I am grateful to be in such a brace.

Further Reading Recommendations

Barth, Karl. *Church Dogmatics, Vol II.2: The Doctrine of God.* Edited by G. W. Bromiley and T. F. Torrance. Translated by G. W. Bromiley, et al. Edinburgh: T&T Clark, 1957.

Bulgakov, Sergei. *The Lamb of God.* Translated by Boris Jakim. Grand Rapids: Eerdmans, 2008—originally published in 1933.

Gore, Charles. *The Incarnation of the Son of God: Being the Bampton Lectures for the Year 1891.* Edited by Christopher Poore. Galesburg, IL: Seminary Street Press, 2021.

Wyschogrod, Michael. *Abraham's Promise: Judaism and Jewish-Christian Relations.* Edited by R. Kendall Soulen. Grand Rapids: Eerdmans, 2004.

Theology, Damage, Affordance

Maxine King

I am new enough to the formal discipline of theology that it still feels presumptuous to call myself a theologian, let alone contribute to a book on the future of theology in The Episcopal Church. This is not to say that Christian theology was ever foreign to me: I lived at a theological seminary as an infant while my parents studied for their ministry, spent a year living abroad in a missionary family, and spent my adolescence as a pious and precocious small-town pastor's kid. However, my first explicit study of theological materials and the first inkling of a theological vocation came long after these childhood exposures to theology.

After leaving the church I was raised in while at college, I had settled into what would be my operating assumption for my coming young-adult years: Christianity was not a real option for me; I could not live within the bounds of its teaching and practice. This was never a decision based on assessing the likelihood of God's existence or the rationality of the resurrection, or anything of that sort. I simply and categorically assumed that my flourishing and even my living at all as a trans person were impossible within the parameters of the Christianity I knew. Facebook messages from those I grew up with in my congregation, warning me that "the devil is going to get you," seemed only to confirm my hypothesis.

Still, I was never very successful at extirpating Christian patterns of thought from my psyche, deeply lodged as they were due to my upbringing as a missionary-pastor's kid. I did make a go at it, though I always maintained a tenuous connection. When I would visit my parents during those years after college, we would often attend an Episcopal service on Sundays, as it offered a kind of neutral ground for continuing our Sunday morning churchgoing routine. (I don't think this is what *via media* was ever supposed to mean, but it worked for us!) During one of these visits, at the Church of the Atonement in Chicago, I wept through the entire liturgy. It perhaps speaks to my failure to remove the vestiges of Christian assumptions that I never even considered making a critical examination of these tears, even though I had been well-equipped to do so by the masters of suspicion from my liberal arts education! These tears did not seem to prompt a decision for critical evaluation as much as they seemed to place a demand upon me: to seek after this God who drew me to cry out to him.

When I returned home after that visit, I looked up the nearest Episcopal church. There happened to be a small parish just a few blocks from my apartment—St. Andrew's, Tucson. (Neighborhood parishes are a providential blessing to the carless in the car-dependent cities of America!) I was fortunate to find there a community in which I could flourish, encounter Jesus, and slowly relearn the basics of Christian practice. The strange new world of the Bible was proclaimed to me, and I found myself caught up in this strange new world during our celebration of the Eucharist.

It was in learning to pray the Daily Office that I first had an inkling of a theological vocation. I still remember being set alight during my initial encounter with the exegesis of Psalm 95 in the Letter to the Hebrews. On one level, I was engaging in the literary criticism of my undergraduate studies in English by reading another's interpretation of a text I had also read, but this was no longer merely an intellectual exercise. Psalm 95 was more than just another poem, for it was, as the epistle's author puts it, living and active. It was a prayer I had made my own by reciting it as the psalmist did, and now I found myself in union with the author and original recipients of the Letter to the Hebrews, who had also prayed and sought understanding of these words.

This prayer-filled communion in which I found myself extended from the biblical world to my own ecclesial world of parish, diocese, and communion, and to the whole number of saints across time and space. And further, God was present as both subject and object of this entire process of writing, interpreting, praying, and living. He was the sanctifying subject of the writing of these scriptural words and their subsequent critical analysis and application in the Church. He was the desired object of the worship that constituted the human participation in the entire process. I was learning that Christian living—and later, theology in particular—involved the incorporation and transformation of my entire self, my soul and body.

It was the theologians of the early church who first captured my imagination as I listened to audiobooks of Gregory of Nyssa, Augustine, and Cyril while packing orders at the tea warehouse where I worked. I was fortunate to come across a copy of Peter Brown's *The Body and Society*, which provided further context to these early Christians' historical setting, especially regarding themes of gender and sexuality—I have yet to stop thinking about his reading of Origen's (alleged) self-castration, making him "a walking lesson in the basic indeterminacy of the body"![1] What most fascinated me about these figures was the way in which the familiarity I had with

---

1. Peter Brown, *The Body and Society: Men, Women, and Sexual Renunciation in Early Christianity* (New York: Columbia University Press, 1988), 169.

their Christianity was refracted through the prism of their distant historical context. Their language and practices bore a family resemblance to those of my childhood and my adult re-conversion, but their history, though not wholly alien, was still a foreign country. The Bible was a polyphonic witness to a transcendent God generating endless surplus meanings rather than serving as a mere instruction manual. Sexual renunciation was joining an angelic alternative to married and propertied society rather than merely achieving virgin purity. The Christianity that once in all its familiarity seemed impossible for me to live within was being made strange, and in its strangeness I was finding Christianity to be newly habitable.

The possibility of formally studying theology first occurred to me at the suggestion of a local priest, who encouraged me to consider going to a seminary or divinity school. Though I had loved school and once thought I would go to graduate school for English, living in poverty after completing my undergraduate degree had made such hopes seem impossible. But my priest told me that her alma mater, Virginia Theological Seminary, was entirely free (including room and board!), even for lay persons without clerical aspirations. At the time, I lacked the stability of a job because of the COVID pandemic, so graduate school seemed newly possible and not an entirely irresponsible decision. I also happened to be making more money on pandemic unemployment insurance than I had at any of my previous jobs, so with those savings, I was able to fund a cross-country move to Virginia, where I began my academic theological education.

Unsurprisingly, it was early Christian ascetics and theologians who continued to excite me at the beginning of my studies. But I began to wonder if my enthusiasm for the foreignness of early Christianity was, in fact, offering a convenient escape from the theological problems that are most pressing to me and our Church today. Did my fascination with its strangeness provide an easy excuse not to bring my whole self and history to the theological task? This is certainly not to say that anyone else's attraction to particular historical periods in theology is a sign of such avoidance, but it seemed like it was at least a temptation for me. I had a nagging sense that I did not yet fully know how to integrate myself and the communities to which I belonged into my growing theological understanding. Moreover, I worried that my interest in these far-off periods might lead to a kind of quietism about the present crises in my church and the world that affected me and those I loved.

During the summer after my first year of seminary, I was singing with my home parish choir on a choral residency at Wells Cathedral in England when I found copies of Karl Barth's *Epistle to the Romans* and *Dogmatics in Outline* in a charity shop. I had made it through my first year without reading more than a few pages of his writing, but I at least knew that he was a central figure in the research of my first theological teacher, Katherine Sonderegger. So, I picked them up to read between rehearsals and Evensongs, and upon reading, I was immediately hooked. Barth placed a radical question mark on the immense beauty of the medieval cathedral in which I was singing. Or, better, this *No!* was directed at my own tendency to mistake the human cathedral for the living God himself—a dangerous tendency all too present for Episcopalians like me who delight in our own religiosity. And further, Barth gave me the theological language and impetus to conceive of my theological task not as a retreat into a pious esotericism. Instead, the task of theology is to participate in the church's necessary criticism of its current proclamation and to ask what it will be tomorrow.

Further, my reading of Barth gave me a theological diagnosis for what I had come to see as a problematic dialectic in contemporary theology's incorporation of trans people into theological reflection. On the one hand, there was a reactionary dismissal of trans life, as described by sexologists and gender clinicians (and, in an odd alliance, certain radical feminists). On the other hand, there was a seemingly more positive appraisal of trans*ness*, though abstracted from the lives of actual trans *people* and made into inert material for a useful theological allegory of a God who crosses boundaries and destabilizes norms. Indeed, my desire to escape to the patristics was partly formed in reaction to this dialectic, as I desperately wanted to flee from being forced into one of these unsatisfying positions. Barth's thoroughgoing realism, blistering critique of abstraction, and emphatic rejection of natural theology all seemed to cut through the false choice of reaction or appropriation. Barth's criticisms even seemed to cohere with the charge that theorists in trans studies made against queer theory's transformation of living trans people into merely theoretical material.[2]

Barth helped me see that this problematic dialectic of dismissal and instrumentalization I had encountered in these theologies about trans people was not merely a political and ethical problem. It also seemed to touch on fundamental theological principles, perhaps even the most fundamental problematic in Christian theology. How can we produce knowledge of a God who transcends all categories of creaturely knowledge and experience? Many theologians have argued that because God is unknowable directly (at least within our earthly existence), our means of knowing and participating in him is achieved through the indirect mediation of fellow creatures. An early instance of this kind of formulation is found in Saint Augustine's *De Doctrina Christiana*. In it, Augustine famously distinguishes between "use" and "enjoyment" to describe the two different relations one can have to any particular thing. Augustine makes this distinction to establish that all other things should be used for the enjoyment of God, who is

---

2. I make this argument in further detail in Maxine King, "Toward a Theology of Trans Opacity: Trans Studies' Critique of Queer Theory in Conversation with Karl Barth's Doctrine of Revelation," *Anglican Theological Review* 106 (4): 430–43. https://doi.org/10.1177/00033286241290236.

uniquely to be enjoyed. For those of us living after Kant's categorical imperative to never simply treat another human as a means (as well as the ever-growing list of historical examples of humans being reduced to use-value for another's benefit), Augustine's formulation seems like it would be dangerous at best or inherently immoral at worst.

Augustine certainly did not mean "use" (*uti*) in the sense of an instrumentalizing use-value. It might be better to understand his system of use and enjoyment as sacramental rather than instrumental: to use a thing in order to enjoy God is to consecrate it to the praise and service of the all-good and loving God. Building on the other famous distinction Augustine makes in *De Doctrina Christiana* between signs and things, one's fellow creature ceases to be merely another thing, but instead becomes a visible sign of invisible grace. In this way, Augustine's distinctions help elaborate the principle in the First Epistle of John that "he who does not love his brother whom he has seen, cannot love God whom he has not seen" (1 Jn 4:20, RSV). Rather than establishing the necessity of Christian instrumentalizing, Augustine's distinction between use and enjoyment can instead claim that any unloving reduction of the visible sibling to mere usefulness forecloses the possibility of a true enjoyment of the invisible God.

While I am generally convinced of this positive ethical reading of Augustine, it does seem to me that his modern critics have perhaps put their finger on one danger inherent in particular forms of Christian theology. And since I've identified this reading as a sacramental one, we might well associate it with what Lauren Winner calls the "characteristic damage" of Christian practices.[3] Winner cautions against the tendency to prematurely celebrate the radical possibilities of Christian Eucharist, prayer, and baptism by demonstrating their historical

---

3. Lauren Winner, *The Dangers of Christian Practice: On Wayward Gifts, Characteristic Damage, and Sin* (New Haven: Yale University Press, 2018).

interdependence with American chattel slavery, medieval pogroms against Jews, and the bourgeois trappings of the nineteenth-century family. While Winner strongly argues that we should not understand our beloved practices as inherently liberatory, neither should we discard them as fundamentally irredeemable. Perhaps the practice of Christian theology has its own characteristic damage: reducing a fellow creature to theological use-value in our attempt to know and enjoy God.

My own initial work in theology, as I've described it here, can be fairly characterized as more *No* than *Yes*, to put it Barthianly. The *No* of ideology critique is certainly always necessary in theology whenever its dangerous practices entail the damage and instrumentalizing of creatures—this *No* is part of the sword that Jesus announces he has brought in the gospel. But I do not think this exhausts its task—certainly not if such a theology seeks to be faithful to the good news of Jesus Christ, in whom all God's promises are *Yes* and who came to give abundant life to all. And even if our human attempt to describe and correspond to this *Yes* will be dangerous and damaged, we must undertake it, albeit with fear and trembling. But if dismissing the possibility of theology is not the road to take, how does one continue to practice theology while recognizing its characteristic damages and inherent dangers?

Having recently begun my Ph.D. at Princeton Theological Seminary, I am still exploring what shape my own positive contribution to theology might take, but I have been excited by recent work in queer and feminist theological methodologies by Hanna Reichel and Natalie Carnes, who have each drawn upon the concept of affordances to name the ways that theological doctrines can be put to use (for good and for ill).[4] This concept, first articulated by the psychologist

---

4. See Hanna Reichel, *After Method: Queer Grace, Conceptual Design, and the Possibility of Theology* (Louisville: Westminster John Knox Press, 2023), especially chapter 7; and Natalie Carnes, *Attunement: The Art and Politics of Feminist Theology* (New York: Oxford University Press, 2024), especially chapter 3.

James Gibson and further developed in ecological and design theory, clarifies an attentiveness to what a particular doctrine makes possible and forecloses. It also recognizes the inherent ambivalence of theological doctrines, in that the same doctrine, in different contexts and for different people can either be seen as building up or destroying charity for God and neighbor.

In encountering Reichel's and Carnes's ideas, I recognized my own theological work in their methodological descriptions. Barth's doctrine of revelation had provided me with a positive affordance from which I could carve out a habitable space for myself (and others, I hope) within a theological landscape that had seemed uninhabitable. This consideration of the affordances that accompany particular doctrines also describes a particular relation the theologian has to the history of theology and ecclesial traditions. On this view, the theologian becomes a kind of discerner of the Spirit's movement in Scripture, the history of doctrine, and the current experiences of bearers of the tradition. Her look backward is not merely to critically evaluate what is orthodox and what is problematic in the past, as if the good and bad of a living tradition could ever be perfectly discerned by our human acts of judgment. Instead, the theologian looks to the past to ask what elements of our tradition offer possibilities for participating in the Spirit's current movement over the waters of chaos to make creaturely flourishing possible.

I have so far outlined my conception of theology on the level of ideas and themes. But the material conditions and the ecclesial setting that make theology possible are equally (if not more!) relevant to the future of theology in The Episcopal Church and to my own future as a theologian. In concluding this chapter, I would like to focus on two pressing institutional considerations that will deeply shape the future of theology in our church.

First, there are the ongoing divisions in the Anglican Communion and the question of The Episcopal Church's place within the

Communion. I am among those new Anglicans who joined The Episcopal Church well after the sharpest internal schisms of the early 2000s and who are in the strange position of having missed the earthquake, but still experiencing its aftershocks. And although I am new to these conversations, it seems that recently there is a not-insignificant number of Anglicans who have begun to speak of these divisions in a different key. Rather than assuming that our proposals can simply eradicate the disagreements (whether through convincing argument or, more likely, mutual excommunication and schism), recent statements have assumed the present and ongoing inevitability of disagreement, at least for the foreseeable future. Rather than enforcing a bland centrist compromise, frankness about Anglicans having two different doctrines of marriage (among other doctrinal differences) might instead enable continued useful argument across theological difference rather than its suppression or supersession.

The 2024 Nairobi-Cairo Proposals from the Inter-Anglican Standing Commission on Unity, Faith and Order offer the most recent ecclesial statement and action that has followed this line of thought. The proposals find an affordance within an Augustinian theology of church division with which they describe our current disagreements and chart a way forward. Their particular address to the church party I am a part of is a wise one that should be received for the future of our theology: "Those who call themselves progressive or liberal should be prepared to grant graciously the degree of seriousness with which their fellow Anglicans take the matters at hand and concede the consequence of some degree of diminished communion."[5] Our theology from the "progressive or liberal" party of The Episcopal

---

5. Inter-Anglican Standing Commission on Unity, Faith and Order, "The Nairobi-Cairo Proposals: Renewing the Instruments of the Anglican Communion," https://www.anglicancommunion.org/ecumenism/iascufo/the-nairobi-cairo-proposals.aspx, §48.

Church need not be accompanied by its all-too-common triumphalism. Our theologies, too, share in the characteristic damages and negative affordances of all Christian works. This humility need not lead us to stop confidently sharing our own readings of Scripture and encounters with God's grace. It should instead free us to make our arguments without needing to destroy our siblings or shore up our position as the *true* Anglicans. As the work of The Episcopal Church continues amid this internal and external division, I hope our theology can be characterized by such freedom and humility.

Second, rapid changes occurring in the landscape of American higher education generally and theological education in particular demand that our imagining of the future of Episcopal theology include these material considerations. While my formal theological training has occurred in the setting of two residential seminaries, Virginia and Princeton, these are sometimes spoken of as the last gasp of an aging system to be replaced by local diocesan schools and part-time hybrid and online training. I am immensely grateful for the residential seminaries that have made my theological vocation materially possible. Residential theological education has given me more stable housing and better health insurance than I ever had as a food service or lay church worker. It has allowed me to have close relationships with faculty whose tenure has given them the time to research and the ability to share in the governance of their institutions. I would not to call myself a theologian without having been formed by the institutions that materially invested in my education.

Yet it is certainly true that theology existed long before the advent of the seminary and the university. And it is equally true that a tenured theological faculty in the ivory tower does not mechanically guarantee a living theology that is faithful to the dynamism of the God we worship. One of the most famous theologians of The Episcopal Church, William Stringfellow—named as perhaps our greatest by no less an authority than Rowan Williams—lacked any formal theological training and was famously suspicious of theology's comfortable residence within the American academy, even preaching a sermon at Duke University Chapel against "the demonic, incarnate and militant, in the authority, tradition, ideology, and institution of the university."[6] Karl Barth (who also lacked doctoral training in theology!) offers a wonderfully biting recapitulation of God's judgment of Israel's religious system in Amos for the theology that delights in the trappings of its academic setting to the detriment of its vital connection to the living God:

> I hate, I despise your lectures and seminars, your sermons, addresses, and Bible studies, and I take no delight in your discussions, meetings, and conventions. For when you display your hermeneutic, dogmatic, ethical, and pastoral bits of wisdom before one another and before me, I have no pleasure in them; I disdain these offerings of your fatted calves. Take away from me the hue and cry that you old men raise with your thick books and you young men with your dissertations! I will not listen to the melody of your reviews that you compose in your theological magazines, monthlies, and quarterlies.[7]

There are important theological reasons not to cling so tightly to our current system of theological education and production as to snuff out the fiery and free movement of the Spirit that makes the human work of theology possible.

---

6. William Stringfellow, "The Wisdom of Being Foolish," in *Sermons from Duke Chapel: Voices from "A Great Towering Church,"* ed. William H. Willimon (Durham, NC: Duke University Press, 2005), 158.

7. Karl Barth, *Evangelical Theology: An Introduction* (Grand Rapids, MI: Eerdmans, 1979), 135–36.

But these reasons are also not sufficient to guarantee that the emerging institutional alternatives to seminaries and divinity schools will necessarily be more attuned to the Spirit blowing where he chooses. I especially worry that our appeals to accessibility or justice in moving away from residential theological education can seem like a coat of rhetorical paint on the standard neoliberal playbook of dismantling higher education. The replacement of salaried faculty with adjuncts is not just, and it only makes the professoriate less accessible. It is a sad but perhaps unsurprising irony that the beginning of a tentative diversification of theological faculties has coincided with widespread adjunctification! For those theological teachers who do not come from wealth, do not have other salaried employment, or lack access to clerical pensions and health insurance, the supposed flexibility of adjunct contracts and the cost-cutting of online education is really just church-sanctioned poverty.

I certainly do not mean to imply that online theological education and local diocesan schools are inherently opposed to the flourishing of faithful theology in our church. I have taught in my current institution's online degree program, and I found it to be a wonderful experience. My class was full of dedicated students whose contexts and situations wouldn't have allowed for their participation in a residential setting. I am grateful for the new theological opportunities that they and others will have in this new landscape. And indeed, it is very likely that these online programs and local formation will be the setting for at least some of my and many of my fellow graduate students' future theological teaching—I write this as someone who has a vested interest in making our online and distance theological education the best that it can be. But if these opportunities are only made possible by the unstable underemployment of theologians, and the loss of dedicated research libraries and other vital resources, these students and our Church and its theology will all suffer for it. If tenured faculty appointments at residential seminaries are only going to persist for the lucky minority, The Episcopal Church will need to find new ways to materially support its other theologians and theological educators.

Yet, whatever the ecclesial and material conditions may be for the theologians of The Episcopal Church, the necessary task of critically evaluating our church's proclamation in light of the ever-free Word of God will continue. Such evaluation will, at times, resemble an ideology critique of theology's characteristic damage, while at other times it will involve identifying doctrinal affordances that enable the creation of habitable theological niches for creaturely flourishing. It will be a human attempt to be guided and governed by the Holy Spirit, who blows where he wills and brings life to the dead. In all this, our theologians and our church will pray to be granted in this world knowledge of God's truth, and in the age to come life everlasting.

Further Reading Recommendations

Crite, Allan Rohan. *All Glory: Brush Drawing Meditations on the Prayer of Consecration.* Cambridge, MA: Society of Saint John the Evangelist, 1947. Available at https://anglicanhistory.org/ssje/crite1947.pdf

Gordon, Colby. *Glorious Bodies: Trans Theology and Renaissance Literature.* Chicago: University of Chicago Press, 2024.

Kempe, Margery. *The Book of Margery Kempe.* Translated by Anthony Bale. Oxford: Oxford University Press, 2015.

Stringfellow, William. *An Ethic for Christians and Other Aliens in a Strange Land.* Waco, TX: Word Books, 1973; reprint, Eugene, OR: Wipf and Stock, 2004.

"He Must Increase, and I Must Decrease": Jesus Christ as the Center of Proclamation

Kara N. Slade

Yesterday

The story of how I became a theologian is deeply uninteresting to me, because I find God endlessly interesting and myself much less so. That being said, here is the story. At the time, the unfolding of my vocation to theological scholarship felt like it happened through a series of accidents. I never thought I would become a theologian until I became one. I thought I would be an engineer who enjoyed church as an essentially recreational activity. From a young age, I had an interest in science, and my industrial chemist father encouraged me to follow in his footsteps. When I graduated from high school and left Florida for Duke University, I had the kind of unshakable confidence unique to eighteen-year-olds that I knew what the trajectory of the future would be. I loved the practicality of mechanical engineering, the reward of seeing ideas and plans become real objects in the world. Mechanical engineering was fun, and I was good enough at it that I was able to stay at Duke for a Ph.D. in the field. I was active in the Episcopal campus ministry, but in reality, church functioned for me as an activity that respectable people did. God existed, I was sure, but as a vague (if ultimately important) being in a vague beyond. I remember telling a friend at the time that believing in the Church was easier than believing in Jesus.

That orientation changed when I was confronted with the reality of my need for Jesus. When I took my first job as a civil servant at NASA, I expected to stay there for decades. Within five years, however, it became clear that the particularities of my position and my own particularities were a bad fit for each other. What started as a problem of professional dissatisfaction became the kindling for a personal conflagration. The less said about the details, the better, but it was a profoundly difficult time. I left without a clear idea of what I would do next, but I had become much clearer about my need for God. I found, as many others have, that when you have nowhere else to turn, your understanding of God becomes much more serious and specific.

A priest at my former parish in Virginia suggested that I consider going back to school to study the ethics of technology. After being rejected by Yale, I returned to Duke in the Master of Theological Studies program. My plan was to complete a two-year master's degree and eventually teach ethics to engineering undergraduates. Like many of my plans, this one also turned out to be wrong. I ended up transferring to the Master of Divinity program and staying on for a second doctorate, this time in theology. It seemed like a stunning accident that in the midst of my studies, the rector of my internship parish suggested I might consider ordination. Despite my initial protestations to the contrary, the Church made me a priest.

I have told the story thus far as a series of accidents, but in retrospect, the tea leaves of Providence were there to read all along. I was extremely active at my childhood parish, taking part in everything from acolytes to youth group. Although I found youth group miserable, I loved serving as an acolyte and I was an insufferable know-it-all in Sunday School. The clearest sign of my later vocation appeared much earlier, however. As a precocious elementary schooler, I often turned to the back of the Book of Common Prayer (1979) during moments of boredom in church. I was fascinated by the "Historical Documents of the Church" section that promised knowledge of things I couldn't yet understand. Again and again, I turned to the paragraph under the heading "Definition of the Union of the Divine and Human Natures in the Person of Christ."[1] I puzzled over what seemed to be the incomprehensible sentences of the Chalcedonian formula. It turns out that since the early 1980s, I have been enthralled by Jesus Christ and how the Church talks about him. One of the great gifts of my life is the fact that I am now paid to be thus enthralled, and to share my delight and wonder with others.

The story of my path as a theologian is also the story of how I became a particular kind of theologian. I could not do what I do without the influence and guidance of my own particular cloud of witnesses, the conversation partners across time and space who have helped me clarify my own thoughts and language. The conversation began in one life-changing semester of my master's program, when I simultaneously took an introductory course in the theology of Karl Barth with Willie James Jennings and a course with Amy Laura Hall that involved a close reading of Kierkegaard's *Works of Love*. In Barth and Kierkegaard, I found what I had been looking for without knowing it: an account of God's action in the world that is relentlessly centered on God's self-revelation and saving work in Jesus Christ. I also found a realism about human sin, the limitations of human knowledge, and the all-sufficiency of grace, such that Jesus Christ cannot be relegated to an optional benefit in a life that is already going well. In this chapter, I hope to give my own account of why the work of theology is important for The Episcopal Church today,

---

1. Book of Common Prayer 1979, 864.

and why I believe that Karl Barth can be a helpful interlocutor for Episcopalians.

The work of theology is to set out sentences in which God is the active subject. However, it does not do so as an abstract exercise. Theology is not a spectator sport. It *involves* us as human beings, but in the first instance, it is not *about* us. It is a task of the Church carried out for the sake of the Church, in service to the work of proclaiming the Word of God. This is a matter of utmost seriousness in which human speech will ultimately fall short. Barth writes:

> [A]s it confesses God the Church also confesses both the humanity and the responsibility of its action. It realises that it is exposed to fierce temptation as it speaks of God, and it realises that it must give an account to God for the way in which it speaks. The first and last and decisive answer to this twofold compulsion consists in the fact that it rests content with the grace of the One whose strength is mighty in weakness. But in so doing it recognises and takes up as an active Church the further human task of criticising and revising its speech about God.[2]

The human limitations of theology, and of theologians, necessitate a constant process of self-interrogation and correction:

> The work in which the Church submits to this self-examination falls into three circles which intersect in such a way that the centre of each is also within the circumference of the other two, so that in view of that which alone can be the centre it is as well neither to affirm nor to construct a systematic centre,

---

2. Karl Barth, *Church Dogmatics Volume I/1* (Edinburgh: T & T Clark, 1975), 10.

> i.e., the centre of a circle embracing the other three. The question of truth, with which theology is concerned throughout, is the question as to the agreement of the Church's distinctive talk about God with the being of the Church. The criterion of past, future and therefore present Christian utterance is thus the being of the Church, namely, Jesus Christ, God in His gracious revealing and reconciling address to man. Does Christian utterance derive from Him? Does it lead to Him? Is it conformable to Him? None of these questions can be put apart, but each is to be put independently and with all possible force.[3]

In all its language, theology works in relationship to and in service of the Word in its three aspects: the Word of God proclaimed in the Church, written in Scripture, and revealed in Jesus Christ. It is an act of witness to that Word that the theologian has herself heard.

As he wrote the *Church Dogmatics*, Barth kept a copy of Matthias Grünewald's *Crucifixion* from the Isenheim Altarpiece above his desk. I keep a copy in my office as well. John the Baptist's anachronistic presence in the painting is a reminder of the theologian's role as witness: to point to the one who reigns from the cross and to say, "He must increase, and I must decrease." As Barth writes, "Witnessing means pointing in a specific direction beyond the self and on to another ... the biblical word comes into play as a word of witness, when and where John's finger does not point in vain but really indicates, when and where we are enabled by means of his word to see and hear what he saw and heard."[4] That relentless pointing to the person and work of Christ is, I think, the greatest gift that a reading of Barth brings to Episcopalians.

---

3. Barth, *Church Dogmatics I/1*, 11.
4. Barth, *Church Dogmatics I/1*, 117–18.

Today[5]

Over the course of my clerical career, I have repeatedly experienced a particular genre of meeting in which a group of extremely accomplished leaders asked each other what they valued most about The Episcopal Church or a particular parish. Probably the most common response, across different events and constituencies, is "community," followed closely by "inclusion." I find it both enlightening and confusing that extremely smart and successful church people consistently struggle to connect their love of the community and its characteristics with the reality of God, or with the difference Jesus Christ makes for the Church beyond that of a salutary moral example. They struggle with the particularity of Christian speech, and perhaps by extension with the particularity of Christianity. The end result can be a church that loudly proclaims its welcome, but lacks a clear and consistent idea of what, specifically, anyone is being welcomed to or why.

A vague humanism is insufficient to sustain the contemporary church in an increasingly challenging context, either in its own life as an institution or as a witness within a pluralistic society. Jesus must be more than a generalized model of the moral life, regardless of how much easier it is to talk about Jesus' teachings—or, at least, the less controversial ones—than about the cross and empty tomb. For us, and for our churches, God is not and cannot be a vague deity who creates and then watches human events from afar. References to "the divine," without reference to who we believe God to be—without being rooted in the particularity of our story—are ultimately uncompelling. We have been shown precisely who God is, in the revelation of Scripture as the Word of God. God is, in the words of my late parishioner,

---

5. Portions of this section appeared in an edited form in "Who is Karl Barth?," *Earth and Altar*, July 31, 2023.

friend, and neighbor Robert Jenson, "whoever raised Jesus from the dead, having before raised Israel from Egypt."[6]

It is as problematic to speak of "the human" apart from Christ as it is to speak of "the divine" apart from the Trinity. Stanley Hauerwas, commenting on Karl Barth's "apocalyptic humanism," writes, "Jesus is no image or symbol of the general reality of the human exactly because he is a singular reality, not an instance of a more universal principle . . . Accordingly, Jesus cannot be judged from some general, ostensibly human point of view, 'but rather every human being must be regarded from the point of view of this particular man.'"[7] Just as God cannot be boiled down to a vague, aloof divinity, the Christian life cannot be reduced to a generalized hope for individual or social improvement for those whose lives are going well. It also cannot be limited to inclusion without an account of holiness, regardless of how nonlinear or recursive the path of sanctification may be. The Christian life promises an utterly transformed life in Christ to those for whom sin, both individual and structural, is real—that is to say, to all of us.

Our current experience as a Church is far from unique in the course of theological and ecclesial history. Karl Barth was trained by theologians for whom the particularity of Christian confession had become decidedly muted. In the early decades of the nineteenth century, Friedrich Schleiermacher gave an account of Christianity that centered human experience and a "feeling of absolute dependence" on God. Meanwhile, he relegated the Trinity to the last chapter of *The Christian Faith*, perhaps the foundational text of liberal theology. The

---

6. Robert Jenson, *Systematic Theology 1* (New York: Oxford University Press, 2001), 63.

7. Stanley Hauerwas, *Fully Alive: The Apocalyptic Humanism of Karl Barth* (Charlottesville: University of Virginia Press, 2022), 26, quoting from Karl Barth, *Against the Stream: Shorter Post-War Writings, 1946–1952* (London: SCM, 1954), 186.

close of the nineteenth century saw Adolf von Harnack's attempt to separate the moral "kernel" of Christianity from the "husk" of unscientific myth. For Harnack, the "kernel" of Christianity was found in a "fellow-feeling" for humanity, unmoored from the truth of cross and resurrection, and an approach to Scripture that placed modern Biblical scholarship over the Word in a position of judgment.

At the outbreak of the First World War, Barth discovered the depths to which this approach proved to be intellectually and morally bankrupt. Harnack, along with 96 other leading German intellectuals, signed a manifesto enthusiastically supporting Germany's war project, which led to a religion of the nation. As a young pastor in the small Swiss town of Safenwil, Barth realized that he had to begin again in his approach to Scripture and theological language. In conversation with his friend Eduard Thurneysen, he developed the ideas that would become his epoch-making commentary on Romans and lead to the rest of his intellectual project. That project would be marked by a rejection of idolatry in all its forms, from National Socialism and the Führer principle to Soviet Communism to American postwar hegemony. It is challenging for contemporary Christians that he rejected all attempts to make even the most noble political projects the goal of theology and the life of the Church. When he writes in 1933 that theology should proceed "as if nothing had happened," it can sound at first glance like an irresponsible denial of the imminent dangers of authoritarianism.[8] However, this controversial sentence is intended to function not as a refusal of politics but as an ordering of politics under the first principles of theology. Jesus is Lord, and this confession of the Gospel entails resistance to all false claims to lordship.

---

8. Karl Barth, *Theological Existence To-Day: A Plea for Theological Freedom* (Eugene, OR: Wipf and Stock, 2011), 9.

The importance of a perspicuous and rightly ordered political theology, as described above, is clear in tumultuous times. Beyond that, however, lie some primary doctrinal assertions that Episcopalians would do well to attend to. First, when we as Christians say "God," we mean the Triune God—Father, Son, and Holy Spirit—who acts in loving freedom. The word "God" refers precisely to the Trinity, and there is no other God-concept or idea that stands behind the Triune God revealed in Scripture and confessed in the Creeds. There is no God-behind-God who can be co-opted into another ideology, only the God revealed in Jesus Christ. The vocation of theology is to speak of that particular God's action in loving relationship to creation. This approach stands in contrast to modern methods that center the thinking, believing, religious human subject. Theology entails us, just as God chooses to be God for us in Jesus Christ. But it is not about us in the first instance. It is about the Triune God, and it does its work in service to the Church's proclamation of God's loving acts.

That proclamation can be summed up succinctly in Barth's 1962 advice to students at Princeton Seminary: "that God is not against them but for them." It can also be summed up by John 12:31–32: "Now is the judgment of this world; now the ruler of this world will be driven out. And I, when I am lifted up from the earth, will draw all people to myself." (NRSV) Far from being bad news for us as creatures, this judgment is the divine *No* to everything that is contrary to God, enveloped in God's gracious *Yes* to us. It is the good news that in freedom, God chooses to create a world whose deepest logic is the covenant of grace between creator and creature. In freedom, God chooses to reveal Godself in Jesus Christ, as attested in the witness of Scripture. In freedom, God chooses to be God *for us* in Jesus Christ, and on the cross, Jesus does in our place what we cannot do for ourselves. From the point of the cross are all things reckoned, and all things seen.

Second, one of the most slippery aspects of Anglican theology in particular is its relationship to natural knowledge and scientific reason. In 2005, The Episcopal Church's Committee on Science, Technology, and Faith released a document entitled *A Catechism of Creation*. While it was concerned for the most part with the laudable goal of environmental stewardship, it also took pains to differentiate Episcopalians from the various permutations of what is generally called "creationism" in the American context. The constructive doctrine of creation it sets forth describes a God who creates "in, with, and under" evolutionary processes of natural selection.[9] To support their argument, they cite Charles Kingsley's words that "God has made a world that is able to make itself," yet without noting the nature of the world that Kingsley envisioned.[10] For Kingsley, natural selection also included the logic of colonial domination, as he wrote in a short lecture entitled "The Natural Theology of the Future":

> Physical science is proving more and more the immense importance of Race; the importance of hereditary powers, hereditary organs, hereditary habits, in all organized beings ... She is proving more and more the omnipresent action of the differences between races, how the more favored race (she cannot avoid using the epithet) exterminates the less favored, or at least expels it ...and, in a word, that competition between every race and every individual of that race, and

---

9. Committee on Science, Technology, and Faith of the Executive Council, *A Catechism of Creation: An Episcopal Understanding*, First Edition Revised June 2005, https://www.episcopalchurch.org/ecojustice/a-catechism-of-creation-an-episcopal-understanding/, 12.

10. *A Catechism of Creation*, 12.

reward according to deserts is (as far as we can see) a universal law of living things.[11]

The act of discerning God's purpose from nature and history is a morally and epistemologically fraught exercise that inevitably brings the biases and sin-soaked limitations of human beings to bear.

Barth knew the temptation of natural theology all too well, and his reaction appeared most famously in his response of "Nein!" to Emil Brunner. Writing later in the *Church Dogmatics*, he would ground his definition of sin in the person and work of Jesus Christ, who reveals the truth about sin. In the second volume of his doctrine of creation, he writes,

> We have only to cease trying to ignore the free grace of God in Jesus Christ. We have only to cease trying to make use of "natural" theology and therefore anthropology. Illusion always results when we seek light on human nature from any other source than the man Jesus Christ. To do so is to trifle with the fact of sin. It is to dig leaking wells. It is to entangle ourselves in conjectures and reinterpretations. It is again to seek final refuge in oblivion.[12]

Barth knew all too well the demonic ends to which an ideologically captive church could deploy natural theology—including, eventually, painting genocide and racial superiority as God's will. The human heart is a factory of idols, as Calvin knew, and reading God out of nature is an especially efficient way to run that factory.

---

11. Charles Kingsley, "The Natural Theology of the Future," in *Scientific Lectures and Essays*, Works of Charles Kingsley 19 (London: Macmillan, 1880), 324.

12. Barth, *Church Dogmatics III/2*, 520.

Finally, in this time as in every, the Church is called to be a Church of witness. We cannot save ourselves, much less the world. In fact, to believe that we can is a form of idolatry. Barth locates the root of sin in the pride of humanity—the human delusion that we can be our own savior—but he also identifies it in humanity's sloth. While we cannot do what God alone can do, nor can we place ourselves in the position of God, we are not absolved of the duty to love our neighbor and to be witnesses in a world that does not yet know that it has been conclusively transformed by God in Christ.

Tomorrow

Several years ago, I had the opportunity to give a lecture to a group of Episcopal clergy on the topic of "formation for the church today." I used a little essay by Robert Jenson called "The Return to Baptism," which appears in his contribution to a volume titled *Encounters with Luther*. Drawing on the Large Catechism, he writes, "baptism is the casting of the old into the waters and the appearance of the new. Not just in Luther, but in the whole tradition, baptism has never been understood as merely the beginning of new life. Baptism is that ending of the old and beginning of the new which is life . . . [T]he old life ends when I submit myself to the waters, and the new self is an eschatological self, a self in the kingdom, a self in the Spirit."[13] While there is an absolute once-and-for-all aspect to the sacramental act, the Christian life after baptism does not exist on an upward trajectory where we never again have to return to these questions. Specifically, he says, "How do we return to baptism?" The answer is simple but

---

13. Robert W. Jenson, "The Return to Baptism," in *Encounters with Luther: Lectures, Discussions and Sermons at the Martin Luther Colloquia 1975-1979*, ed. Eric W. Gritsch (Gettysburg, PA: Institute for Luther Studies, 1982), 218.

wrenching: "Give up your past life again to the judgment of God, as you did when you first gave up yourself to the waters," where in the pattern of the sacraments we apprehend again "the death of the old and the birth of the new."[14] There is no room for a narrative of progress here, and no room for a theology of baptism that marks a beginning but not an end, a welcome without true transformation. Here, the old Adam must die, and die, and die again.

When I said these things out loud in front of a group of Episcopal clergy, the result was interesting to say the least. Some people thought it was exactly right. "Why don't we hear more of this from the pulpit? I need to hear this," exclaimed the one layperson in the room. But one priest said he was "shocked" (in a negative sense) to hear someone talk about sin and judgment so vehemently in a "progressive" context. I'm sure he wasn't the only one. I replied that if we talked about it more, perhaps it wouldn't be so shocking. I should have been less obnoxious in my response, but I do agree with the principle behind what I said. However, this is the gift that pastor-theologians like Jenson and Barth gave to us, and to me: the gift of truthful and courageous speech about the reality of God and the reality of the human condition, the gift of the true story in a world that has lost its story.

It is my earnest prayer that the future of theology, both within The Episcopal Church and beyond it, will be *theological*. That is to say, theology should be about *God*, and not a form of psychology, sociology, or politics shouted in a loud voice. At the same time, a theological worldview centered on God's action in the world permeates every aspect of how we live our lives: personal, familial, political, and cultural. Furthermore, theology cannot exist without the Church. On all these points, Jenson and Barth continue to speak to us together against some of the most troubling, and not particularly new, currents in the discipline.

---

14. Jenson, "The Return to Baptism," 217.

One of the most whimsically true instances of this kind of theological speech can be found in Jenson's book for children (and grownups), *Conversations with Poppi About God*—an extended interview with his eight-year-old granddaughter, Solveig. At one point in their dialog, Solveig and Poppi (Jenson) are talking about the Nicene Creed, and in particular about the line "through him all things were made." Solveig says, "Well, I would like to say that Jesus is not the one who wrote the many movies Daddy is writing. He did not write your systematic theology." Jenson responds, "That's certainly true. But that's the same point we had earlier, isn't it? In one way, we do what we do, but we would not do it if it were not for God."[15]

The most pressing question for The Episcopal Church today is perhaps the same question that it has always been. To use Jenson's language, would we do it—whatever "it" may be in our ecclesial life—if it were not for God? What difference does God make? More to the point, what difference does Jesus Christ make, not as a vaguely good idea or an inspirational model, but as the Savior of the world and head of the Church? What difference does baptized life in Christ make to the Church as a body of people who are made a new creation in Jesus Christ? These have always been questions that confront the Church, but perhaps they confront us now more than ever.

Further Reading Recommendations

Barth, Karl. *Dogmatics in Outline*. Translated by G. T. Thompson. London: SCM Press, 1949. Also available in more recent editions.

---

15. Robert W. Jenson and Solveig Lucia Gold, *Conversations with Poppi about God: An Eight-Year-Old and Her Theologian Grandfather Trade Questions* (Grand Rapids, MI: Brazos Press, 2006), 140.

Barth, Karl. *Homiletics.* Foreword by David G. Buttrick. Translated by Geoffrey W. Bromiley and Daniel E. Daniels. Louisville: Westminster/John Knox Press, 1991.

Jenson, Robert W. and Solveig Lucia Gold. *Conversations with Poppi about God: An Eight-Year-Old and Her Theologian Grandfather Trade Questions.* Grand Rapids, MI: Brazos Press, 2006.

Ramsey, Michael. *The Christian Priest Today.* London: SPCK, 1972. Also available in more recent editions.

The Promise and Perils of Theological Imagination in The Episcopal Church

Scott MacDougall

Becoming Episcopalian, Becoming a Theologian

I decided to become a trained theologian shortly after I became an Episcopalian. Really, I decided to become a trained theologian *because* I became an Episcopalian.

As far back as I can remember, there was never a time when I was not actively pondering questions related to the character and identity of God. Because I was raised as a member of an active, churchgoing United Methodist family, I naturally framed my concerns in Christian terms. As a child, I did so vaguely and intuitively. By high school, I was doing it explicitly and anxiously. Even when the answers I was receiving to my inquiries caused me to move further and further away from a specifically Christian commitment to a more general philosophical and cultural appreciation for the religious impulse, my viewpoint on "the transcendent" retained a distinctly Christian cast. Whether studying other faiths or reading about comparative religion, philosophy of religion, or the history of religion, my early formation as a Christian shaped how I thought about it all. Even my work in theater when I was just out of college had a Christian theological undercurrent: I conceived of my small company as a quasi-monastic community, emphasized the parallels between performance and liturgy, and considered the development and presentation of those performances as types of prayer.

It was when I took the initial steps to re-engage with Christianity as an actual practitioner, rather than as someone regarding it from a safe intellectual and aesthetic distance, that I turned to theologians. I had discovered The Episcopal Church and was convinced by the shape of its corporate life and practices that it offered something profound, something true. Before I could go further, however, I needed to understand how Christian theologians in general and Anglican theologians in particular brought together the scriptural witness, human knowledge and experience, and the insights and practices of Christians through time to articulate a vision of truth, meaning, and value capable of producing individual and corporate lives that manifested those same truths, meanings, and values. Like many others, I had firsthand acquaintance with the death-dealing power of theology. I wanted to be convinced of its life-giving potential so that I could trust and commit to the way of life that The Episcopal Church appeared to offer.

As my understanding of Christian theology deepened, so did my relationship with The Episcopal Church. I learned that theology casts a disciplined vision of who God is, who we are, and how we might live given those realities. I started to see how our individual and shared lives as Christians test those visions, sometimes confirming them, sometimes falsifying them, and sometimes suggesting possibilities for revising them slightly or developing radically new ones. Soon, I could hardly think of anything that excited me more than considering the implications of the dynamic interplay between a Christian theological imagination conditioned by its foundational sources and the lived practice of Christian faith in the form of love for and service to both God and the world.

I couldn't take Christianity seriously without taking theology seriously. But neither could I take seriously the demand that Christianity makes on us without reconsidering my relationship to theology. As I tried to better integrate the various aspects of my life, I began to ask myself about the use of my time and energy. This is what led me to seek theological training. I thought that, given a proper schooling and tools, my lifelong struggle with theological questions could serve The Episcopal Church by equipping me to help others contend with them, too. I enrolled in an M.A. program focusing on Anglican theology at the General Theological Seminary with the intention of continuing for a Ph.D. in systematic theology and eventually teaching theology in an Episcopal seminary (and, if I were lucky, one day serving as editor of the *Anglican Theological Review*). I wanted to help form clergy able to nurture the theological imaginations of their parishioners, just as mine had been nurtured by my parish priests. I wanted to help Episcopalians discover and live out deep, Jesus-shaped, gospel-inflected meaning in practicing their vocation to love God and neighbor in all the many aspects of their daily lives.

Eventually, I taught theology at an Episcopal seminary and even served as Co-Editor-in-Chief of the *Anglican Theological Review*. I don't know to what extent I contributed to building up Episcopal Christians in the practice of their faith as I had set out to do, but I remain utterly convinced of the necessity of the work. Who we understand God to be and the form that our lives take are inextricably linked. We are commanded to love God and neighbor with our whole heart, soul, and mind (Lk 10:27, Mt 22:37; see also Deut 6:5). This is not possible without a critical working view of who the God we love is, who we are, and what Christian love looks like. Theology is not optional but required for discipleship, in all its dimensions: intellectual, practical, and spiritual.

Theology and Theological Imagination

In my view, Christian theology can be defined relatively—and deceptively—simply. Theology[1] is an intellectual and spiritual discipline that puts the scriptural witness, human knowledge and experience, and the deep history of God's relationship with God's people into conversation in order to produce a coherent, compelling, and faithful account of Christian truth that both shapes and is shaped by Christian practice in a specific time and place.

This Christian account of what is true and meaningful is the vision that constitutes a theological imagination. *Imagination* is not used here to indicate something that is "made up" or "only in one's mind." Instead, it points to the thoughtful, reflective, and critical position one has attained through prayer and study, based on one's commitments and supportable arguments, rooted in appropriate sources, about what is right, good, and true. It is a well-reasoned perspective—not a mere opinion—that describes how one *imagines* (i.e., *supposes on good grounds*) God and the world to be.

At first, this might make theological imagination sound like a type of philosophy dressed in religious clothes. In some ways, it is, which is hardly surprising, given that philosophy and theology were not separate endeavors until relatively recently. However, a theological imagination is not the same thing as a philosophy. That is not only because theological imagination is explicitly Christian in a way that a philosophical outlook—even one espoused by a Christian—is not obliged to be. It is also because, in addition to the rational and logical capabilities of the intellect, theological imagination involves the aesthetic, affective, and somatic registers. These are elements that

---

1. For ease of readability and because the Christian context is clear, I don't always qualify *theology* with *Christian* here, even though I technically should, since how I define and discuss theology does not always apply to the theologies of other faiths.

shape a theological viewpoint but are not always capturable in discursive, linguistic terms, thereby rendering concepts fully legible to the intellect alone, as philosophy requires.

What is important to note about this is that, while theological imagination should not be taken to suggest that we can simply conjure up what is true about God and the world from the fantasies of our own minds, on the one hand, neither can we simply rationalize or argue our way to that truth, on the other. Beliefs are certainly integral to theological imagination. But so are experiences of beauty, love, and embodied, creaturely life, which warrant those beliefs. Because we are bodies—beloved flesh—we can only know God in the ways God has given us to know anything at all. This includes the intellect. But it also includes our other ways of knowing: by sense experience, prayer and contemplation, worship, work, service, relationships, and interactions of all kinds. A full theological imagination is held together by a web of beliefs and arguments. However, it also demands, for instance, not only a conceptual account of beauty but an understanding of divine reality informed by encounters with it; not only clarity about the proper object of our love but an understanding of divine reality informed by participation in loving it; not only an affirmation of creaturely existence as a gift but an understanding of divine reality informed by living fully as flesh, here and now, and not as if there were something, somewhere, or someone else we were meant to be.

I have started to veer away from defining theological imagination in general toward describing the features of my own in particular. I'll return to the definitional task by adding that different expressions of Christianity operate with different theological imaginations. They are communities animated by specific Christian visions of how reality is constituted. Moreover, specific theologians or groups of theologians within those communities can offer additional theological imaginations that might be more or less in line, or more or less in tension, with those of their home communities.

While this might seem obvious, its implications might be less so. The question of how to judge "good" and "bad" theology, for example, becomes more complicated when making that call relies less on, say, evaluating the method of scriptural interpretation employed alone, or assessing the extent to which a view supports certain central tenets of the faith alone, than it does on understanding how that theological position fits within an entire theological vision as conceptualized and lived by actual Christians. This is not to say such judgments cannot or should not be made. On the contrary, discernment between "good" and "bad" theology is a critical imperative. Without exaggeration, it is a matter of life and death. What it is to say is that discerning the difference between "good" and "bad" theology requires a holistic, multi-factor diagnosis based on an examination of the health of the entire theological imagination of which it is a component, which takes time, sensitivity, skill, empathy, and humility.

The Three Questions of Theology

Ultimately, a theological imagination results from a struggle to reckon as thoroughly as possible—intellectually, practically, and spiritually—with three essential questions:

1. Who is God?

2. Who are we?

3. How then are we to live?

The Questions and Scripture

The first place we go to answer these questions is scripture. There is not a shred of scripture that does not engage one or more of these questions. There are passages that answer them directly. For example, portions of the Hebrew prophetic literature and Paul's letters expound on God's identity explicitly. The creation accounts in Genesis tell us something about who we are, signaling that, whatever else we may be, we are a creation of God's beneficence and are invested with a special role in the world. A number of texts in the Hebrew scriptures and the New Testament provide principles for how to live well as God's people.

In some ways, however, these are exceptions rather than the rule. More often, we do not find in the biblical texts propositional replies to our theological inquiries. The psalms and the wisdom literature, for example, frequently answer the three questions somewhat obliquely, by praising God, lamenting before God, struggling to be faithful to God, and so on, illuminating answers to theology's three core queries slantwise, not head-on. Even when a text does not seem to answer any of the questions, it might actually be addressing them all. Think of the Song of Songs and the Revelation to John. One might need to wrestle with those writings to receive the blessing of their answers. The effort, however, will be repaid because every scriptural text relates to one or more of them and, therefore, is meant to give that insight to us.[2]

Above all, scripture illuminates who God is, who we are, and how we should live in light of those identities less by way of uttering propositions than by providing a narrative, by presenting a story. Similarly

---

2. This is not, I hasten to add, to say that scripture's answers to these questions are uniform or uncontestable. They are neither. Here, I am only making a case for maintaining scripture as our central and primary source for doing theology.

to Jesus' liberal use of parable in teaching, a massive proportion of the Hebrew scriptures and, most crucially, the Christian gospels (including the Acts of the Apostles), take the form of stories about the relationship between God and human beings, stories that are far less interested in *telling* us who God is, who we are, and how we should live in light of those identities than in *showing* us those things. Moreover, the extra-biblical story of the Bible itself, the history of how its various texts were produced, collected, and canonized, and what this tells us about how our forebears in the faith experienced, understood, and related to God, is itself part of the overarching narrative scripture provides to answer the three core theological questions.

There is no greater power shaping theological imagination than the narratives that have grounded our answers as God's people to those three core questions over time and across space. To be sure, we have answered them in different ways at different times and in different places, as is only right and good. Yet, the stories that have animated our faith and practice—our theological imaginations—have provided our most fundamental point of orientation in how we have answered them.

The Questions and Theology

Just as there is no piece of scripture that does not in some way address the three basic questions, there is no area of Christian theology that is not tasked with bringing all of our God-given ways of knowing to interpret the scriptural witness to answer them.

Who is God? This is the basic, foundational question for theology, one that has long been treated most explicitly under the theological heading of the doctrines of God, Christ, the Holy Spirit, and—when viewed in their unity—the Trinity, as well as creation, providence, salvation, and eschatology.

Who are we? This is the foundational question for theological anthropology, which seeks to articulate the nature and character of humanity as a beloved creation of God, while also describing and accounting for sin and grace.

How should we live? Just as the second question tends to be answered with reference to the first, so the third is best answered in light of the second. Theologically, this question is addressed by a host of disciplines: ecclesiology, liturgical theology, and sacramentology; Christian theologies of religion; moral theology and ethics, including political and liberation theologies (construed broadly); and many of the various trajectories on the wide spectrum of practical theologies.

This categorization of the areas of theology is crude and misleading. Even if it seems to do so at first glance, no part of theology truly answers only one of the questions. It would be absurd to think, for example, that the doctrine of God tells us nothing about who we are or how we are to live, that theological anthropology has nothing to do with God's identity or our lived reality, or that ecclesiology has nothing to say about God's nature and character or our own. The point is that theology, like the scripture to which it responds and with which it is in intimate dialog, is ultimately only and always about these three questions, even when it seems like it isn't.[3]

The Relationship Between the Questions and Theological Imagination

The basic vocation of the theologian—which means, of all disciples of Jesus—is to identify the God whom we worship, strive to understand ourselves in relation to that God, and draw out the concrete, practical implications of this for conducting ourselves accordingly. We do that

---

3. And even when theologians forget that it ought to be!

always rooted in what I've called "the scriptural witness." What we take that witness to be constitutes the vision that lies at the heart of our theological imaginations. Through a recursive movement between the biblical texts and how we understand and interpret them using the full range of the ways we know things, and in conversation with the ways that our forebears in the faith have attempted to address these three questions, we build up an account of the scriptural witness to God's identity and our own and of what these realities call us to be and do.

Turning to my own theological imagination by way of example, I think we mistake God's identity if it is not characterized by naming what God has done, is doing, and will do; that we do not properly understand ourselves apart from how we are positioned in the unfolding story of our relationship to the God who has done, is doing, and will do those things; and that we cannot discern how to make our way through this complicated, beautiful, and tragic world as Christians except by discerning and acting in ways that seem most aligned with who God is and with who God created us to be, and with who God promises we will one day become. That is, we are only able to grasp all of this—to the limited extent we are able to grasp it this side of the fulfillment of all things—by inhabiting—intellectually, practically, and spiritually—the narrative that grounds what we as Christians understand to be the Really Real. That is what I mean by the scriptural witness.

What do I think is the content of that witness? What is the metanarrative that orients my perspective and determines my theological imagination? Developing some ideas I once put forward in a Good Friday sermon, it runs something like this:

> In the beginning, God created out of nothing something other than God to love for its own sake. God granted freedom to

that creation, freedom to evolve, experiment, and become. A small part of creation developed the ability to know and love God in return. But it did so imperfectly, unable to love itself, others of its kind, the rest of creation, or, above all, God with the fullness of communion that God is and has desired for creation from the beginning.

After repeatedly attempting to reveal to these creatures how to know and love God and themselves better, God entered into creation itself, taking on the material condition of human flesh. Jesus of Nazareth was and is the epitome of God's self-revelation. Through human words, actions, and relationships, God graciously displayed in our own terms—*as us*—who God is, who we are, and how we are to live.

The more that, in showing this, Jesus attracted the poor, oppressed, and despised, the more he challenged the prevailing views of what constituted goodness and truth, the more resistance grew. The tangle of misplaced priorities, deep anxiety, and false desires that wounds and scars this broken world rose up in its totality against God's self-offer. God's creation tortured its maker to death.

Yet, even then, the God who created all that is out of nothing, brought new life out of the nothingness of death. In the resurrection, God overruled the rejection of communion and flourishing, sealing the promise to bring all of creation it to its perfection, into undreamt-of new life beyond brokenness, suffering, and even death, all on account of the unfathomable, inexhaustible love that God is.

By placing ourselves at the disposal of God the Holy Spirit, who makes Christ present to, in, and as us when we gather in Jesus' name, and who inspires our daily existence and practices, our lives are conformed to the pattern of Jesus' life. We, too, are enabled to show in our words, actions, and relationships, who God is, who human beings are, and how we should live in light of those realities. We are granted the capacity to love God and neighbor. We are filled with hope for the final fullness of communion, and are compelled by that hope to strive to mirror those conditions now, in matters big and small, to the utmost of our strength, knowing we will never do so fully on account of the brokenness of sin, the bondage that presently constrains creation. In the future of complete freedom, God will overcome all the obstacles to communion raised by sin. That full freedom is what we call salvation. That final state is the Kingdom of God. The divine establishment of the Kingdom of God is the completion of all things in love and blessing that Paul wrote about as God being All in all (1 Cor 15:28).

This is the story by which I orient myself, first, simply as a Christian, and then, also, as a theologian. This "scriptural witness" summarizes what I think the Bible tells us about God and God's relationship with creation in general and with people in particular. It is only what the creeds affirm. It is nothing more than what the Christian church has always maintained, even if inflected differently on account of how I have been shaped personally, including by my historical time and place, with the insights and limitations that come with those circumstances.

When I engage in theology, when I attempt to present a clear and precise account of what I believe to be true regarding a particular theological conundrum, I strive to answer the questions posed by the situation by grounding the inquiry in this narrative.

Assessing the Theological Health of The Episcopal Church

I think the Anglican tradition's greatest gift is the particular sensibility of its theological imagination.[4] Drawing on the resources of the broad, small-C catholic Christian tradition, it does not prescribe what people must believe but instead pushes the boundaries of Christian theological imagination out as far as possible, opening up a wide space within which Anglican theological belief and practice can reasonably roam. Those boundaries, named by the Chicago–Lambeth Quadrilateral,[5] are set by the canonical scriptures, the ancient creeds, the practices of baptism and eucharist, and the office of the episcopate, "locally adapted," and are informed—but not predetermined by—the thought and practice of Anglicans and other Christians throughout the ages. The Anglican theological sensibility thus maintains a high regard for the believer's own freedom of theological conscience. With that freedom, however, comes responsibility: if the church is not going to tell believers what to think or how to act, it is incumbent upon the faithful to work those things out for themselves. Ideally, of course, they receive resources for that by way of Christian formation, which occurs through regular participation in corporate worship, sharing an ecclesial life with others, and the guidance of skilled teachers and pastors. Ultimately, however, Anglicans each bear responsibility for developing the capacity to discern with wisdom how to navigate the circumstances of their complex lives in a manner that comports

---

4. For more, see Scott MacDougall, *The Shape of Anglican Theology: Faith Seeking Wisdom*, Brill Research Perspectives in Theology, ed. Stephan van Erp (Leiden: Brill, 2022).

5. For the texts of those important documents, see the 1979 Book of Common Prayer, 876–78.

with their best understanding of who God is, who they are, and how they are then called to live.

Unfortunately, the leadership of The Episcopal Church has too often failed to take its role in developing the theological capacity of its congregants seriously enough. I have heard too many bishops, priests, respected lay leaders, and even seminary professors speak of theology as a threat to us, because it is supposedly too divisive, legalistic, academic, "impractical," or irrelevant. I have heard exhortations not to preach theologically or provide theology in formation sessions because theology is "alienating" or "unwelcoming." Former Presiding Bishop Michael Curry popularized the phrase, "If it's not about love, it's not about God." I have listened to several sermons delivered by influential figures that improperly used this claim to counsel setting theology aside because it is not sufficiently "about love." This is shockingly anti-intellectual for members of a denomination who pride themselves on not having to "check our brains at the door." It also weirdly pits theology against love, as if they were at odds, and maybe even mutually exclusive. Theology that is not about love, given that its subject is the God who is love, is not theology, just as a love that is mistaken about who God is, who we are, and how we are to live toward God and our neighbor is not love, not a Christian form of it, anyway. From denominational communications to parish preaching, there has sometimes been a shying away from theology in The Episcopal Church, save, perhaps, for vague gestures toward "the Baptismal Covenant" that rarely do justice to the theological radicality of its strenuous and demanding vows.

This institutional devaluation of theology has affected our seminarians. In the time leading up to the pandemic, but even more explosively afterward, a number of students in my theology courses reflected these theological antipathies. Added to that were, first, the wider cultural dismissal of expertise, leading some to proclaim they had no need for any theology they didn't enter the seminary with, and, second, a suspicion fostered by the academy and society that any normative discipline like theology could only be a mechanism of domination rather than a gift for liberation, leading others to decry theology as hopelessly retrograde and oppressive. When professors and seminary administrators are content to let students maintain these attitudes and undermine pedagogical attempts to challenge students to open their perceptions to wider theological vistas, teachers of the discipline are left without room to teach, theology becomes an exercise in validating the unformed and uninterrogated views students already happen to hold, and new priests who continue the derogation of what should be extolled are ordained to serve our people. The loss of formational opportunity is tragic, to say nothing of its effect on the health of the Christian faith and practice that result from it.

Among Episcopalians who do retain a high regard for theology, it can be a reductive one. Some, for instance, read theology or theology-adjacent material, such as spirituality literature, as a kind of Christian self-help program for personal improvement. Others maintain that theology is valid only when it underwrites the pursuit of a certain form of social justice. Still others wield the supposedly unassailable, unquestionable theological formulations of past centuries, which they call "orthodoxy," as a sword against error.

We do not do theology to cultivate ourselves, even if it does have that effect. We do not do theology to motivate work for social justice, even if speaking properly of God, humanity, and world entails a moral call to active and vigorous involvement in caring for the vulnerable. We do not do theology in order to acquire a set of time-less, universal propositional truths, even if no theologian would deny the importance of speaking rightly of God. When those second-order goods become ends in themselves, they become idols. They no longer refer to the living God but to an ideology. Something other than God—be it self-improvement, social justice, or orthodoxy—has captured theology and inverted the order of things. We do not improve ourselves, seek social justice, or maintain orthodoxy to identify God, understand ourselves, and draw practical implications from this for our lives, but precisely the reverse. We attempt to identify God, understand ourselves, and draw practical implications from this for our lives and, *in so doing*, enrich and nourish ourselves, enter into serving others in solidaristic and costly Christian love, and speak of God with our words and lives truthfully. The emphasis is placed on the right things by preserving their proper order, by living out of the story that animates us.

The reduction of theology to lesser goods is also a reason why it is important not to trust those who call themselves "prophetic" or "orthodox," which happens with startling frequency in The Episcopal Church. Like "beautiful," these are descriptors one should never apply to oneself but leave to others to assign to them. Those who claim to be either prophetic or orthodox, rather than allowing prophecy or orthodoxy to blaze forth unmistakably from their words and actions, are almost always neither one nor the other. Their protests to the contrary notwithstanding, their theologies are ultimately in service to some extra-theological agenda, not to a humble, stumbling quest to articulate God's identity and our own and to specify a vision of what these imply for how to love God and neighbor in a Christlike form.

In my view, limited as it is, too much of The Episcopal Church (and not only our church, of course) has lost sight of the thing that lies at the core of Christian faith and practice: theological imagination. Theology is how people make meaning and find value as Christians in a world that often seems devoid of both. It raises up the common story that we inhabit together as followers of Jesus. It gives us the tools we need to fight back against both death-dealing cultural currents, such as ecocide, political and social violence, and every form of dehumanization, and twisted versions of our faith, such as the prosperity gospel, Christian nationalism, and reactionary neo-traditionalist anti-modernism, all of which are, yet again, ideologies rather than theologies. Without good theology being regularly on offer, it's no wonder that so many people, even in our churches, were shocked when Bishop Mariann Budde preached mercy for the oppressed, fearful, and marginalized from the pulpit at Washington National Cathedral. "Wait," some exclaimed, "Christians are allowed to say that?" Without a well-formed theological imagination, what answer will our people give to the preachers who have started calling empathy an anti-Christian evil, a ploy of Satan? What will they say that isn't either mere sentimentality or a rehash of Enlightenment human-rights discourse if they cannot articulate how an empathic imperative is an entailment of who God is, who we were created to be, and what the call to relational communion connected to those realities demands of us? That our clergy are too often derelict in their duty to form the theological imaginations of those they are called to serve is nothing less than pastoral malpractice.

However, there is some good news here, and it is this: It has become increasingly evident that those in The Episcopal Church who assert that offering theology to the people is a surefire way of pushing them out the door are very, very wrong. Do parishioners want to be told what to think or bludgeoned with catechetical formulas? Absolutely not. Nor should they be. I know firsthand, however, from my own work preaching, speaking, and leading workshops that a massive percentage of Episcopalians are positively famished for the meaning-making possibilities that good theology provides, for the resources it supplies for articulating and living their Christian commitments in profound and not superficial ways, and for taking up the responsibility of doing exactly that. I have seen this hunger with my own eyes, over and over again.

Why should this be surprising? Christianity is, by its very nature, a religion based on the command to witness to the birth, life, ministry, death, resurrection, and continued presence of Jesus of Nazareth in words and deeds, acts of worship, service, and love. It shapes those witnesses to inhabit the world in a distinctive way, with a characteristic sense of value and meaning. This is compelling to people not only because it is beautiful but also because, for those who hold it, it is good and true. While sometimes daunted by the challenge, the project of coming to better understand who God is, who they are, and how they fit into the story of God's relationship with God's people and God's world inflames and excites them. Working at the level of the national church and speaking and teaching at diocesan and congregational gatherings in order to invite everyday Episcopalians into that adventure and equipping them for the journey is now the sole focus of my work as a theologian.

Further Reading Recommendations

Griffiss, James E. *The Anglican Vision.* Cambridge, MA: Cowley, 1997.

Marshall, William. *Scripture, Tradition and Reason: A Selective View of Anglican Theology through the Centuries.* Blackrock, Ireland: Columba, 2010.

McMichael, Ralph, ed. *The Vocation of Anglican Theology.* London: SCM, 2014.

McIntosh, Mark A. and Frank T. Griswold. *Seeds of Faith: Theology and Spirituality at the Heart of Christian Belief.* Grand Rapids: Eerdmans, 2022.

Douglas Adams, Chuck D, and the Making of a Theologian

Jason A. Fout

It is a frightening thing to discuss how one becomes a theologian. It is frightening for a couple of reasons. First, as a theologian who has learned a great deal from Karl Barth, and as someone whose undergraduate training was in analytical philosophy, I've learned to be skeptical of autobiography—and more broadly, "experience"—as theologically significant. For example, I don't think that my believing in God is significant for understanding God. I could be an unbeliever, and you or I could still be working to understand what Christians are responding to in their lives, and what they believe about that. That there is a God to believe in is not created by my believing: I believe because there is such a God. And Lord, help my unbelief! So when I do theology, I tend to focus on *who* we believe in, in the first place. The question of who it is that believes this may also be interesting and important. But if someone is doing theology, and it sounds too preoccupied with what *we* do or who *we* are, then I start to get a little worried.

It's also frightening for another reason. Frankly, it's embarrassing. To survey all the twists and bumps in my path: the false certitudes so easily defeated, the self-righteousness so deftly punctured, the awkward ways in which the Holy Spirit was at work drawing me into this life and vocation, all show me as utterly contingent, tentative, finite, sinful, and subject to external pressures. In other words, it shows me as completely human. But as frightening as that is, it is at least truthful and may yet serve to call attention to the One who calls us.

The joke I like to tell about my upbringing is that my father was a nonpracticing Methodist, and my mother a nonpracticing Presbyterian, and between the two of them, they couldn't decide which church to not bring me up in. It was in high school when I decided, with great solemnity, that I was an atheist. This made eminent good sense. After all, religion was a sham, disproved by evolution (I was a freshman at the time, as you can tell), and religious leaders were charlatans, while their followers were dumb sheep. In retrospect, I suppose, it is easy to see how I was setting myself up to later become a Christian, and not long after, a leader in the church, even a priest, and eventually a theologian. This kind of juvenile, arrogant, self-assured dismissal was surely the kind of pride that "cometh" before a fall (Proverbs 16.18). Now, clearly, there are mature and demanding materialist and atheistic perspectives. Those were not mine.

I came to faith a couple of years after becoming an atheist. Partly it was through the gentle witness of a group of good friends, and partly it was because my mind and imagination were opened up through reading literature. Now, often when someone says such a thing, they go on to talk about reading refined, "canonical" works of literature, rooted in high culture. Or, if not, perhaps they encounter C.S. Lewis, or J.R.R. Tolkien, Shusako Endo, or maybe Anne Lamott. Not me. For me, it was Douglas Adams.

Douglas Adams (1952–2001), for those unfamiliar with him, was a self-described "radical atheist," a passionate environmentalist, and an author whose titles include *The Hitchhiker's Guide to the Galaxy* (a gonzo science-fiction comedy series that he thought up while lying drunk in a field in Austria). Originally intended to be a three-book story arc, it eventually spread to five volumes, thereafter known as the "five-part trilogy" in just the kind of playful nonsense that Adams so loved.

As a "radical atheist," Adams was pleased to pepper his books with lighthearted, skeptical, and atheistic references, no matter how implausible. For example, in *The Hitchhiker's Guide to the Galaxy* (the first volume of the eponymous series), Adams describes something known as a Babel fish, which, once implanted in one's ear, serves to translate all of the languages in the universe, so that one may understand another's speech instantly. Now it is clear, given the anticipated travels around the universe, just what role this element will play in the story. But Adams really digs into what he sees as the implications: "...it is such a bizarrely improbable coincidence that anything so mind-bogglingly useful could have evolved purely by chance that some thinkers have chosen to see it as the final and clinching proof of the non-existence of God."

> "The argument goes something like this: 'I refuse to prove that I exist,' says God, 'for proof denies faith, and without faith I am nothing.'
>
> "'But,' says Man, 'The Babel fish is a dead giveaway, isn't it? It could not have evolved by chance. It proves you exist, and so therefore, by your own arguments, you don't. QED.'
>
> "'Oh dear,' says God, 'I hadn't thought of that,' and promptly vanished in a puff of logic."[1]

Of course, no part of this is anything other than light, comical absurdity. I share it only to reflect that, of all possible books that

---

1. Douglas Adams, *The Hitchhiker's Guide to the Galaxy* (New York: Pocket Books, 1981), 61. Subsequent references will be provided parenthetically in the main text.

might have contributed to my coming to faith, this wasn't an obvious choice.

As I mentioned above, it was particularly at an early point in my high school career that, having grown up with no particular faith of any kind, I learned more about evolution and, in the process, adopted a breezy scientism and thoroughgoing materialism, held with the kind of certitude that one would expect at that age. There was obviously no God or gods, and the sooner we got over such projections, the better. Entire faiths and cultures could be critiqued and dismissed easily from this perspective, often on the back of a shallow and rather wooden characterization of whatever belief was in my crosshairs. This was the context in which I encountered *The Hitchhiker's Guide to the Galaxy*. I greeted passages such as the above with a smile, and Adams's reference to the fictional best-selling book *Well, That About Wraps It Up for God* with a knowing chuckle. I picked up Adams's book and read it with a mix of rather concrete thinking and empathy, a combination that, to my surprise, set me up for the work of the Holy Spirit. To show how, it would be worth giving a brief overview of the beginning of the book.

It begins in "the uncharted backwaters of the unfashionable end of the western spiral arm of the Galaxy" where we find a "small unregarded yellow sun," around which orbits "an utterly insignificant little blue green planet whose ape-descended life forms are so amazingly primitive that they still think digital watches are a pretty neat idea" (3). From the beginning, the book places the earth and its inhabitants on a vast canvas, de-centering it.

More specifically, the story focuses on Englishman Arthur Dent, who is enraged by the imminent destruction of his house by the local planning authority to make way for a bypass. Representatives from the authority insist that he should have spoken up earlier in the process since the plans were on public display. It emerges that they were on "public display" in the authority's office—in an unlit cellar, at the bottom of a locked filing cabinet, housed in a disused restroom, "with a sign on the door that said *Beware of the Leopard*" (10).

Arthur is lying in the mud between a bulldozer and his house, trying to stop the destruction, when his friend Ford Prefect walks up and invites him for a drink. (Ford is actually an alien from the planet Betelgeuse, and not, as Arthur thinks, an out-of-work actor from Guildford.) The occasion for the drink is that the world is about to end. More specifically, a fleet of spacecraft piloted by an alien race known as the Vogons would soon arrive to destroy the planet. It happens that the earth had been slated for destruction to make way for a hyperspatial express route, the plans for which had been on public display in the local planning department on Alpha Centauri for fifty years. When they arrive and the earthlings protest that they had never been to Alpha Centauri, they are met with a scoff: "I'm sorry, but if you can't be bothered to take an interest in local affairs that's your own lookout." And later, "Apathetic bloody planet. I've no sympathy at all" (36). Whereupon the earth is utterly and unceremoniously destroyed. It is not only the earthly local planning authorities who are officious and dismissive.

I can't fully explain why the book affected me so, but I remember being stunned and even disoriented by the destruction of the Earth. Everything I knew, took for granted, understood myself by, planned for, remembered—gone in an instant. It was only a daft novel, but this really hit me. However, this was not, it turns out, the end of the story for Arthur and Ford: using a device Ford had, they hitched a ride on the Vogon destructor craft, and the rest of the book features a series of wildly improbable comic events.

Along with being stunned by the destruction of the earth, it is the wildly improbable nature of the subsequent events that left a mark on me. Indeed, so many of the plot points of the story rest on happenings so utterly improbable as to be virtually impossible, yet their very improbability (and hence, actual possibility, no matter how minute) is trumpeted throughout. Central to the plot is a spacecraft named The Heart of Gold, which is powered by an Infinite Improbability drive, every bit as absurd as it sounds.

At one point, when Arthur and Ford are thrust by the Vogons into outer space without space suits, we are told that, if you hold a lungful of air, you can survive in the vacuum of outer space for about thirty seconds. Alas, "with space being the mind-boggling size it is the chances of getting picked up by another ship within those thirty seconds are two to the power of two hundred and sixty-seven thousand seven hundred and nine to one against" (36). Nevertheless, our two protagonists *are* picked up—after twenty-nine seconds—by The Heart of Gold, which happens to be piloted by an old friend of Ford's and his girlfriend, an earthling whom Arthur had previously met at a party in Islington. What's more, by a "totally staggering coincidence," the numerical odds of them surviving in space were identical to the telephone number of the flat where Arthur had met this girl. This is just one example of the sort of absurd plot twists that fill the series.

The effect of all of this on me was profound. The book imaginatively cleared away all that was known, and thrust me into a universe seemingly governed by science but not moored to cold, unthinking causality, instead rejoicing in sheer absurd improbability: and the improbabilities were not merely funny, but life-giving. The uncaring, deadly, silent emptiness of space was instead a site where nearly anything could happen against all odds, most likely something good and comical. For all of Adams's profession of atheism, there seems in many ways a very hopeful sort of *providence* found in these novels. This is even clearer because those who benefit from these improbabilities—such as Arthur and Ford, near death—are most often those in greatest need, incapable of helping themselves but blessed by goodness nevertheless.

As art and literature do, *The Hitchhiker's Guide to the Galaxy* spoke to and shaped my imagination. And the Holy Spirit—unbeknownst to me at the time—was using it to help me edge my way into faith, and eventually, to become a theologian. In particular, it helped me move from thinking of the world as a place of ironclad causality, dominated by the survival of the fittest, to seeing the sheer wonder and goodness of this place we are in. Instead of taking the Earth for granted, I began to see it as a gift and a place where perhaps those serendipitous "coincidences" could happen. For me, the world was charged, if not yet with the grandeur of God, at least with a goodness, where coincidence or surprise might become a blessing.

I was drawn into faith a year or so after reading *The Hitchhiker's Guide*, and following that, became more and more interested in philosophy and theology. As I grew as a theologian, the doctrine of creation *ex nihilo* has become particularly important to me, and to my teaching. The doctrine of creation is less about *how* creation came to be (much less *when*), and more about the relation of creation to God.

It might be easy to think of the relationship between God and creation as one of a "greater" and a "lesser" over which the "greater" exerts power. But this is wrong. There is no creature over which to exert "power" apart from God's act to create and sustain.[2] This relationship is not about power, but about love. In fact, a friend of mine is fond of saying that instead of calling it creation *ex nihilo* (out of nothing), it would be just as fitting to call it creation *ex amore* (out of love).[3] Everything that is exists out of the sheer freedom of God's love. All of which indicates that creation is not therefore an agent

---

2. For more on this, see Rowan Williams, "On Being Creatures" in *On Christian Theology* (Oxford: Blackwell, 2000), 63–78.

3. See Jacob Sherman, "Creation: An Act of Love," in *The Church Times*, 19 February 2016, at https://www.churchtimes.co.uk/articles/2016/19-february/features/features/creation-an-act-of-love.

"over against" God, competing for scarce resources: it is not that, for humans to act, God must curtail God's act, must "make space" for creation. Humans are only capable of acting *because* of God's act. This is *not* an agonistic relationship in which for one to "win," the other must "lose."

If you are worried about a relationship of "dependence" on God—we've all encountered bad human relationships of "dependence," or even bullying—you might think of our dependence on God as analogous to the kind of dependence we have as humans on language. We are utterly dependent on language to express ourselves verbally. This dependence does not hold us back or keep us down; because we are dependent on language, we *may* speak and express ourselves. We wouldn't somehow be "free" apart from that, except to be free from all verbal expression. An even closer analogy to what I'm saying about God would be to talk about existence: each of us—it's maybe funny to say—depends on existing in order to be. That dependence isn't a matter of being dominated by another or closed down in our agency: it is the very condition of our being free and being agents in the first place. We are not free to be other than creatures, which is another way to say that we are free to be God's beloved creatures and let God be God.[4]

God's power in creating is therefore unlike any human use of power. It does not dominate or subdue. It orders the creation without that order being an expression of neurosis or anxiety. Creation is also contingent. It is changeable, dependent, it may cease to exist, it might not have been made in the first place. God alone is not contingent in this sense. All of which suggests that creation is, at bottom, a gift.

---

4. Indeed, the creature may glorify God and participate in God's glory, as I argue in *Fully Alive: The Glory of God and the Human Creature in Karl Barth, Hans Urs von Balthasar, and Theological Exegesis of Scripture* (Edinburgh: T&T Clark, 2015).

God does not create in order to "get something" from us—so when, for example, we do not particularly love God, it does not make God cranky and in need of affection. God's love does not fail; God does not fail. God is not "lonely." God does not need us to complete some "project"; we do not "add" something to God. Another way to put all of this is that, for God, the creation is free to be the creation. We are created in pure generous superfluity: the creation is a gift. And therefore, it is grace.[5]

This way of looking at creation is also anti-dualistic. Some ancient creation stories maintained that there was some kind of pre-existing "stuff" which a god or gods then came to, lending it form. This ends up being a telling of the story in which rather conventional power is used to wrangle something else into shape. But this is not creation *ex nihilo*. This perspective insists that *the whole* is created by God, not only the "form" (or the "soul" or the "mind") with the physical or bodily being "of the earth," of a "lower nature," or not from God.

All of this suggests that the creation is not just "neutral," not *just there*. It is good (and very good; Gen. 1:31, NRSV). There is no isolable aspect of creation which can be said not to have been created, which is not good but merely neutral, or maybe in itself wicked or chaotic. This also means that there is no part of creation which is beyond God's care, God's love, or the possibility of God's redeeming.

Finally, creation is not merely a place of ironclad causality, understood solely through an amoral materialism; as *good*, and as the creation of *this God*, there is a moral structure or valence to "how things ought to go." Although it is certainly a good creation of a good God, it is also the case that not all coincidences are blessings, not all accidents are happy, and that many "good" human creatures are nevertheless

---

5. The words "gift" and "grace" are very closely related, although this is clearer in the Greek of the Bible, and in Latin.

bent on acting wickedly, being created by and creating systems which perpetuate wickedness on a large scale. It took me a while before I began to really wrestle with this last point.

Augustine, in his *Confessions*, told of encountering a child singing "Tolle! Lege!" ("Take! Read!") Taking this as a command of sorts, he picked up the Bible and read from Romans 13:13–14, hearing it as a direct address to himself, feeling contrition, and being converted. Another key moment in my becoming a theologian is less a matter of "Take and read" and more a matter of "Take and listen." I still remember it vividly: I was driving one evening in the summer of 1989, when I first heard "Black Steel in the Hour of Chaos" by Public Enemy.

As a typical, somewhat conservative white Christian growing up in the northern suburbs of Chicago (I had come to faith about two years prior), I had heard of rap and hip-hop but was not particularly tuned into the genre. I clucked my tongue and worried about the lyrics but didn't really know the artists or the art well, much less the situations they arose from; in large part, this reflected my own racial and cultural isolation.

The song blared on the radio with the force of a meteor landing. It starts with spoken word samples and then shifts to a heavy driving beat, accompanied by a high-pitched piano sample that communicates power, anxiety, tension, extending throughout the piece. At times, Flavor Flav speaks in the rap as though he were on a telephone. And then comes Chuck D's relentless, deep, booming voice, telling the story of a man imprisoned for resisting the draft.

The man wouldn't fight to protect a nation that never "gave a damn" about the speaker and his people, and the rap tells of his imprisonment and his efforts to escape to freedom. The prison where he's thrown is a "hell" governed by "a swarm of devils." Incarcerated, he is "rotting," men are packed four to a cell "like slaves"—in fact, prison is a form of "slavery, organized." To his captors, he is "not a citizen."

The man begins planning an escape, waiting for a corrections officer to fall asleep on the job so he can seize the guard's gun—the constant refrain, echoed in the title, of "going for the steel." He gets an opportunity and does just that. In order to escape to freedom, he instigates a riot in the prison. He counts six officers in the prison: should he kill them on his way to freedom? He decides, "I'll give them a chance because I'm civilized." This is a real challenge because of the dehumanizing conditions in the prison: "As for the rest of the world they can't realize / a cell is hell, I'm a rebel so I rebel / between bars got me thinkin' like an animal." The man and fifty-two others escape to the prison courtyard. Once there, they are met with gunfire and the man realizes that the prison is a machine created to dehumanize and kill him ("If I come out alive then they won't come clean"—he'll either be killed now or the authorities will lie about him and make his situation worse, likely killing him later).

At this point, the lyrics become chaotic and jumbled, reflecting a break-in to the prison from outside by the S1Ws (short for Security of the First World). The S1Ws were a group that, at one time, provided security for Public Enemy and were later incorporated into the band itself, being advocates for social justice and change. The prison is now lying in disarray, the men have escaped, and the listener is likewise invited to follow.[6]

For me, this was not only culturally and racially foreign, but uncomfortably direct, uncompromising, and unsettling. I was upset, offended. Six minutes of relentless, hard rhyming and truth-telling left me indignant and exhausted. I can't remember anything else I listened to that day, or subsequent days, but that left an indelible

---

6. Interestingly, the song implies that the men escape, but the end of the video superimposes images of Chuck D being placed in a noose, suggesting that, inevitably, the system wins and the man is put to death.

mark on me. It haunted me.[7] I came back to it eventually, perhaps by way of listening to "Fight the Power" from the *Do the Right Thing* soundtrack and thinking that I should give Public Enemy more of a listen. Over time, I came to see it not as a tale of lawless violence, but of desperation rooted in extremely dehumanizing conditions—conditions which were in no way restricted to the prison. To respond, to escape, to work for freedom from inhumanity, is to lay hold of one's God-given human agency. Instead of a visceral reaction to their music, I grew in appreciation of the band and their message. Thankfully, the Holy Spirit was not done with the work of making me into a theologian. Learning to listen to voices that were not my own, not from my community, voices that maybe troubled me, was a part of that work.

Perhaps predictably, the book *God of the Oppressed* by James H. Cone had a similar effect on me when I first read it in February of 1996.[8] It was the first work of Black Theology that I had read, perhaps the first genuine work of contextual theology that I had encountered at all. I remember wrestling with the work mightily—my old copy has extensive notes in the margins and endpapers—feeling challenged, disoriented, and convicted. I didn't want to read anymore, but I also couldn't look away. I kept reading. And over time, Cone became a welcome, always helpfully challenging voice in my own work and life. His searingly honest book *The Cross and the Lynching Tree* is a perennial fixture on my systematic theology syllabus.[9]

Together, these and other works helped me to come to terms with my own racist assumptions, imbibed from my white suburban upbringing, and to begin to recognize racist systems and those who

---

7. The song is found on Public Enemy's album, *It Takes a Nation of Millions to Hold Us Back* (Def Jam, 1989).

8. James H. Cone, *God of the Oppressed* (New York: Seabury Press, 1975).

9. James H. Cone, *The Cross and the Lynching Tree* (Maryknoll, NY: Orbis, 2011).

benefit from and those who suffer from them, and that God was committed to redemption not only in a spiritual sense, but also in a material sense: God's mission in the world is holistic, bringing liberation from oppression—and, at least in some ways, I am among those who oppress. Instead of being separate and being able to cluck my tongue in judgment on a racial "other," I was now connected, ineluctably, through this shared history of suffering and oppression. And even while I had responsibility, I was also the product of a sinful and broken system.

Earlier in my growth as a theologian, through the absurd writings of Douglas Adams, I was able to come to imagine the world as creation: as life-givingly dependent on God, as completely contingent, as utterly a gift, and as good, such that we might even look for mind-bogglingly improbable things to happen as blessings. Later, through the challenging voices of Public Enemy and James Cone, I began also to imagine that good creation as fallen, tinged throughout with sin and brokenness, beset with suffering and injustice on a wide basis.

Sometimes students are surprised that I teach the doctrine of Original Sin in my systematic theology class. But I take it that the Christian faith is not merely about *sins*—individual wrong acts we've done—but about *sin*—the condition that affects us all, in various ways, which exceeds individual acts we have committed, and affects not just people but the whole creation. Put one way, the fallenness of the world is a thorny problem, not something that, if we just had sufficient buy-in and energy, we could fix easily with the right kind of project or two (or the right artificial intelligence engine). We cannot excuse or justify suffering and oppression, especially when we are not ourselves suffering or oppressed. But the remedy for it will always be worked by sinful and fallen humans, even when it is those who are suffering and oppressed doing such work.

When we consider it this way, Original Sin has less to do with exegesis of a passage in Genesis or convincing others that they're sinful, and more a matter of simply observing that we ourselves, and others, and pretty much everything is broken and not the way it is meant to be—not the way God intends. We don't need to worry about pinpointing a "time" when humanity fell, because the story of Adam and Eve helps us to see that it goes all the way back. We cannot conveniently blame someone in our midst. (Indeed, the story of Adam and Eve also stubbornly resists *explaining* sin: it just shows it.)

The brokenness and sin that we inherit from Original Sin mean that we are always "wounded healers" in Henri Nouwen's memorable phrase. Frederick Buechner explores this in his novel *Brendan*, which he quotes in his magnificent memoir *Telling Secrets*. Describing Brendan, Buechner says the Irish saint wandered to the ends of the earth in search of paradise. Having never found it, near the end of his life, he returns home looking for better ways to serve Christ. "He meets the Welsh historian-monk Gildas one day, and when Gildas stands up at the end of their interview to dismiss him, the narrator of the novel, a friend of Brendan's named Finn, describes what happens to him:

> For the first time now, we saw he wanted one leg. It was gone from the knee joint down. He was hopping sideways to reach for his stick in the corner when he lost his balance. He would have fallen in a heap if Brendan hadn't leapt forward and caught him.
>
> "I'm as crippled as the dark world," Gildas said.
>
> "If it comes to that, which one of us isn't, my dear?" Brendan said.
>
> Gildas with but one leg. Brendan sure he'd misspent his whole life entirely. Me that had left my wife to follow him and buried our only boy. The truth of what Brendan said [that

we were all deeply wounded] stopped all our mouths. For a moment or two there was no sound but the bees.

"To lend each other a hand when we're falling," Brendan said. "Perhaps that's the only work that matters in the end."[10]

I think there is great wisdom here: "to lend each other a hand when we're falling." This isn't a paternalistic "I'm fine but I'll help you when you fall." Rather, we each lend each other a hand when each of us is falling. Because we're always falling (in some way) that's the only condition under which we could ever lend a hand anyway. This is compassion in the face of a broken world and suffering. We are wounded healers; we lend each other a hand when we are falling, in the midst of this astonishing, wondrous, good creation.

Theology comes foremost from the encounter with God in Jesus Christ and the Holy Spirit: in a sense, it is a traditioned, reflective response to this reality. At the same time, theology is never done in isolation from God, as though this "response" were somehow apart from God and God's agency: theology is not merely a human work. We who follow Jesus undertake this as one way of loving, following, and serving God; and as we do it, we not only grow in understanding but also in maturity. Apart from God, the good news of Jesus, and the work of the Holy Spirit, the church is nothing, and so this kind of theological reflection ought to be broad-based and not merely the precinct of scholars. That's not to say that there is no place for trained specialists, such as myself and the other contributors to this volume. There certainly is. An analogy might be that of health: each person is responsible for their own health, but trained specialists such as physicians or counselors can help us to do it better, and help us if we are suffering or "stuck."

---

10. Frederick Buechner, *Telling Secrets: A Memoir* (New York: HarperOne, 1992), 87–88.

At the same time, even as we need health specialists, so also do we need theologians. It is essential that the church encourage those who would dedicate their lives to theology in pursuit of serving God's people. These individuals would help the church attend to its believing, confessing, and preaching, its prayer and spirituality, and to God and God's ways with the world. And they might, as I have tried to here, help us see more closely the wonder and goodness of creation, as well as its suffering and brokenness.

Further Reading Recommendations

Ford, David F. *The Shape of Living: Spiritual Directions for Everyday Life.* With a new foreword by Susan Howatch. Grand Rapids: Baker Books, 2004.

Kilby, Karen. *God, Evil, and the Limits of Theology.* London: T&T Clark, 2021.

Williams, Rowan. *Resurrection: Interpreting the Easter Gospel.* 2nd ed. London: Darton, Longman, & Todd, 2014.

Zahl, David. *The Big Relief: The Urgency of Grace for a Worn-out World.* Grand Rapids: Brazos Press, 2025.

An Anglican Theology of Hope for a Common Future

Joy Ann McDougall

Discovering Theology, Anglican Traditions, and The Episcopal Church

It was the spring semester of my freshman year when my history and politics professor in Yale College's Great Books program, Frank Turner, observed that I seemed to turn all my political philosophy essays into ones about theology. He was right. In the fall, I had chosen to wrestle with the two cities in St. Augustine's *De Civitate Dei*, and in the spring, I challenged Karl Marx's diatribe against religion as the opium of the people. Truth be told, I wasn't aware at the time that there was such a thing as theology. But on his recommendation, I signed up the following fall for Hans Frei's class on Early Modern Christian Thought. There, I encountered the writings of Bunyan, Locke, Kant, and Kierkegaard, among many others. I became fascinated by Frei's unfolding narrative about what had happened in this modern period to the reading of Scripture, the understanding of Christian faith, and what it meant that religion was being placed within the limits of reason alone.

Although I was a newcomer to academic theology, that wasn't the case with the church. Raised in a Congregationalist church in Forest Hills, New York, I had attended Sunday School since kindergarten, led our church youth group, and built houses one summer with Habitat for Humanity in Americus, Georgia. But it was in Frei's lecture hall that I first realized how I could combine my Christian faith with formal academic studies. And I was off and running. The following year, I wrote my first research paper on F. D. Maurice and the Christian Socialist movement, and a second on the Barmen Declaration and the Confessing Church in Germany during the Nazi period. Finally, I wrote my senior thesis on faith and reason in the writings of Kierkegaard and J. H. Newman. Tellingly, it was Newman's *The Grammar of Assent* with its defense of the illative sense, the tacit knowledge that we rely on for religious certitude, that prevailed.

And yet, I still hadn't joined The Episcopal Church. I had attended an Episcopal parish while at Yale Divinity School and was slowly becoming familiar with the Book of Common Prayer and the Sunday liturgy. But after completing my master's degree, I went to study Protestant theology in Germany, where I attended Lutheran worship services and evening prayer at St. Michael's, the Jesuit church in Munich. I finally stopped straddling denominational fences during my Ph.D. studies, as I read more Anglican theology, primarily contemporary works by James Griffiss, Rowan Williams, and Kathryn Tanner. Most importantly, however, I became a colleague and friend of fellow student Mark McIntosh, to whom this book is dedicated. From our first meeting, I admired how Mark seamlessly wove together a vibrant spirituality with rigorous academic theology, both of which were anchored in his deeply rooted commitment to the word and sacraments. Mark was wise, kind, and humble—virtues that inspired my vocation as a theologian at the time and continue to do so today. I have much to thank Mark for: a directed study we took together on patristic and medieval Trinitarian theology, his invitation to Rowan Williams' Lenten Series at St. James Cathedral in Chicago, and most of all his hard-earned wisdom about raising children and the patient work of theology. After a long season of discernment, I was received into The Episcopal Church in 1996 at the Church of the Epiphany, a struggling parish on the economically blighted West Side of Chicago, with two friends and mentors, Mark and Kathryn Tanner, as my presenters on either side.

There are many reasons why I found a home in The Episcopal Church, but it was what Frei has called its "generous orthodoxy" that attracted me most of all.[1] Here was a tradition that was anchored firmly in the historic creeds and liturgy of the early church, but also open to debate and reform in light of new scientific, moral, and theological challenges. Just as importantly, I realized that as an Anglican theologian, I could—to borrow a baseball metaphor—"switch-hit," that is, call alternately upon resources from Protestant and Catholic traditions to do the work of theology. This Anglican switch-hitting became especially helpful as I began teaching systematic theology in a broadly ecumenical and racially diverse United Methodist divinity school located in the Deep South: The Candler School of Theology of Emory University. There, I discovered that many of my evangelical-leaning students, be they non-denominational, Baptists, Methodists, or Korean Presbyterians, shared my passion for Karl Barth's Reformed theology. Meanwhile, my Episcopal and Roman Catholic students (and a swathe of the others) were taken with Rowan Williams's richly spiritual theology and Karl Rahner's appeals to a world saturated with God's grace. Happily, my students found common ground and inspiration to strive fiercely for racial,

---

1. Frei coined this term in his response to Carl Henry in Hans Frei, "Response to 'Narrative Theology: An Evangelical Appraisal,'" *Trinity Journal* 8. N.S. (1987): 21–24 (cited on 21) and reprinted in Hans W. Frei, *Theology and Narrative: Selected Essays*, ed. George Hunsinger and William C. Placher (New York: Oxford University Press, 1993), 207–12 (cited on 207–208).

gender, and economic justice as they waded into different streams of Protestant and Catholic political and liberation theologies.

The Anglican tradition, with its mélange of Protestant and Catholic sensibilities, is often criticized for lacking a distinctive confessional tradition or, even worse, appearing as a contemporary version of the lukewarm church of Laodicea. That is not at all what I experienced in The Episcopal Church—either in my parishes in Chicago and Atlanta or my work with Candler's Anglican-Episcopal Studies Program. There I witnessed a vibrant faith rooted in a life of prayer and the study of the Scriptures, and a church with a social conscience attuned to the needs of the least, the lost, and the left out. Moreover, I deeply appreciated The Episcopal Church's reasoned approach to faith that accepts challenges from other sectors of society. And I cherished a tradition that celebrated not only the liturgy but also the sacramentality of the world through artistic expression. Speaking now as a systematic theologian, I found in the Anglican tradition an ease with doing theology both "from above," beginning with revelation and established doctrines, and "from below," grounded in the lived experiences of people and the ordinary realities of the world.

Practicing Systematic Theology as an Anglican and Feminist

My understanding of the theological enterprise has been deeply informed by my cross-training in different theological approaches, first by the Barthian-influenced Yale School of Theology, and subsequently by the Tillichian-influenced correlationist and liberation approaches that I encountered at the University of Chicago. The same was true of my time in Germany, where I chose to attend two opposing Protestant faculties at the Universities of Munich and Tübingen. In Munich, I studied with the inheritors of the liberal Protestant traditions of Schleiermacher and Troeltsch and listened to Wolfhart Pannenberg as he unfurled his magisterial systematic theology for the first time. Coming from my Barthian training in theology, I was initially perplexed by Pannenberg's insistence that faith seeking understanding (*fides quaerens intellectum*) required doing apologetics with the full range of sciences, in his case, cultural anthropology, modern psychology, and quantum physics. Soon, however, I was intrigued by his intricate trinitarian theology and efforts toward achieving a rapprochement between his Lutheran tradition and that of Roman Catholicism. A few years later, in Tübingen, I moved decidedly back in the other theological direction, studying with the other leading post-Barthian Protestant theologian in Germany: Jürgen Moltmann with his left-wing Reformed political theology, his urgent appeal to a suffering God, and his spirit-filled theology of hope. Eventually, I found that Moltmann's trinitarian theology of love, with its spirit of freedom and commitment to the Trinity's practical significance for the life of faith, matched closely my Anglican conviction, and it won the day.[2]

Given this crisscrossing of different theological approaches, I do not hold to a foundationalist understanding of systematic theology, one in which a philosophical framework provides the ground-level for theological construction. But neither do I eschew critical correlation approaches that look for touchpoints in human experience to explain the claims of revelation. Instead, I find myself often switch-hitting again among neo-Barthian, liberal, and liberationist approaches in my teaching and scholarship. In doing so, I seek what William Placher championed as the "middle ground," entering a genuine conversation with other disciplines that respects both the pluralism of the

---

2. For more detail, see my *Pilgrimage of Love: Moltmann on the Trinity and Christian Life* (New York: Oxford University Press, 2005).

ideological marketplace and the truth claims of Christian traditions.[3] I pursue what Frei called "ad hoc apologetics," engaging other disciplines (in my case, most often political philosophy, hermeneutics, and gender studies) insofar as they support or else offer ideological critique of Christian claims.[4] Steering such a middle course, synthesizing different theological standpoints and methods, does not mean landing nowhere theologically. Rather, this is a characteristically Anglican way of theologizing, a *via media* that invites theological comprehensiveness and seeks a mean between extremes. As such, my practice of the Anglican *via media* does not seek a weak compromise in systematic theology, but as Paul Avis put it, "attempt[s] to reconcile opposites and to transcend conflicts in a manner that is both 'progressive' and 'innovatory.'"[5]

As I will illustrate below, I practice systematic theology as a *public* theology, one which addresses the three overlapping publics of church, academy, and wider society. Three primary commitments animate my work: first, to affirm the sovereignty and unsurpassable love of God, the redemptive work of Jesus Christ's life, death and resurrection, and the life-giving presence of the Holy Spirit who promises to make all things new; second, to work alongside scholars from other disciplines and sectors of society in pursuing knowledge and truth with integrity; and third, to respond with creativity and faithfulness to the pressing

---

3. For William Placher's careful description of this "middle ground" in theological method, see chapter 7: "Conversation: A Pluralism Open to Voices of Tradition," in his *Unapologetic Theology* (Louisville: Westminster John Knox, 1989), 105–122.

4. For more on Frei's term, see William Werpehowski, "Ad Hoc Apologetics," *The Journal of Religion* 66 (1986): 282–301.

5. Paul Avis, "What is Anglicanism?," 468–69 as quoted in Scott MacDougall, *The Shape of Anglican Theology: Faith Seeking Wisdom* (Leiden: Brill, 2022), 44. See MacDougall's fuller discussion of theological comprehensiveness and *via media* as two boundary markers of Anglican identity, both with a history of various interpretations, also in *Shape of Anglican Theology*, 36–46.

social ills and political demands of our day. My version of public theology is at once practical and praxis-oriented; that is, it stays close to the ground, meeting persons of faith in their everyday lives and calling for the church to address the world's needs, most especially the travails of the disenfranchised and destitute.[6]

Within this broad Anglican vision of the theological enterprise, let me say a word about doctrine. I treat classical Christian doctrines as normative but also as capacious frameworks for articulating one's faith claims. In my classroom, I present doctrines as conveying firm truths for believers to root their lives in, while insisting that persons of faith embody these doctrines in unique ways within their life situations. On this point, I draw from Reformed theologian Serene Jones's image of doctrines as "dramatic scripts," that individuals improvise on even as we know that these scripts shape and perform us as much as we do them.[7] To borrow another of Jones's metaphors, Christian doctrines offer "cartographies of grace," maps through which persons of faith chart distinctive pathways as they experience the vicissitudes of their lives.[8] Quite traditionally, I treat the Scriptures and historical Christian traditions as the lifeblood of doctrines; they provide diverse and at times conflicting truth-claims that need to be adjudicated anew in different contexts and circumstances. This does not mean that Christian theologians, clergy, and laypersons alike should treat historical traditions as a grab-bag to pick and choose from willy-nilly. As I remind my students in systematic theology, our task is to wrestle

---

6. My vision of systematic theology as public theology closely resembles Kathryn Tanner's take on the task of systematic theology. See, for example, Kathryn Tanner, *Jesus, Humanity and the Trinity: A Brief Systematic Theology* (Minneapolis: Fortress Press, 2001), xiii.

7. Serene Jones, "Theological Anthropology," in *Essentials of Christian Theology*, ed. William C. Placher (Louisville: Westminster John Knox Press, 2003), 142.

8. Serene Jones, *Feminist Theory and Christian Theology: Cartographies of Grace* (Minneapolis: Fortress, 2000).

with the full witness of Scripture and tradition as well as with diverse life experiences in crafting theological claims. Even if doctrines have a certain historical fluidity, they must nonetheless cohere with one another to offer a plausible vision of God, the self, and the world.

Along with being an Anglican and a systematic theologian, I am also a committed feminist theologian. I affirm the central feminist critiques of the patriarchy, sexism, and androcentrism which are deeply embedded in our Scriptures and traditions. All too often, I espy to my dismay the same forces alive and well today in local Episcopal parishes and diocesan structures, despite our official teachings and best efforts to the contrary. Furthermore, it is impossible to disregard the tacit acceptance of misogyny tied to a culture of hyper-masculinity afoot in the United States today. Against this backdrop, I identify myself with those Roman Catholic, Protestant, and Anglican feminist theologians who affirm their particular traditions but look to reform them by appealing to diverse women's experiences, feminist interpretations of Scripture, and feminist and other critical theories.[9] Reform-minded feminist theologians do this work not only to overcome patriarchal structures and ideology within their communities of faith, but to foster the full flourishing of all persons in the wider society.

Beyond this reformist agenda, I deliberately locate myself within the broader global feminist theological movement, searching for family resemblances among women's experiences of patriarchy and sexism, while also acknowledging the intersectional realities that thread through different cultural imaginaries and create distinctive

---

9. This reformed camp includes a broad spectrum of so-called second- and third-wave feminist and womanist theologians, such as Katie Cannon, Rebecca Chopp, Shawn Copeland, Elizabeth Johnson, Serene Jones, and Amy Plantinga Pauw. Despite the significant theological differences among them I would place Anglican and Episcopal theologians, such as Kelly Brown Douglas, Sarah Coakley, Ann Loades, Kwok Pui-lan, Kathryn Tanner and Ellen Wondra within this broad feminist reformed camp as well.

challenges for achieving gender justice. I search for solidarity with global women's movements in resisting different forms of gender oppression that block women's vision of themselves, their gifts of grace, and their vocations. As an Anglican and feminist, I pay attention especially to the work of women across the Anglican Communion who expose and seek to remedy gender-based inequities in healthcare, education, and material resources. And I discern other signs of hope throughout the Anglican Communion in women's leadership development, successful campaigns for women's ordination to the priesthood and the episcopate, and in women's organizations such as the Mothers' Union that have embraced global partnership across eighty-three countries.[10]

An Anglican Theology of Hope for the Future

We live today in precarious times. Many of us are watching in alarm as the post–Second World War world order that has kept the peace in the United States and Europe is being overturned, and our democratic institutions appear on life support. In the United States, we are experiencing political tribalism and unprecedented uncivil discourse. The situation is not all that much rosier on the ecclesial front. For more than a generation, the Anglican Communion has been riven by fractures between its more liberal churches, largely located in the Global North, and the more conservative and rapidly growing Anglican churches of the Global South, particularly those in Africa. Major divisions over questions of ecclesial authority, issues of sexuality, and the right interpretation of Scripture have cut to the heart of Anglican

---

10. For an excellent introduction to Anglican feminist initiatives and women's organizations across the Anglican Communion, see the essays collected in *Anglican Women on Church and Mission*, ed. Kwok Pui-lan, Judith A. Berling, and Jenny Plane Te Paa (New York: Morehouse Press, 2012).

identity and have threatened the unity of its global communion. On my home front, The Episcopal Church faces its own major challenges: declining church membership and shrinking finances have forced the closing of local parishes and the curtailing of diocesan and national budgets for significant ministries. In times such as these, the stakes for Anglican theology and the Episcopal church to define its identity and to demonstrate its relevance couldn't be higher.[11]

With these concerns in view, I offer three recommendations for the future of Anglican theology and for energizing the life of The Episcopal Church today. Each of my proposals addresses the overlapping publics of the church, the academy, and the wider society. Each seeks to meet in explicitly theological terms the twin crises of identity and relevance that I see facing Anglicanism today. My hope in making these recommendations is to strengthen the ties between the church, the academy, and the wider society, and to create an Anglican theology of hope for their common future.

Taking the World Christian Turn in Anglican Theology

My first recommendation for Anglican theology is to become "polycentric" in its self-understanding—what I elsewhere have called taking the World Christian turn.[12] Instead of treating British theological traditions as the lodestar for the Anglican Communion, a polycentric approach to Anglican identity examines closely the distinctive

---

11. For the classic formulation of the twin crises of identity and relevance, see Jürgen Moltmann, *The Crucified God: The Cross of Christ as the Foundation and Criticism of Christian Theology* (San Francisco: HarperCollins, 1991), 7–24.

12. On "taking the World Christian turn" and its implications in systematic theology and Anglican identity, see my editorial introduction, "Changing Landscapes and New Horizons: The Changing Maps of World Christianity," in *Theology Today* 71 (July 2014): 159–63. For a polycentric approach to Anglican tradition, see Kwok Pui-lan, "Postcolonialism and Anglican Theology," *Anglican Theological Review* 106 (2024): 139–55.

ecclesiologies, rituals, and liturgical traditions of its regional churches and teases out threads of unity amid their profound differences.[13] A chorus of contemporary Anglican theologians insists that a polycentric approach to Anglican identity is the *sine qua non* for the Anglican Communion's future viability. Most notably, Kwok Pui-lan has encouraged Anglicans to cultivate a "postcolonial imagination" to overcome the cultural hegemony of the English tradition in interpreting Anglican history and its theology.[14] What does a postcolonial imagination entail? First, it means taking seriously the "hybridity," "the collisions and coalescence of two cultures," which the different branches of the global Anglican communion display.[15] As Kwok points out, hybridity is not new to the Anglican tradition; it has been at the heart of Anglicanism since the time of the Elizabethan Settlement between medieval Catholicism and continental Protestantism. Given the changing demographics of the Anglican Communion, with now more than half of Anglicans currently living in Africa, Anglican theology needs to embrace fully its hybrid identity, especially across the geographical and cultural borders of the Global South.

A polycentric approach to Anglican theology means more than a geographical de-centering of historic British traditions. It seeks a cross-fertilization of theological ideas, rituals, and liturgical practices across the diverse cultural contexts and communities that

---

13. For an example of a polycentric approach to Anglican theology and traditions, see the essays collected in *Beyond Colonial Anglicanism: The Anglican Communion in the 21st Century*, eds. Ian T. Douglas and Kwok Pui-lan (New York: Church Publishing, 2001). This volume includes various contextual ecclesiologies across the Anglican Communion, while identifying threads of unity among them.

14. Kwok Pui-lan, "Postcolonialism and Anglican Theology," 139. For a full-length treatment of her postcolonial approach to Anglican tradition, see Kwok Pui-lan, *The Anglican Tradition from a Postcolonial Perspective* (New York: Seabury Books, 2023).

15. Kwok, "Postcolonialism and Anglican Theology," 145.

constitute the global Anglican Communion. Such an exchange needs to highlight the gifts of different cultural contexts in which Anglicanism has flourished and identify the current theological and existential struggles of its member churches. Cultivating such a robust theological exchange resists parochialism setting in across the Anglican Communion and forges a more complex sense of its unity, however fraught with tensions that task might be. In sum, I hope that Anglican theology can take this World Christian turn in its self-understanding, not by washing away its historical origins, but by more fully realizing its historical identity of inclusivity and comprehensiveness.

Practicing Anglican Theology as Public Theology

My second recommendation builds on the first. The future of Anglican theology rests on its offering an explicitly *public* theology that confronts the wider world's social ills and injustices. I pose this challenge because I see a perennial risk within Anglican theology to romanticize its past and retreat to a narrow understanding of its traditions to shore up its identity. Certainly, historical Anglican resources and characteristic patterns of theologizing are central to Anglican identity. And yet, Anglican traditions have equally important historical precedents for practicing a bold public theology that addresses the moral and political challenges of its day. To take one well-known example, Anglicans can look to the Christian Socialist movement in nineteenth-century England as a theological resource for their public witness today. A leader of the Christian Socialist movement, F. D. Maurice, joined an incarnational principle with an eschatological vision to address the desperate conditions of the poor in his time. Maurice saw Jesus' incarnation as ushering in the Kingdom of Christ on earth, a kingdom built on the social harmony and fellowship of all persons. The church, he contended, is tasked with witnessing to that Kingdom, engaging in social reforms to overcome the divisions between the prosperous and the working poor.[16]

Just as in Maurice's time, Anglican theology, and The Episcopal Church in particular, need to redouble their efforts to address the deep economic divides, racist policies, and moral crises eroding our common life in the United States today. Let me offer two examples of contemporary authors, Jennifer McBride and Kelly Brown Douglas, who put core Anglican principles to work to address the social and political crises of our times. Interestingly, both are Anglican priests and theologians, but neither wears their Anglicanism as a badge of their identity. Rather, their Anglican identity appears in the incarnational (kenotic) and sacramental theologies that fund their social vision. Both of their works prove instructive for what a bold but also broad-based Anglican public theology might look like today.

In her book *Radical Discipleship: A Liturgical Politics of the Gospel*, Jennifer McBride offers a potent theological argument for a "lived theology," a theology of "reduced distance" between oneself, the disciples of Jesus, and all those persons relegated to the margins of contemporary society.[17] Anchored in an incarnational theology, one in which McBride recalls that "God has reduced distance... and teaches us how to live embodied lives," *Radical Discipleship* is a moving personal account of McBride's seven-year engagement with different communities living on the margins—first, as a teacher and director of the Certificate in Theological Studies sponsored by Candler School

---

16. For a more detailed discussion of the theological underpinnings of F.D. Maurice's Christian socialism, its weaknesses, and legacy within Anglicanism, see Kwok, *The Anglican Tradition from a Postcolonial Perspective*, 67–77.

17. Jennifer McBride, *Radical Discipleship: A Liturgical Politics of the Gospel* (Minneapolis: Fortress Press, 2017), 23.

of Theology at the Arrendale women's prison in Atlanta; second, her year-long journey with the Open Door Community, an intentional community patterned after the Catholic Worker movement that served the homeless, and those newly released from prison for nearly forty years in midtown Atlanta; and finally, her extraordinary journey of accompaniment of Kelly Gissendaner, the only woman in Georgia to be executed in 2015.[18] McBride's book is at once a memoir of her ongoing conversions as she practices her lived theology, and a bold invitation to her readers to join her in her pilgrimage of prophetic and radical discipleship today.

Using the liturgical calendar as her theological compass, McBride takes us into the rhythm of life at the maximum-security women's prison, as she studies theology texts alongside women hungering for their voices to be heard, their self-worth to be affirmed, and searching for glimmers of hope and restorative justice within their prison walls. McBride doesn't take her readers alone on this pilgrimage of faith into the prison. No, she has in her backpack the works of Dietrich Bonhoeffer, Martin Luther King Jr., and Jürgen Moltmann, who together have inspired her incarnational and earthed witness to what radical discipleship looks like today. In Advent and the Christmas season, we go forth with the Open Door Community as they celebrate their Eucharistic liturgy of the Christmas boxes, which are taken to the death row inmates and "permanents" at the Jacksonville State prison. We journey through the Lenten season of repentance, Holy Week's time of trial and atonement, only to re-discover the liberation in Christ at Easter now experienced through the voices of women in the prison whose spirits have been freed while their bodies remained bound. Having been accompanied through this liturgical politics of the gospel,

---

18. McBride, *Radical Discipleship*, 84.

McBride enjoins her readers to go forth and practice their own radical discipleship, one of prophetic witness and compassion to the least, lost and the left behind.

A second example of bold public theology is Kelly Brown Douglas's *Stand Your Ground: Black Bodies and the Justice of God*.[19] Douglas decries the culture of violence perpetrated against the African American community in general and the fearmongering about young Black men in particular. Her book lays bare the racist history behind recent "stand-your-ground" laws and the police brutality that has led to a string of murders of young black men from Trayvon Martin to Michael Brown. In the wake of such crimes, she calls upon persons of faith to stand *their* ground in solidarity with mothers' deep grief in the loss of their sons and daughters, and to join protest movements that defend the dignity of all persons as created in the image of God. In the prophetic black faith traditions of Jarena Lee, Martin Luther King Jr., Howard Thurman, and James Cone, among so many others, Douglas urges churches today not just to save souls, but to do justice. For this Episcopal priest and womanist theologian, Jesus as God-incarnate—who breaks into the world, tends to the marginalized and the excluded, and exercises only non-violent power—represents the true justice of God. Douglas calls the church to live out of this memory of Jesus, turning its faith into action to make that justice real in the midst of the world.

Reimagining a Feminist Theology of Sin and Grace

My third and final recommendation relates to my own constructive feminist theological project, tentatively titled, *Rising with Mary:*

---

19. Kelly Brown Douglas, *Stand Your Ground: Black Bodies and the Justice of God* (Maryknoll, NY: Orbis Books, 2015).

A Feminist Re-imagining of Sin and Grace. In my view, there is a pressing need for a feminist re-imagining of a theology of sin and grace within Anglicanism today. Even if Anglicans may not have a single historically settled position on these doctrines, a full-bodied theology of sin and grace is at the heart of Anglican liturgies and the everyday practices of Anglicans worldwide. Sin and grace are not simply topics confined to theological anthropology, but they thread throughout the doctrines of God, creation, soteriology, and pneumatology.[20]

The other reason for a feminist reformulation of these twin doctrines is that classical formulations of sin often "miss the mark" in diagnosing the nature of women's bondage to sin. What do I mean by "missing the mark"? Simply stated, feminist theologians have argued that traditional depictions of sin in terms of a Promethean ego presume a measure of agency and will to power that many women do not possess. Such a titanic view of self misdiagnoses the problem of sin for women, which often appears as its very opposite—too little self or else its dissolution into a web of relations to others. Root metaphors for sin in terms of the rebellious will and over-reaching pride are not just a wrong diagnosis, but they also generate false guilt and shame in women, which have debilitating if not death-dealing consequences in their lives.[21]

---

20. Simeon Zahl describes sin and grace as the "load bearing" doctrines of the faith in Protestant theology: see his article "Sin" in *The Oxford Handbook of Theological Anthropology*, ed. Jens Zimmermann, Ashley Moyse and Michael Burdett (Oxford: Oxford University Press, forthcoming). Serene Jones makes a similar case for the doctrines of sin and grace as the linchpin of Luther and Calvin's theologies and her own. See her chapters on lived grace and sin in *Feminist Theory and Christian Theology*, 49–68; 94–125.

21. For an overview of these second-wave and third-wave feminist critiques of classical doctrines of sin see my chapter "Feminist Theology" in *The Oxford Handbook of Systematic Theology*, ed. John Webster, Kathryn Tanner, and Iain Torrance (Oxford: Oxford University Press, 2007), 672–73.

My feminist work seeks to reverse the tide against such misunderstandings and misuses of sin-talk. In my view, earlier efforts to "add and stir" feminist insights into traditional theologies of sin anchored in the dynamics of the will are inadequate to the task at hand. I propose instead a different tack: first, to revise the classical symbol of the condition of sin, "the bondage of the will," by placing it within the visual sphere—what I term a gendered "bondage of the Eye." With this metaphor, I describe sin as a deep deception, a closing of one's eyes or else having one's vision blocked to the beneficence of God, the goodness of oneself, and of others. Such deceptions can be rooted in subtle and invisible forces such as gender stereotypes and sexist prejudices that circulate in our cultural imaginaries. But deep deceptions can stem from long-preserved patriarchal structures and institutions that stand in the way of women realizing their full potential and even their failing to accord others the dignity that they deserve. The fallout from such a blocked vision of God's beneficence and one's created goodness is a second bondage, what I term "bondage of the I," in which women become imprisoned by debilitating deceptions about who they are, or else are deprived of critical resources—adequate education, healthcare, or the economic means to flourish.

In keeping with this feminist re-imagining of sin, I propose a companion theology of grace. Here, the gift of grace begins with a clearing of one's vision, in particular, the dissipation of gender-based deceptions, and the discovery of one's truest identity through encounters with the living Christ. Put differently, I suggest a feminist reading of the traditional *via salutis*, the journey from conversion to new creation.[22] I traverse this feminist journey along three narratives

---

22. For an excellent feminist interpretation of conversion, see Elizabeth A. Johnson, *She Who Is: The Mystery of God in Feminist Theological Discourse* (New York: Crossroads, 1992), 62–65.

from the Gospel of John, in which Jesus and women exchange intimate friendship, compassion in their deep sorrow at the cross, and ultimately rise into newly found freedom for themselves and in the world. These astonishing "exchanges of grace" describe a dynamic becoming in Christ, in which women are at once the recipients of a healing and life-giving grace and become its purveyors to the world.[23] I invite contemporary women to find themselves afresh in these biblical stories and in a feminist interpretation of grace that conveys to them their created dignity (original grace), their strength in community with one another, and ultimately the fullness of a new creation. To return to my language of sin, women are, through the gift of grace, released from the "bondage of the Eye/I," to discover a spirit of freedom and hope for themselves and the world. Such a re-imagined feminist theology of grace testifies to the promises made to women and to all of humanity by a God of extravagant and vulnerable love, a gifting God who calls each of us by our very own name and claims us as one of God's own.

To conclude, let me recall the original impetus behind my three recommendations for the future of Anglican theology, namely, to address the twin crises of Anglican identity and its relevance for the life of faith. Each of my recommendations addresses the question of Anglican identity by recalling first its historic traditions: its principles of *via media* and comprehensiveness, the Anglican legacy of engagement in social reform, and by turning to the doctrines of sin and grace at the heart of our liturgy and the ordinary practices of faith. I also urged Anglicanism to remain a *living* tradition: to embrace its hybrid identity in a new global way, to respond to the acute social ills and

---

23. I am borrowing this term from the Festschrift of the same title in honor of Ann Loades, *Exchanges of Grace*, ed. Natalie K. Watson and Stephen Burns (London: SCM Press, 2008).

moral crises of our day, and to reimagine its language of faith so as to overcome its gender prejudices and to actively support women's pursuit of their vocations with the utmost freedom. To revitalize Anglican identity in these ways can, in my view, restore churches' profound theological and social relevance. Moreover, inviting Anglican theologians and Episcopal churches to come together across the three publics of church, academy, and the wider world makes good on the incarnational theology that is the heart of Anglican tradition. And it is to practice an Anglican theology of hope for a common future in which all will flourish.

Further Reading Recommendations

Douglas, Kelly Brown. *Stand Your Ground: Black Bodies and the Justice of God.* Maryknoll, NY: Orbis Books, 2015.

Jones, Serene. *Feminist Theory and Christian Theology: Cartographies of Grace.* Minneapolis: Fortress, 2000.

Kwok Pui-lan. *The Anglican Tradition from a Postcolonial Perspective.* New York: Seabury Books, 2023.

McIntosh, Mark A. *The Divine Ideas Tradition in Christian Mystical Theology.* Oxford: Oxford University Press, 2021.

Toward An Embodied and Transformative Theology

Olufemi Gonsalves

And so, dear brothers and sisters, I plead with you to give your bodies to God because of all he has done for you. Let them be a living and holy sacrifice—the kind he will find acceptable. This is truly the way to worship him. Don't copy the behavior and customs of this world, but let God transform you into a new person by changing the way you think. Then you will learn to know God's will for you, which is good and pleasing and perfect. (Romans 12:1–2, NLT)

The human body is a text, and storytelling begins with and in the body. My soul's story is fully seen and understood through this earthly vessel. In contrast to the traditional Western approach to theology and logic, based on Cartesian dualism, which expresses a detachment between the mind-soul and the body-flesh, my Black woman's body is essential to my theological story as a means of knowing. Motivated by a love ethic of healing and wellness for the world, the womanist logical approach is embodied and holistic. My Black woman's body in a pulpit preaches without the use of words. My body tells my story within God's story, as my life is intertwined in God's divine and everlasting existence. This is not only true regarding my identity and the body I claim, but it is true of every living thing created by God. Our bodies talk, they preach, and they sing. They are a fleshy quilt, reflecting a complex and somewhat hidden narrative called the *imago Dei*.

I am a womanist public theologian whose research centers on the intersection of theology, the arts, and mental health. I exegete culture and varieties of art forms, such as Black women's fashion and literature, through a womanist lens as an expression of public discourse to create ways of theological meaning-making in the realm of mental health policy and neuroethics. Public theology aims to serve the common good, countering the idolatrous and diabolical, anti-moral imagination as revealed in haunting spirits of addiction to privilege and the need for domination, which are at the heart of bias, stigmatization, and oppression in the West.[1] Celebrating the more recent understandings of the *imago Dei* as diunital and relational, my research argues that Black women's fashion, in all its incarnational expressions, flourishes as a liberative tool in presenting what bell hooks identifies as the oppositional gaze in the face of the terror of white supremacist cultural normativity.[2] These liberative expressions of the *imago Dei* act as models for the development of mental health hermeneutics and policy-making.

As a Black woman and fourth-generation Episcopalian, I am aware of the tension between our tradition's spirit of white normativity and the ever-growing diversity in its midst. I am aware

---

1. Frank A. Thomas, *How to Preach a Dangerous Sermon* (Nashville: Abingdon Press, 2018), xl. Thomas argues that true Christianity positions itself against racism, misogyny, patriarchy, LGBTQIA-phobia, blame, discrimination, and scapegoating.

2. bell hooks, *Black Looks: Race and Representation* (New York: Routledge, 2015), 128.

of the fear of failure and shame that is often projected onto and inadvertently absorbed by marginalized bodies.[3] It is common among white-dominant churches to engage in worship practices that are, according to Fulkerson and Shoop, grounded in a disconnect between the lived-out embodied existence and a theological understanding of human bodies.[4] This marginalization and *othering* of the body is what I refer to as a dismemberment between the multiple aspects of human life. As a womanist public theologian, I live in a diunital universe among those who live according to binary logic, and I find this simultaneously challenging and invigorating. I live an embodied, interdisciplinary existence of fluidity. The line between the sacred and secular is often invisible. I work for the common good, seeking an embodied theological understanding of the image of God and a transformed beloved community. Thus, I am a theologian who practices the hermeneutics and exegesis of art, biblical texts, and culture because I envision a Church that is transformed in mind and body, embodying an ever-transformative theology.

I use the prophetic moral imagination of public theology from a womanist perspective. The major themes of my work are womanist axiology and African hermeneutics, public theology in the context of fashion and mental health policy, aesthetics and fashion as a liberative tool, and a response to the terror of white supremacist ideologies. Overall, this is Womanist Care. The Black woman's body as an artifact and the doctrine of the *imago Dei* set the scene. These two elements guide and drive my research.

---

3. Emma Ineson, *Failure: What Jesus Said About Sin, Mistakes and Messing Stuff Up* (London: SPCK Publishing, 2022), 32.

4. Mary McClintock Fulkerson and Marcia W. Mount Shoop, *A Body Broken, A Body Betrayed* (Eugene: Cascade Books, 2015), 43.

Becoming and Embodying Theology

The seedlings of my transformation toward becoming a theologian were planted, watered, and sown in the Episcopal churches of my childhood in South Florida. My mother, grandmother, great-aunt, and great-grandfather were choirmasters and organists in this tradition. It was at Saint Ann's, Saint Andrew's, and the Church of the Transfiguration that I fell in love with God and all the expressions of God, especially the expression of God as Jesus Christ. Each church offered an embodied style of worship and provided spiritual and emotional refuge from cultural and racial bias for its congregants. The Black Church experience within the Episcopal tradition has always been a place of empowerment for my kinfolk and me.

The churches of my youth did not seem to operate within an "us versus them" mentality. The clergy, irrespective of their socio-political and cultural background, cared deeply about the people and their plight in public life. They interacted with the community, shared themselves while valuing the individual stories of the community, as well as the overarching narrative of the people, as sacred. We were not just close as a parish, but we also had close relationships with other parishes of Caribbean heritage in our diocese. I experienced an embodiment of liberation theology years before I attended seminary or studied the works of James Cone, Gustavo Gutiérrez, and Katie Cannon. And in retrospect, I realize that Christian theology is about liberation. This liberation is not only regarding freedom for the oppressed and the oppressor alike, but it is also about empowerment. God did not set us free so that we can be powerless, fruitless, and of no earthly good. We have been given the Holy Spirit, who blesses us with gifts to serve the body and with the fruit of the Spirit to reflect Christ to the world. The churches of my childhood were powerfully connected with the Holy Spirit. The community expressed the fruit of the Spirit and identified their spiritual gifts, using them to bless and empower others. Despite the racial and cultural biases and socioeconomic struggles they faced in daily life, they were empowered by their church community to seek justice in an unjust world.[5]

I suspect that I became a theologian long before I knew what theology was or what theologians do. Insights blossomed while attending confirmation classes at the Church of the Transfiguration in Miami Gardens, Florida, where my uncle Elisha S. Clark Jr. was the rector. In the late 1970s, it was a small community of people of Bahamian heritage and the surrounding neighborhood, then called Opa Locka. For me, church was always home. It was home because I was surrounded by people who looked like me, who encouraged me, and who supported me in my spiritual formation. It was a "high church" and only boys could serve as acolytes. Yet, as a young Black female, I knew that God had set aside unique places for me. So, I made sure to immerse myself in the Book of Common Prayer, mainly the sections we used in the weekly services and those we had to study for confirmation. I did not know or care that males of European descent crafted the contents of the book. All I knew was that I experienced God's love leaping off the pages and subsequently holding me lovingly captive. Although I was ten years old, this embodied theological experience empowered me.

I was empowered to no longer mimic whiteness as a guarantee of immunity from racial ridicule in those places that were overwhelmed with bias and exclusion in my childhood. Although terrorized by it, the spirit of white supremacy I encountered as a youth, in tandem with the empowerment I gained from attending The Episcopal Church of my preteens, somehow shaped, trained, and formed me as an exegete.

---

5. Wylin D. Wilson, *Womanist Bioethics: Social Justice, Spirituality, and Black Women's Health* (New York: NYU Press, 2025), 107.

Exegesis became my tool of survival, from mere survival to overcoming, and from overcoming to flourishing. As I moved forward in my theological journey, I discovered the phenomenon of Black women's narratives as hermeneutical responses to white normativity. There are interpretive skills one develops when one has to engage in the daily practice of "reading the room," which involves assessing the cultural attitudes of the people and their intentions toward you. My experiences with racialized sexism shaped and formed me as a specialist in the practice of interpretation. I not only enjoy the practice of unpacking the meaning of texts, culture, and life, but I also enjoy rethinking how texts, bodies, and art give voice to diverse stories among us. As a womanist theologian, I not only expand on practices understood in the West, but I also challenge them by crafting approaches of my own, those that prioritize my lived experiences and ways of knowing. In short, I love the art of what Renita Weems coined as "tinkering."[6]

I tinker and challenge because much of traditional Western theological interpretation views human life within God's story through a narrow scope, missing the multiple layers of human identities. The problem reveals itself in the application. It is "when" and "where" I find how the single story harms the whole of the beloved community. It was when I embarked on applying an interpretation cultivated from the perspective of a cis-gendered straight, able-bodied, elite white male that I found out that the clothes did not fit, especially around those parts that make me an unapologetically Black woman. Looking back at my time at Church of the Transfiguration, the theology of that space fit because the people made it so. They framed the liturgy in the African spirituality and cosmology that they embodied as

---

6. Renita J. Weems, "African American Women and the Bible" in *Stony the Road We Trod*, ed. Cain Hope Felder (Minneapolis: Fortress Press, 1991), 58.

Bahamian people. As Alasdair MacIntyre says, "Stories are lived before they are told."[7] I lived my younger days as a Black liberation, decolonial-postcolonial, and womanist theologian long before I knew these concepts had names or had any inkling what they meant, and I had no premonitions letting me know that I would later read and retell scripture for the sake of doing Womanist Care, the ongoing act of dialog between womanist theologians and pastoral caregivers known as empowered co-journeyers. The Womanist Care practice of *re-tale-ing* is a liberative act toward reconciliation.[8] *Re-tale-ing* is how I practice public theology and narrative ethics.[9] To present a Christian response to major ethical issues in the public sphere requires a definitive understanding of the doctrine of the *imago Dei* as its essential, fertile soil.

We cannot understand or imagine a concept until we have the right metaphor to perceive it.[10] This is particularly so when grasping an understanding of the *imago Dei*. Much of what I observed along my journey explored little regarding metaphorical language but focused, in the literal sense, on human agency and human domination over other species in creation. Metaphors imply that there is synergy, while the literal explanation related to Cartesian dualism, which focuses on human capability framed in structures of individualism, is static.

---

7. Cited in Karla F. C. Holloway, *Private Bodies, Public Texts: Race, Gender and a Cultural Bioethics* (Durham: Duke University Press, 2011), opening epigraph. Holloway notes that Black women's stories occur in private spaces, and no particular path is sketched for ethical inquiry concerning Black female bodies.

8. S.R. Toliver, *Recovering Black Storytelling in Qualitative Research* (New York: Routledge, 2022), xxxvii.

9. Weems, "African American Women and the Bible," 61. Weems notes that retelling, or my term *re-tale-ing*, the Bible is a hermeneutical strategy for those raised in an aural tradition, especially Black women in the United States.

10. Diarmuid O'Murchu, *Quantum Theology* (New York: The Crossroad Publishing Company, 2004), 58.

Although it proposes that there are potentialities for human beings, those potentialities apply to specific aspects of certain humans. This issue, a need for meaning-making regarding the *imago Dei*, is what inspires me to tinker, to be a theologian. I am tenaciously seeking metaphors that give voice to those who live on the margins and beyond, those who live with neurological and psychological disorders and disabilities. I became a theologian because I am in love with God. Moreover, I am passionate about the practice of meaning-making that creates a more widely accessible story of God, especially for the "forgotten ones."

Womanist Public Theology: A Project of Process and Purpose

Theology has been a language of the few, namely, academics and clergy. While public theology and biblical interpretation have been given opportunities to engage public spaces other than the academy, seminary, and the preacher's study in the past, it appears that churches today are not familiar with either practice. Public theology, a term often defined by the ministry and public discourse of Martin Luther King Jr. and other leaders in the Black Christian experience, is very much misunderstood today, and some believe it refers to white evangelical males doing theology in public.[11] Further, I dare not mention to everyone I meet that I am a womanist public theologian, because the term "womanist" exacerbates the already confused listener. Although womanist thought and womanist theologies are commonly known among Black women in universities and seminaries, I have found that many of my non-Black colleagues do not know much about

---

11. Stephen Burns and Anita Monro, *Public Theology and the Challenge of Feminism* (London: Routledge, 2015), 72.

womanism. They assume that it refers to all Black women who embark on the theological project. In addition, I find that many have forgotten that theology is a creative, colorful, and perhaps never-ending project. This is what I was told during the first week of my first term as a theology student. Soon after, I discovered a large chasm between what I was told and the actual practice. Oddly, it was in those spaces where diversity was lacking, and where I was the outsider within, that I realized how much diversity mattered.[12] I became aware of the power and influence I possess as a Black woman theologian in white dominant spaces, particularly in the church and seminary settings. We are like the group of blind monks examining an elephant depicted in Itcho's painting.[13] Every perspective has a story and contributes to the larger story. The more those around me expressed some fear of my Black woman perspective, the more I fiercely dug my high-heeled shoes into the journey toward meaning-making that embodied a Black woman's story of God.

Womanism is inclusive. It creates metaphors that transcend gender, cultural, economic, racial, and societal norms. It embodies a Luxocratic vision. In the essay "An American Credo," Pauli Murray states, "When my brothers try to draw a circle to exclude me, I shall draw a larger circle to include them."[14] Murray's words are prophetically inclusive, resonating with the inclusive voice of womanism that would be named some forty years later by literary genius Alice Walker. Just as stories are lived before they can be told (MacIntyre), ideas and concepts are lived out and expressed long before they are

---

12. Barbara C. Harris and Kelly Brown Douglas, *Hallelujah, Anyhow* (New York: Church Publishing, 2018), 31.

13. This refers to a well-known Buddhist parable that was illustrated by painter Hanabusa Itcho (1652–1724).

14. Pauli Murray, "An American Credo" in *Common Ground*, Vol. Winter, 1945, 22–24.

named. Murray's words were embodied in the life of Zora Neale Hurston, whose life and storytelling inspired Walker to transform the term "womanish"—a term used by Black women to describe an attitude that reflected agency and autonomy—to "womanism." While womanism deals with the attainment of agency concerning Black womanhood, it also aims to address the need for equal access to opportunities for all people. It cares deeply for the commonweal.

Womanist logic and axiology are diunital, presenting an oppositional gaze in the face of dominator culture's dualistic and binary approach to meaning-making. It looks at the oppressive antimoral imagination in the eye and offers a public critique from a positionality of the Black woman as spectator. It transforms the auction block into a pulpit, a platform. Womanist logic is narratival, experiential, ecological, moral, emotional, and communal and embraces the mystical aspects of human life.[15] Gracefully overlapping and interacting with womanism, public theology is prophetic, multilingual, multidisciplinary, and multi-contextual, strategic, innovative, and liberative. Born out of the need for a prophetic voice in the public sphere, characteristics of public theology are in the work and ministry of Martin Luther King Jr. It addresses the anti-moral imagination in both public and private spheres. This voice has four elements: (1) the capacity to envision equality and to embody this vision, (2) the use of empathy or emotion as a catalyst for change, (3) the use of sacred texts and storytelling as sources of wisdom, and (4) the use of poetry and other artistic expressions to inspire hope.[16] These elements are essential in working with a trauma-sensitive hermeneutic toward decision-making in

---

15. Layli Phillips Maparyan, *The Womanist Idea* (New York: Routledge, 2012), 41.

16. Thomas, *How to Preach a Dangerous Sermon*, 17.

mental health policy.[17] And it all comes to fruition through my interdisciplinary, pluridisciplinary, hermeneutical reflections on Black women's fashion and literature.

In my story, God sews like an expert seamstress and tailor. She does not need any measuring tape. Westernized reason alone presents a flat and static existence, a narrow understanding of the *imago Dei*. It speaks of one ability that may be visible and present in some members of the beloved community. It leaves many of God's beloved outside the gates. God's upside-down kingdom is fully expressed through Jesus Christ and debunks any ideologies that leave some in and others out. In my childhood, I often found myself in trouble with teachers and other adults in authoritative positions due to an internal compass that moved me to consider those who are overlooked. Once more, I had yet to know what public theology was or what public discourse was, but I was living the story before it could be told. Even then, the common good meant something to me. I tinkered with the protocols and policies that were in place to find ways toward change. Reasoning is not solely a mind–soul occurrence. Our lived experiences produce knowledge, too. My whole being thinks and reasons. I am not because "I think." I am because God is. God clothed herself as the burning bush, saying, "I am that I am," not "I think that I am."

The word "process" in this section's title refers to our ever-transforming understanding of God, as there is so much more to understand, see, and experience in God's story. In real time, this cycle of verbs operates in reverse. We experience or live out something, see, and then come to the place of understanding. This is an embodied knowing, to be clothed in understanding, a move toward a Luxocracy.

---

17. Jennifer Baldwin, *Trauma-Sensitive Theology* (Eugene: Cascade Books, 2018), 79.

We are moving toward the goal of being shaped or transformed so that the clothes fit. The fact that these words came from the ideas of a womanist does not mean they do not apply to all who do the creative work of theologizing. However, I have observed that many do theology while looking back, reading the text through a rearview mirror, not allowing themselves to be fully clothed, but simply opting to don a baseball cap or a stylish, classic Kangol. Nostalgia feels good, but a little bit of tinkering in a world that requires so much more will not do. Hermeneutics cries out, "All theologies are contextual. Context, in all its directions, matters."

If all theologies are contextual, then they ought to engage in ever-transformative dialog just like Jazz playing over the chord changes of the big narrative, which is salvation through Christ Jesus. He said, "See, I am making all things new" (Revelation 21:5). Joel B. Green observes that "our neurobiological profile is itself in a state of ongoing formation and reformation."[18] We must keep up with Christ, allowing God to change how we think, while experiencing the contextual elements of this world. Through Christ, we are liberated from the oppressive, single story of a privileged few, which belongs to the dominator culture around us. Addiction to privilege and the need to assert dominance have no respect for persons and go hand-in-hand, as privilege has the power to injure its subordinates while also reaping the benefits of being oblivious to the occurrence of such injuries. The system maintains itself due to social narratives rooted in victor-victim binaries.[19] Theology, like God, must see the visible and invisible, the seen and unseen.[20]

---

18. Joel B. Green, *Body, Soul, and Human Life* (Grand Rapids: Baker Academic, 2008), 87.

19. Kwame A. Appiah, *The Lies That Bind: Rethinking Identity* (New York: Liveright Publishing, 2018), 148.

20. Baldwin, *Trauma-Sensitive Theology*, 78.

Dr. King warned against the danger of an addictive commitment to power.[21] In his sermon "The Drum Major Instinct," he stated, "The drum major instinct can lead to exclusivism in one's thinking."[22] Jesus also challenged the self-proclaimed religious folk regarding their need for dominance over others and their addiction to privilege, as they sought the high and favored seats among their community. The addiction to privilege and the need for dominance are forms of *othering*. It is a means of securing certain identities by stigmatizing, alienating, and disempowering others.[23] Seeing the visible and invisible, Pauli Murray embodied the womanist public theologian's response to such systems. Womanist public theology uses the Master's tools, the prophetic, liberative, and empowering imagination of Christ, to dismantle the master's house of injustice, unfair access to opportunities, and dominator culture.

The Word is active and alive. Theology imagines that we are in the process of a synergy between the biblical text and the world we live in. Doing theology in the present for a world that is long past and gone will not take us there. Like the Word, theological practice must be active and alive. Theological engagement of the present time is moving beyond the act of showing partiality in what issues it will consider for public discourse. It will no longer label some ways of meaning-making as "contextual" and too disruptive, too challenging to see. I envision theological discourse that no longer disassociates itself from the body, singular or as the body of Christ. This embodied theology considers the lived experiences, ways of knowing, or epistemologies, of bodies unseen as well as the seen.

---

21. O'Murchu, *Quantum Theology*, 140.

22. Martin Luther King, Jr. "The Drum Major Instinct" in *A Testament of Hope*, ed. James M. Washington (New York: HarperCollins, 1986), 263.

23. Charles K. Bellinger, *Othering: The Original Sin of Humanity* (Eugene: Cascade Books, 2020), 3, 41.

Toward an Embodied and Transformative Theology

Romans 12:1–2 offers hope, as it speaks to the transformation of Christ's body toward God's beloved community. The author assumes that the audience has grappled with their identities as people created in the image of God. Sown and sewn, planted and carefully knitted, they are bound to God and one another just as the community of trees has vertical and horizontal connections. As above, so it is below. In this reality, there is no need to conform to the world's illusion of power and control, to the addiction to privilege and the need to dominate others.[24] "Conform" is such a volatile word and concept, and from the lens of a Black woman, it equates with silencing. As a public theologian, I envision a more robust practice of theology in the public sphere and a deeper concern for those whose expression of the *imago Dei* challenges cultural normativity. There are aspects of our tradition that hold mysteries we cannot fully understand. There are no metaphors that could fully trace the meaning of those mysteries. Yet, I envision a broader understanding, a meaning-making phenomenon within our tradition. As some of us are called to do the work of theology as vocational practices, all are theologians. All creatures have a relationship with God and with creation. I define this to be a way of giving our bodies to God, surrendering our whole selves in relational service to God. Whether the relationship can be seen and measured by the human eye or if the relationship is far off and estranged, hidden and invisible, it is there.

In studying the hidden life of trees, Peter Wohlleben finds himself in an encounter with a tree stump that appears dead to the human eye but is alive due to its relationship with the surrounding trees.[25] He has

---

24. O'Murchu, *Quantum Theology*, 139.

25. Peter Wohlleben, *The Hidden Life of Trees* (London: William Collins, 2016), 5.

been forced to recognize that there are relationships among the trees that he could not see as a creature who lives above the soil, on the earth. Trees represent an unfolding mystery. I unpack the metaphor of trees and the Ubuntu theological perspective of the *imago Dei* in my research.[26] Although the metaphor may not fully explain the *imago Dei* in all its depth and breadth, the metaphor captures the communal aspect of what it means to be created in God's image. It also runs counter to the theme of individualism, which primarily focuses on the abilities of the individual, especially the Cartesian concept that centers on the human ability to reason. Romans 12:1 says, "Give your bodies to God because of all he has done for you." (NLT) It is about God's abilities, not our individual capabilities and intellectual prowess.

The metaphor of trees centers on the likeness of God within the collective, the body, and the beloved community. As individuals, not all of us can reason due to neurological disruptions. Nor are we all able to express love according to society's definition, and according to Paul's understanding of the fruit of the Spirit in Galatians, due to the lack of self-regulation associated with some mental disorders. Not all will have the creativity of Billy Strayhorn, Joni Mitchell, and Franz Liszt. However, in 1 Corinthians 12, it says that the Holy Spirit gives spiritual gifts to us individually in service of the body, the beloved community, for the common good. And like trees, the mutual interdependence or holonomy of the community benefits all, especially the voiceless and/or silenced members symbolized by Wohlleben's tree stump.[27] Thus, I more readily see the image of God in us as a body, hidden and intertwined beneath the soil, rather than in me alone.

---

26. Michael Battle, *Reconciliation: The Ubuntu Theology of Desmond Tutu* (Cleveland: Pilgrim Press, 2009), 126.

27. O'Murchu, *Quantum Theology*, 58.

Conclusion

We are because God is. Relationships, seen and unseen, visible and invisible, matter. Womanist public theology engages in discourse for the common good, and I became a theologian because I desire to respond to important ethical and moral issues in all spheres as a means toward an inclusive, embodied understanding of the image of God, the beloved community. My research aims to develop a meaning-making or hermeneutics that *re-tales* biblical texts as liberative tools for engaging mental health public policy. The voices of those who live with mental health disorders and disabilities due to emotional trauma and neurological disruptions are often unheard and unseen in the Church and other public spaces. Reading biblical texts that inspire inclusion and support for those challenged by mental disability, rather than vilification through misunderstanding, is essential to moving toward a tangible beloved community.

An embodied and transformative theology is an ongoing process.[28] Jazz legend John Coltrane worked endlessly to transcend his previous solos. Also, he transcended the desire to copy the behaviors and customs of other musicians in his world. Like Trane, we must keep working to move beyond the desire to mimic the behaviors and customs, addiction to privilege, and need for domination of the world, but be transformed into a new people. An embodiment of a transformative theology means that we are constantly being renewed in our bodies/brains, and minds/souls. Finally, there can be no liberation without community.[29] An embodied theology means that when the

---

28. Embodiment refers to how an idea, belief, or concept is lived and the movement/process toward becoming imitators of Christ, not particular to physicality and physical ability, prowess, and power.

29. Audre Lorde, *The Master's Tools Will Never Dismantle the Master's House* (New York: Penguin Books, 2017), 18.

sins of the addiction to privilege and the seemingly insatiable need for domination draw a small circle of exclusion, we, the embodiment of Christ, must always draw a larger circle to embrace all, especially those who are often overlooked and unseen.

Further Reading Recommendations

Baker-Fletcher, Karen. *Dancing with God: The Trinity from a Womanist Perspective.* St. Louis: Chalice Press, 2006.

Douglas, Kelly Brown. *What's Faith Got to Do with It? Black Bodies/Christian Souls.* Maryknoll, NY: Orbis Books, 2005.

Kim, Sebastian C. H. *Theology in the Public Sphere.* London: SCM Press, 2011.

Peppiatt, Lucy. *The Imago Dei: Humanity Made in the Image of God.* Eugene, OR: Cascade, 2022.

Theologizing and Organizing Together: Constructing Liberative Anglican Ecclesiologies

Francisco J. García Jr.

Tracing the roots of my pathway to studying theology and identifying as a theologian, I identified a series of core moments or choice points that I identify as theological acts—"God" moments where theology/the divine/Spirit acted upon me and/or I acted in response to something occurring in my life and community. I offer here five "acts" that have shaped me and my theological trajectory in significant ways.

Act 1: Activist Origins

My first theological act came out of a moment of righteous indignation as a freshman in high school in a working-class suburb of Los Angeles County. In the middle of an English class, I heard my teacher, whom I had respected and admired up to that point, defend a proposed state law that would prevent undocumented families from accessing essential public services—even to the point of preventing kids from attending public schools. A few additional elements made it worse: my classroom was filled with kids like me—a majority Latine-immigrant classroom. Worse still was this teacher's use of Christianity to justify xenophobic policies under the pretext of "faith, law, and order." I didn't have all the words, or critical analysis at the time to articulate my feelings or to muster a response in class, but as the son of Mexican immigrants—and as a young Chicano Roman Catholic who grew up learning about the social teachings of Jesus and faith-rooted Mexican-American community leaders like Dolores Huerta and César Chávez—it was personally and spiritually troubling. Everything inside of me told me that I couldn't remain silent. That latent sense of rage and confusion that I felt in hearing blatant anti-immigrant rhetoric from a teacher whom I had previously respected and trusted, and the wave of protest that was emerging in schools and communities across California, propelled me into activism at the age of fourteen and led me on a years-long path of exploring the intersections between faith, justice, and collective action. Without knowing it precisely, I felt the spirit of God guiding me to question the theological and political frameworks that marginalized my community as well as others. I joined my classmates in rallying outside our school to proclaim the human dignity of our families and all who might be cast as less than for lacking a piece of paper. I call this my first theological act because, in the tradition of liberation theology, formal theological reflection is considered a *second-order* activity—a "reflection on practice in the light of faith" as noted by Gustavo Gutiérrez, one of the foundational liberation theologians on whose shoulders we all stand, and whose work I am forever mining for deep reflection and application.[1]

---

1. Gustavo Gutierrez, "The Task and Content of Liberation Theology," in *The Cambridge Companion to Liberation Theology*, ed. Christopher Rowland (New York: Cambridge University Press, 2007), 27.

Act 2: Walk Out

A few years later, I engaged in another act of theological questioning when I walked out of a mass (in the parish I had grown up in) upon hearing what I experienced as a narrow-minded sermon. The priest spoke of a teenage girl's decision to have an abortion as a sin, without regard to the socioeconomic contexts that led to her pregnancy and abortion. As I reflected on what I was hearing, something didn't sit right with me. What I heard from this preacher was an abstract dehumanization of a young, nameless girl. She had been made a theological pawn. I knew that I could no longer remain in that parish and began searching for a different spiritual home. As Gutiérrez notes, theological challenge comes from "the *non-persons*—those who are not recognized as people by the existing social order: the poor, the exploited, those systematically and legally deprived of their status as human beings, those who barely realize what it is to be a human being."[2] Despite the disempowered nature of this girl in the sermon, like the many nameless women in the Bible, I felt her spirit counter-preaching to me subversively, rounding out her story in an act of re-humanization. "This priest doesn't speak for me," I heard. "He doesn't know me or own my story. Keep searching for God's truth." Here, the principles of love, justice, and mercy were speaking to me. Many years later, I would read the provocative words of theologian Marcella Althaus-Reid, who examined how even in progressive, liberationist circles, "the suffering arising from gender and sexual discrimination" was thought to be "of a second order."[3]

---

2. Gutierrez, "The Task and Content of Liberation Theology," 28.

3. Marcella Althaus-Reid, "Demythologizing Liberation Theology," in *The Cambridge Companion to Liberation Theology*, ed. Rowland, 126.

Act 3: Eco-Maya-Liberation Spirituality in Yucatán

Another key moment on my theological journey occurred in Mexico as I studied abroad for a semester during my undergraduate years. During my fieldwork in rural, indigenous Maya communities in the Yucatán, I was introduced to a grassroots liberation theology in practice through an innovative eco-cultural-spiritual justice project. I encountered a community of university students and faculty trained in agronomy/agriculture working with Catholic priests and several Maya villages to cultivate sustainable agricultural practices in the region. The two priests involved in incubating the project had committed themselves to a ministry of presence and accompaniment with local Maya communities for years and had earned their trust and respect. What they heard from the communities was that they were facing a combination of food insecurity, economic precarity, and a loss of indigenous traditions. Working with local community leaders and the university, they developed an ecological school that addressed all these concerns—training young people in the latest sustainable agricultural practices to support local employment and food sources, while also honoring their Maya culture and spirituality, which was a blending of indigenous spirituality with Catholic teachings and practices developed over 500 years. I heard testimonies about the deep spirituality of the land and of God's preferential option for the poor. More importantly, I saw these beliefs and values lived out in practice in an intentional community. The community was modeled after and inspired by the *Comunidades Eclesiales de Base* (Base Ecclesial Communities) that emerged across Latin America in the 1960s to 1990s, but rooted in local indigenous contexts. As Alexia Salvatierra and Brandon Wrencher note, BECs sought to be "a Church of and with the poor" and one "that incarnates and achieves holistic justice."[4] It was here that I began to witness and experience the presence of a liberating God, one who accompanied the people on their journey for life, livelihood, and meaning. Still, this kind of community and spirituality seemed unreachable when I returned to the United States.

Act 4: A Dear Teacher Shows Me the Way Home

My experience in the Yucatán predated my arrival in The Episcopal Church by five years, when my interest in connecting faith, justice, theology, and organizing began coalescing more intently. Critical on this path was learning at the feet of a true hero of the faith-rooted struggle for freedom, the Rev. James Lawson (1928–2024), who indirectly guided me to my first Episcopal parish: All Saints Church in Pasadena. From the early days of the Black freedom struggle (what many know as the Civil Rights Movement) through the 2000s, Lawson was a cornerstone of people's movements rooted in the philosophy, theology, and practice of nonviolence. In Los Angeles, Lawson played a crucial role in training primarily immigrant, Latine, and Black workers in the hotel and janitorial industries in the way of nonviolence as they fought for living wages and human dignity in their workplaces. I was fortunate to take an inaugural course with him on Nonviolence and Social Movements as a young graduate student at UCLA, and every time I heard him speak, I felt like I was going to church (in the best sense of this meaning). Every class was both a mountaintop experience,

---

4. Alexia Salvatierra and Brandon Wrencher, *Buried Seeds: Learning from the Vibrant Resilience of Marginalized Christian Communities* (Grand Rapids, MI: Baker Academic, 2022), 10–11.

while also being encouraged and guided down the mountain to put the teachings to work. When I asked him about churches that preached from the pulpit what he was teaching us in class, he mentioned a few places, one of them being All Saints Church. I had forgotten all about the church for a few years until I found myself in a spiritually and politically challenging moment in life and desperately needed a spiritual home. I retrieved All Saints from my memory after an internet search of "peace and justice" churches, and it showed up on an interfaith coalition webpage. I had not attended church regularly for several years, and I went to church that weekend.

After the first service, I knew that it would become my spiritual home. I was hungry for God, for theological discourse, and for channeling my faith into social action. All my prior experiences were laying the groundwork for this season. All aspects of my life—personal, professional, spiritual, and political—had become aligned. Over a period of a few years, my interest in deep theological exploration grew right alongside a growing sense of a call to ordained ministry. From the first sermons that I heard from the pulpit, theologically rich and justice-minded ideas and stories were shared that resonated with me. Immersed in all forms of church life ministry, I found an embedded theology that supported, challenged, and sustained me for the work. I was introduced to the works and witness of Thomas Merton, William Sloan Coffin, Desmond Tutu, Abraham Joshua Heschel, Dorothy Day, and others. More importantly, I found myself in a community that sought to live out what was being preached.

Act 5: From Union Organizer to Labor-Community Priest

The theological impact of my introduction to The Episcopal Church was not insignificant. Working as a union organizer, I felt passionate about racial and economic justice and making a tangible impact on people's lives. At the same time, I began to experience burnout with the working hours demanded of me. Being in the church provided both a theological language and a place of respite to discern how best to channel my efforts in the world. As my spiritual life and my organizing life began to fuse over a number of years—through pastoral accompaniment with both parishioners and workers—I discerned a call to become a priest in The Episcopal Church. While in seminary, I continued to work as a union campaign director and contract negotiator for two years. In my final year of seminary, I accepted a call to work at my sponsoring parish and facilitated efforts in justice ministries as well as in Latine/Hispanic ministries. While at All Saints, I helped launch various community campaigns, including an immigration ministry and a community coalition to support a living wage in the city. I also served as the primary pastor to the Latine and Spanish-speaking congregants at the church. Later, I accepted a call to Holy Faith Episcopal Church, where I served as rector to a working-class, multi-ethnic, and multilingual community, and worked on issues of housing displacement, police accountability, and other justice issues facing our predominantly Black and Brown community.

I share this narrative of my journey from young activist to organizer and later clergy because it directly leads to my becoming a theologian. I have been engaged in organizing and justice work for over twenty years. I became a theologian to reflect upon and amplify this work for a new season of theologically grounded ministry and teaching focused on organizing. I have been challenged and strengthened throughout my years in multi-vocational ministry, and in many ways, the work is continuously beginning anew.

The Theological Enterprise: Core Themes

Radical Roots

Part of my understanding of the theological enterprise is to restore its risky, radical nature, to bring it to the place where it exercises "judgment" on pressing issues of injustice based on the core teachings of the gospel. By "radical," once again I draw from Gustavo Gutiérrez's work, wherein he states that to claim the radical nature of a theology of liberation is to "doggedly plunge to the root" of the Christian faith, based in God's love and solidarity with "the least of these among us" as stated in Matthew 25.[5] Anglican community theologian Kenneth Leech speaks of this in his own way, asserting that "genuine orthodox theology must be involved, committed, partisan. A theology which is disconnected from the world is not Christian theology at all."[6] In saying this, I am not adopting the approach of "Radical Orthodoxy" often associated with John Milbank and others. Rather, my interest is in reclaiming the theme of liberation as central to the biblical narrative broadly, and to Jesus' teaching and witness more specifically. In this claim, I draw on several generations of liberationist theologians across many continents whose work easily encompasses sixty years. James Cone and Gustavo Gutiérrez served as the catalysts for the theological fervor that was

---

5. Gustavo Gutiérrez, "Option for the Poor," in *Mysterium Liberationis: Fundamental Concepts of Liberation Theology*, ed. Ignacio Ellacuria S.J. and Jon Sobrino S.J. (Maryknoll, NY: Orbis Books, 1993), 239.

6. Kenneth Leech, *Doing Theology in Altab Ali Park* (London: Dartman, Long, and Todd), 71.

already "in the water," inspired in large part by revolutionary and social movements of the time. Within the Episcopal/Anglican tradition, there are a number of liberation and justice-oriented theologians who have made and are making significant contributions, chiefly among them Kwok Pui-lan, Kelly Brown Douglas, Carter Heyward, Patrick Cheng, Esther Mombo, Jenny Te Paa Daniel, and the aforementioned Kenneth Leech. The seeds of justice-oriented theologies can also be seen in the works of earlier Anglican/Episcopal thinkers and practitioners— some of those voices that I draw from in my work are Verna Dozier, F. D. Maurice, William Stringfellow, Pauli Murray, and Vida Scudder. All of these thinkers in some way point to the radical/rooted nature of Christian praxis, of which Gutiérrez speaks.

Borderlands-Migrant Identities, Latine Spiritualities, and Culture

Given this call for a radical understanding of theology, I cannot understand the theological enterprise apart from the context of the world in which we live, and the particular social location where I find myself. I am a son of working-class Mexican immigrant parents, a child of the *borderlands*, a place of hybridity that includes but transcends geography as first articulated by Chicana feminist writer and social theorist Gloria Anzaldúa some decades ago.[7] My parents grew up in serious urban poverty on the Mexican side of the California/Baja California border. They migrated (separately as they grew up in different regions) to the Los Angeles area in the early 1970s but had traveled back and forth many times before at a time when the border region was more porous, although still dangerous for migrants. Growing up, we made frequent trips across the border to visit with my paternal grandmother

---

7. Gloria Anzaldúa, *Borderlands/La Frontera* (San Francisco, CA: Aunt Lute Books, 1987).

and aunts, uncles, and cousins. My *abuelos* (grandparents) were salt-of-the-earth people, from rural villages (*ranchos*, they called them) in central and southwestern Mexico. My maternal *abuelo* was an agricultural laborer working alongside the *braceros* (agricultural laborers on short-term seasonal contracts approved by the U.S. government) in Texas, but he didn't have papers. He was deported during the heightened anti-Mexican, xenophobic hysteria that gripped the Southwest in the 1950s, which eventually led to an official government mass deportation program, openly called "Operation Wetback."[8] I grew up in a bicultural, borderlands reality—hearing and speaking mostly Spanish at home, English at school. Growing up in a Mexican-Latine Roman Catholicism, Spanish was my spiritual and cultural mother tongue. I recall the vivid imagery of my maternal *abuela's* altar, replete with crucifixes, *Santitos* ("Little" Saints, a term of endearment), and the *Virgen María de Guadalupe* (Our Lady of Guadalupe). My *abuelo* was a devout attendee of the morning rosary and mass at the local Roman Catholic church. The migration narrative, and the lived material and spiritual realities of intergenerational immigrant and mixed-status families, figure prominently into my theological praxis, and I seek to theologize from this place to arrive at approximations to the larger implications for church and society. As Latina ecclesiologist Natalia Imperatori-Lee states, "a narrative ecclesiology invites a telling of church history from the perspective of the marginalized, the despised, and the forgotten, and discovers the universality of the church in the particularity of those experiences."[9]

---

8. Juan Gonzalez, *Harvest of Empire: A History of Latinos in America* (New York: Penguin Books, 2022), 232. See also Erin Blakemore, "The Largest Mass Deportation in American History," last modified June 30, 2025, accessed May 1, 2025, https://www.history.com/articles/operation-wetback-eisenhower-1954-deportation.

9. Natalia Imperatori-Lee, *Cuéntame: Narrative in the Ecclesial Present* (Maryknoll, NY: Orbis Books, 2018), 147.

Everything's Contextual! Toward Constructive Theologies

For this reason, some might call me a "contextual" theologian, or the kind of theology that I do as *contextual theology*, but I would disagree with that view. One of the tasks that I identify with in the theological enterprise is to work toward a common understanding that all theology is contextual. Karl Barth, Dietrich Bonhoeffer, and Friedrich Schleiermacher all had contexts, some of which are conveniently ignored. What has often occurred is that theologies done from a non-white, non-male background, or by someone who is centering matters of race, class, gender, sexuality, or concrete social issues affecting communities experiencing oppression, are considered contextual, while other theologies that are more abstract or less specific about particular social contexts or identities are considered the "real" or more "rigorous" theology. Yet, so-called contextual theologies are dealing with God and all the various doctrines, albeit in nontraditional ways.

A number of theologians have been engaging with the notion of "constructive theology" for several decades now—the most notable being the "Workgroup on Constructive Christian Theology." As members of the Workgroup note, their understanding of constructive is to go beyond descriptive or historical views of theology, but to try to "understand and construct [theology] in the present, to imagine what life-giving faith can be in today's world."[10] I would identify liberationist theologies as falling within constructive theology. Constructive theology seeks to deconstruct dominant forms of theological thinking, retain what is useful and relevant, and reconstruct fresh forms of

---

10. Serene Jones and Paul Lakeland, "Introduction: Theology as Faith in Search of Understanding," in *Constructive Theology: A Contemporary Approach to Classical Themes* (Minneapolis: Fortress Press, 2005), 2.

theological praxis. As Jason Wyman notes, while dogmatic theology has been focused on articulating the correct dogmas/doctrines (primary beliefs) of Christianity, and systematic theology has sought to organize Christian doctrines into an orderly system, "constructive theology emphasizes the contingent, transient, impermanent, and ultimately constructed reality of any theological speech, insisting on foregrounding the imaginatively constructive work that is truly at the heart of theology." Constructive theology engages traditional theological dogmas/doctrines but offers a present and future-oriented perspective.[11]

My Theological Contribution—Constructive, Liberationist, Ecclesiological

Over the years, I have come to the conclusion that my role in the church and in the world of theological education is to develop and contribute constructive and comprehensive theologies and ethics rooted in the spirit of faith-inspired social movements, community and labor organizing, and the liberative theological traditions found within the United States and Latin America. These theo-ethics emerge as an amalgamation of my own social location and are also rooted in the struggles, experiences, and stories of the communities that I have come from and have accompanied for many years. These communities and experiences are primarily based in working-class, immigrant, communities of color in terms of my upbringing and labor-community organizing; and multi-racial, intergenerational faith communities where I have pastored in The Episcopal Church. My research has been particularly focused on how faith emerges for

---

11. Jason Wyman, "Constructive Theology: History, Movement, Method," in *What is Constructive Theology? Histories, Methodologies, and Perspectives*, ed. Marion Grau and Jason Wyman (London: Bloomsbury Publishing, 2020), 10.

working-class Latine immigrant communities outside of traditional church entities, and workers more specifically, as they fight for their rights at work—leading to the emergence of what I call the *ekklēsia trabajadora del pueblo*, a working people's ekklēsia. In this work, I provide a concrete application of theologian Joerg Rieger's re-framing of Paul Tillich's notion of what is of "ultimate concern" in religion/theology—namely, that labor struggles and the unequal class relations that impact all of our lives should be considered in the ultimate category.[12]

Through my research, writing, teaching, and organizing, my work seeks to equip people within The Episcopal Church and across faith traditions, as well as interested community partners, with the theological and practical tools needed to address pressing issues of systemic racism, economic exploitation, and other forms of injustice, hatred, trauma, and suffering in their midst. I believe that a great majority of the solutions can be found in developing a cohesive sense of (organized) community that is rooted in neighborhood institutions and community relationships—civic, secular, and religious. These lessons can be gleaned from examining the role of faith and spirituality in the major social movements of our time, such as the Black freedom struggle, the Chicano movement, movements for gender and LGBTQIA equality, the labor and immigrant rights movements, and other movements for liberation. Because communities of faith were engaged in these movements as well, informal and at times formal theo-ethics are embedded in these movements. There are tangible lessons to learn by reengaging in the study of these and other movements, while also developing new strategies and theologies for our time.

---

12. Joerg Rieger, *Theology in the Capitalocene: Ecology, Identity, Class, and Solidarity* (Minneapolis: Fortress Press, 2022), 99–101.

My Vision for the Future of Theology in The Episcopal Church

Expansive Ecclesiology

I am at heart an ecclesiologist, focused on what it means to be and do church in our present age, and in the relationship between the grassroots church and the work of organized communities organizing for social change outside of church contexts. As I have expressed earlier in terms of my research and practical organizing and ministry interests, my hope is that theological reflection in The Episcopal Church is done in a collaborative relationship with these grassroots realities of church and community life, particularly with communities that have been relegated to the margins. Congregations and church leaders would benefit greatly from exploring faith practices and ecclesiological expressions outside of the institutional forms of church; the entire church benefits once we begin to see more clearly the faith and agency of working-class immigrant communities within the church and community. In addition, both trained and budding theologians in the church can continue to expand our understanding of the ecclesiological landscape both through on-the-ground ethnographic research, and in the collective (*en conjunto*) construction of more imaginative theo-ethical expressions of the church.

Theologies En Conjunto

One of the lessons that I draw from Latine theology in the United States, and that also works well with constructive theological approaches, is the notion of doing theology together in community—*en conjunto*. My hope is that we abandon the days of doing theology from our individual armchairs in isolation from each other, and that we take seriously the notion that the work of theology is actually understood as *theologizing*—an active, engaged process done in community. A high hope I have is that, like the notion of *liturgia*, theology becomes the work of the people. In the spirit of Latine theology *en conjunto*, I hope that such an open and collaborative theological approach can move deeply through Episcopal contexts, beginning with Episcopal Church communities on the margins. From here, theologizing, connected to social action, can move into all the polity structures of The Episcopal Church.

Theologies and Ministry Practices for the Common Good

I am under no illusions that theologizing and organizing in this way is easy. My assessment is that the majority of the church is neither theologically nor practically equipped to move from ideas about justice and liberation to sustained, organized action. Many churches in the United States context—whether large or small, whether predominantly white, Black, Latine, Asian, immigrant, or mixed—are struggling with survival in different ways. While there was a moment during the pandemic when the church was "cracked open," as the Rev. Stephanie Spellers addressed in her insightful book—and people understood the church as *not the building* by necessity—it seems that those lessons have been quickly lost.[13] The need or the perception of the need to increase people in the pews on Sundays to sustain aging buildings, or just to maintain the production of Sunday worship, is incessant. Institutional self-preservation is a powerful force that must

---

13. Stephanie Spellers, *The Church Cracked Open: Disruption, Decline, and New Hope for Beloved Community* (New York: Church Publishing, 2021). I was fortunate to engage in an intellectual dialog with Spellers in a round table convened by the *Anglican Theological Review*. See Francisco García, "Let the Cracking Open Continue: Believing in Kenosis, Practicing Solidarity for the Common Good," *Anglican Theological Review* 105 (2023): 322–26.

be challenged in order to move the church toward faithful transformation rooted in the common good (involving and positively impacting/benefiting people beyond the parish) beyond the walls of the church and its institutional forms. This work can only take place when it is grounded theologically and practically in the relational work of community building and organizing. By turning our theological attention to organized people of faith at the grassroots level and the spiritual practices and ethical actions that occur there, we can help nurture the emergence of a vital Episcopal ecclesiology "from below" that may better equip faith communities for the liberative work of the gospel.

Further Reading Recommendations

Gutiérrez, Gustavo. *The Power of the Poor in History.* Maryknoll, NY: Orbis Books, 1983.

Imperatori-Lee, Natalia. *Cuéntame: Narrative in the Ecclesial Present.* Maryknoll, NY: Orbis Books, 2018.

Leech, Kenneth. *Doing Theology in Altab Ali Park.* London: Darton, Longman & Todd, 2006.

Rieger, Joerg and Kwok Pui-lan. *Occupy Religion: Theology of the Multitude.* Lanham, MD: Rowman & Littlefield, 2012.

The Water of Life: Baptismal Faith, Theological Plumbing, and Encounter with the Living God

Kelli Joyce

Becoming a Christian

I was baptized into the Body of Christ on September 27, 1998, just shy of the half-birthday (all-important at that age) that would have made me five and a half years old. I had been a faithful church attendee for my entire life up to that point, more or less literally: I was born on one Sunday morning, and my parents took me to church for my baby dedication the following Sunday. We lived across the country from all our family, and so my parents would regularly mail my grandparents cassette recordings of me singing as a two- and three-year-old. On one of these tapes, recorded before my third birthday, I sang the names of all the books of the Bible from memory, stumbling only on the pronunciation of the same names—I'm looking at Haggai here—that still give me trouble to this day. I mention all this not because this is a personal essay and therefore an opportunity for sharing cute anecdotes, but because these stories of my upbringing illustrate the extent to which all my thinking and knowing and speaking have been shaped by the Church and by Holy Scripture from the very beginning. I did not come to know Christianity; I came to know everything else from *within* Christianity, through it and in its light.

My baptism as an almost-five-and-a-half-year-old took place in the Southern Baptist tradition, one that is often described as requiring "adult baptism," but which, at least in my experience of it, was much more concerned with "believer's baptism." It was a personal affirmation of belief, not age, that was the standard. (That said, my young age upon requesting baptism did mean, to my childhood delight, that I got to meet with the pastor so he could determine whether my turn to Christ was of my own initiative, or if I simply wanted to please my parents.) It is somewhat strange now, as a scholar studying the theology of baptism from a decidedly Anglican point of view, to think back on my own. What I now believe happened on that Sunday in September is not what any person in the room at the time, myself included, thought was happening. No one believed my sins were being washed away, no one believed I was dying and rising with Christ as I was immersed in those waters, no one believed I was being reborn of water and the Spirit or being mystically united to the Body of Christ across time and space. For us back then, baptism was the first public act of obedience to Christ on the part of someone who had already been fully justified and united to Christ by virtue of what they confessed with their lips and believed in their heart: in other words, by praying "the sinner's prayer." No one in that room believed anything was *happening* in my baptism. And yet, nevertheless, it was.

When I became a teenager, in some ways I leaned even further into my life in the Church, into a life in which all knowing that was worth knowing was knowing in and through the truth of the Gospel. I memorized Bible verses competitively, frustrated Sunday School teachers and Youth Ministers alike with endless questions, and read apologetic works so that I would "always be ready to give a defense to everyone" who might ask me the "reason for the hope" that was within me (1 Peter 3:15). At roughly the same time, I was coming to the exceedingly unwelcome realization that I was a lesbian.

Becoming a Theologian

This realization was, in retrospect, the cause of my first unwilling steps toward becoming a theologian. Every tool I had ever been given and every skill I had practiced was designed for the task of defending the faith from external adversaries. Suddenly, I found myself in need of a way to defend *myself* against the doctrines of the community that had been the air in my lungs. I had two subsequent realizations: I needed to know how one could discern the truth of God's will. And I needed to learn Greek. At that time, I still believed as my congregation had taught me about baptism; it was, therefore, unavailable to me as a rock on which I might ground my indelible belonging to Christ and to the Church. When my youth pastor told me, at the end of a series of meetings during which I laid out my carefully crafted theological arguments in my defense, that he believed I was "predestined to hell" if I was truly unable to cease being a lesbian, a rock for grounding that belonging emerged instead from my parents' response. They were furious with him. Not because they were already affirming; that took more time. But because, to them, my profession of Jesus Christ as my Lord and Savior was as stable a foundation as anyone could wish for. Even when they still believed what *they* had been taught about what constituted sin, they also believed that no sin could damn one who was washed in the blood of the Lamb.

Their anger toward him moved me further down the path toward active engagement with theology. I was sixteen years old, newly licensed to drive, and they gave my sister and me permission to look for another church and join its youth group. We found our way to an American Baptist congregation that had been formally and openly affirming since the turn of the millennium. The adults I met there encouraged the curiosity and questions that my childhood congregation had found so distressing. They were the first to suggest to me that I might consider ordained ministry, or at least seek out formal theological education. They put works of theology into my teenage hands that I had never imagined: liberation theology, process theology, feminist theology. I had never known a community like that congregation, and have never known its equal since. They loved me, and they were persuaded that God loved me; they believed God had a good plan for my life and were invested in seeing it come to pass.

I asked the senior pastor to rebaptize me not long after we began attending. He kindly but firmly told me that he could not; each of us is born where we are born, for good and for ill, and then must choose where to go from there.

Becoming an Episcopalian

Where I chose to go, after no small amount of time spent fighting it, was to divinity school. It was there that I first encountered The Episcopal Church, and it was there that my understanding of the theological enterprise began to change. Thanks to the Episcopal seminary that was attached to my ecumenical divinity school, for the first time in my life, I had the opportunity to pray Morning Prayer in community and receive the Eucharist daily. My childhood congregation had administered the ordinance of the Lord's Supper quarterly; the American Baptist congregation that sent me to divinity school had offered it weekly as part of their contemporary worship service. In both cases, the theological focuses were the traditional Baptist ones: a corporate memorial of the passion and resurrection of Christ and a meal of fellowship among those who believed in Christ. The Prayer Book's assertion that in Holy Communion I was being given true spiritual food and being affirmed as a living member of Christ's own Body was transformative for me. I found my Baptist self worshiping with the Episcopalians more days than not. That same first year of seminary, I also had a memorable spiritual experience concerning baptism. During group spiritual direction, we read the gospel passage in which Jesus admonishes his followers to let the little children come to him and not to hinder them. In the moment that I heard it, though the words were entirely familiar, I felt an overwhelming sense of certainty that I could no longer object to the practice of infant baptism.

I mention these experiences with the sacraments not only because sacramental theology has since become my field of study, but also because it was in coming to an understanding of Christianity as a sacramental faith that I came to an understanding of theology as more than a rhetorical sword and shield to be used to defeat others and defend myself. As a child, theology had been a tool that existed to serve the apologetic and evangelistic enterprise. As a teenager, it had been a strategy for self-protection from those who told me the Church did not and could not have room in it for me. And it is certainly true that theology in a polemical key has a long and distinguished history within the Church. But as I began to engage with the sacraments through contact with The Episcopal Church, another possible register opened up before me: a theology of encounter with God, for the sake of that encounter itself.

I was confirmed at the end of my first spring semester at seminary, and the following summer, I would find a home in the Diocese of Arizona, a community that welcomed and nurtured me even though at that time I had never lived within its borders. At that point, I had no plans to pursue theological study as anything other than something that was a part of my formation for ordination, or my life as a Christian seeking understanding of faith. Maybe as a hobby. Even when I undertook further graduate study in theology at Durham

University following seminary, I wasn't thinking of academic theology itself as a part of my vocation in its own right. I had no plans to become a theologian.

Becoming a Theologian (Again)

There really is something, though, to the saying that we plan and God laughs. I was ordained in 2018 and planned to do nothing but parish ministry from there onward. But family circumstances, the Coronavirus pandemic, and promptings of the Spirit that would not be ignored forever all led to my applying to Vanderbilt in 2021 to undertake doctoral studies in sacramental theology. My (re)turn to academic theology following ordination was in part an extension of my early-seminary desire to better understand what I experienced in the sacraments: to better know the One whom I met in them and to be better prepared to explain the meaning that I have found in them to my friends and relatives in non-sacramental traditions.

I had come to believe that God's gift of the sacramental mediation of grace was a reflection of how God relates to creation more broadly—and specifically, of the relationship between and union of Word and Matter that lies at the heart of Christianity. Language and the material world are both fundamental elements of God's creation, and the development of the process of creation itself is undertaken by means of both God's speaking and God's shaping of already-created matter into something new.

Theology, too, is undertaken by means of both words and material action. In the field of liturgical theology, this reality is often expressed by speaking of "primary theology," which is to be found in liturgical-sacramental practice itself, and "secondary theology," which consists of various verbal reflections upon primary theology.¹ This framework is often expressed by way of reference to the aphorism *lex orandi, lex credendi*. The "law of prayer" is taken to be primary; the "law of belief" is subject to it. The presumed nature of the hierarchical relationship between these two "theologies" has been helpfully critiqued for its historical and theological shortcomings: it tends to assume that there is a single pre-existing thing called "liturgy" that is "a given ... handed to us ready-made" and which functions to shape the (secondary) theological imaginations of Christians in a way that is basically "unilateral and not at all what we might call interactive or multivalent."² Put another way, we must take care not to let any logical or temporal priority which embodied forms of Christian life and worship may have over doctrinal reflection upon them calcify into a distorted misunderstanding which "reduces theology to a doctrinal explication and defence of an irreformable liturgy."³

Rather than selecting one of these two theological modes to prioritize as the truer or nobler endeavor (and the other mode as, by implication, derivative at best and superfluous at worst), the key is to recognize that both are expressions of a single calling given to all Christians: to "proclaim by word and example the Good News of God in Christ."⁴ The whole of human history is within the realm of

---

1. Joris Geldhof, "Liturgical Theology," in *Oxford Research Encyclopedia of Religion*, 2015, https://doi.org/10.1093/acrefore/9780199340378.013.14.

2. Paul V. Marshall, "Reconsidering 'Liturgical Theology': Is There a *Lex Orandi* for All Christians?," *Studia Liturgica* 25, no. 2 (September 1995): 134–35, https://doi.org/10.1177/003932079502500201.

3. Maxwell E. Johnson, "Liturgy and Theology," in *Liturgy in Dialogue: Essays in Memory of Ronald Jasper*, ed. Paul F. Bradshaw and Bryan D. Spinks (Collegeville, MN: Liturgical Press, 1993), 224.

4. *The Book of Common Prayer and Administration of the Sacraments and Other Rites and Ceremonies of the Church: Together with the Psalter or Psalms of David According to the Use of the Episcopal Church* (New York, NY: The Church Hymnal

God's concern and God's action; theology is considered speech and considered action within history in light of the revelation of God in Christ. Theological trouble arises when one aspect of any whole is made absolute, or even simply over-weighted. An undue or exclusive emphasis on the divinity or humanity of Christ at the expense of the other nature is the swiftest path to Christological heresy. *Sola fides*, taken out of its proper soteriological context, can quickly become the very antinomianism against which Paul warns in Romans 6. An inverse focus on good works alone risks the pitiless rigor of classical Pelagianism. Christian theology is most faithful to its task when it witnesses to the fullness of God's nature, character, and activity in history rather than tidily resolving dialectical tensions by choosing to deny one or the other of their poles.

The union of verbal form and physical matter is, virtually as a matter of definition, the prerequisite for sacramental encounter with Christ. The baptismal formula recited without the imposition of water on an unbaptized person is as sacramentally useless as the water of an ordinary bath would be without the words and the intention necessary to make it a sacrament of the Church. In a similar way, an academic theology that reflects on Scripture, doctrine, and ethics cannot stand on its own as an end in itself; the need for rigorous scholarly reflection on the "nature of one's Christian commitments" arises not as an idle curiosity, but because of how often one finds that "Christian life is made up of countless occasions in which one must decide the acts,

---

Corporation, 1979), 305. The Baptismal Covenant, a new addition to the baptismal liturgy of the 1979 Book of Common Prayer, reflects this holistic understanding of the theological significance of both word and matter, belief and action, as implicit in the meaning of baptism into Christ's Body. The Baptismal Covenant begins with a credal declaration of the Christian faith in the words of the Apostles' Creed, then proceeds to a set of vows concerning the appropriate conduct of a Christian life: worship, prayer, repentance, evangelism, service of neighbor, and pursuit of justice are emphasized without distinction.

beliefs, and attitudes that really are in keeping with one's Christian commitments."[5] Conversely, even if it were possible to meaningfully speak of what it would mean to live a life of Christian virtue in the total absence of any reflection upon the content of that category, there is a real sense in which virtuous living can only "*matter* Christianly" insofar as it is undertaken with an understanding that the acts of justice or morality in question are related in *some* way to the person and work of Jesus Christ.[6]

Which is not, of course, to say that the Christian virtue of a good work depends on the actor's possession at all times of a front-of-mind awareness of the theological framework within which their action occurs. The ability to recognize, if asked, the fact *that* one's Christlike action is connected to one's faith in Christ himself is crucial for all Christians. The articulation—in a systematic, internally-consistent and lucid way—of the precise nature of that relationship is also a necessary task, but the need is only that such work be done by *someone*.

This brings me to a metaphor that I have often used with students when they arrive for the first discussion section of Introduction to Christian Theology. It is not uncommon for them to be skeptical of the very idea of theology itself, or at least of its more academic manifestations. Often, they explicitly or implicitly see earnest investment in the answers to doctrinal questions as a hallmark of fundamentalism and a threat to the appropriate level of investment in justice work in the world. And so, to provide another possible perspective on the theological enterprise, I often begin our first session together by telling them about the community college courses that I took in Building and Construction Technology when much of my priestly

---

5. Kathryn Tanner, *Jesus, Humanity and the Trinity: A Brief Systematic Theology* (Minneapolis, MN: Fortress Press, 2001), xiii.

6. Linn Marie Tonstad, *Queer Theology: Beyond Apologetics*, Cascade Companions 40 (Eugene, OR: Cascade Books, 2018), 6. Italics original.

work in the parish was put on hold during the coronavirus pandemic. In the course of my study of construction science, I became persuaded that the Christian life was rather like a home, and academic theology much like the textbooks from which I was learning the basic principles of residential electricity and plumbing and framing.[7]

Living in a home seldom requires any particular knowledge of the codes and skills that led the house to be built in the precise fashion that it was. Even a home that is totally "custom" is customizable only within parameters established by engineers and architects to protect the safety and, to a lesser degree, comfort of those who will live in it. The ordinary life that is lived in a properly-built home depends on "a fairly complex system which is usually unnoticed, but which sometimes goes wrong."[8] Although one obvious function of this metaphor is to legitimate the appropriateness of "specialists with painfully acquired technical knowledge" in the realm of doctrinal theology, it also serves to illustrate the need for continuing learning on the part of the "experts" from the experiences of using the systems they have created.[9] After all, the word "plumbing" itself is an etymological reflection of a famous example of the need for ongoing development of new standards in response to new information: the use of lead pipes in new construction has been totally discontinued, and where old installations exist, they continue to pose real danger to those who drink from the water that passes through them.

There is real value in the development of a body of knowledge concerning the underlying principles and best practices that make

---

7. When I shared this metaphor with a friend who has training in philosophy, they pointed me toward a well-known article in that field which uses very similar imagery. Mary Midgley, "Philosophical Plumbing," *Royal Institute of Philosophy Supplement* 33 (1992): 139–51, https://doi.org/10.1017/s1358246100002319.

8. Midgley, "Philosophical Plumbing," 139.

9. Midgley, "Philosophical Plumbing," 139.

our homes work properly and, ideally, keep us safe within them. That knowledge, however, is always in service of the daily life lived by those who dwell in the home that is built. Indeed, the standard practices and regulations that govern the work of the plumber or the electrician were developed in response to the needs of those who use them. The electrician and the theologian alike depend on insights and skills handed down to them by others, while also developing insights of their own through study and experience. Neither innovation nor the preservation of tradition is inherently the proper approach; what is handed down must be considered both seriously and critically. What is necessary in one context may not work in another; adapting theological language appropriately to its context is as crucial as considering the climate when choosing which material to use as a water supply line.

Understood rightly, academic theology is not a distraction from the political, social, liturgical, and moral action to which each Christian is called. It explains what lies underneath them. While such knowledge may seem expendable when things are going well (given that "systems of ideas which are working smoothly are more or less invisible"), an awareness of the structure of and connections between the doctrines of Christianity is an invaluable tool for both diagnostics and repair when things have gone wrong.[10] *That* things have gone wrong is often more than evident to the untrained eye—for example, it was their own experiences of the gospel of Christ and of the wicked sinfulness of slavery, and not formal theological education, that led enslaved Africans in the United States to the conviction that their liberation was God's will. Christians who acted boldly to free themselves, loved ones, and strangers from slavery were embodying theological truth in so doing, as were those who published compelling theological

---

10. Midgley, "Philosophical Plumbing," 143.

accounts of the illegitimacy of non-abolitionist Christianities. (These two categories are by no means mutually exclusive.)

This pragmatic approach to the project of academic theology provides a framework in which students' legitimate concerns for matters of justice and liberation need not be seen as in competition with the affirmation and explication of Christian doctrine. Insofar as the gospel reveals God's self-giving opposition to the powers of Sin and Death and his action in history to bring about the reconciliation of the whole cosmos to himself and of human beings to each other, it is a basis for active Christian opposition to any personal or societal practices that undermine the flourishing of creation as a whole and in its constitutive parts. To acknowledge that the content of the gospel demands such a commitment to a life lived on the side of liberation and reconciliation is not to reduce Christianity to a set of political causes. Rather, it is to engage in an honest attempt to faithfully follow Jesus Christ, known by us in Word and Sacrament, and to serve as his Body in the contemporary world, whatever the need may be. In an age where wickedness and the powers of Sin and Death make open use of the powers of government, however, this broader calling will be of necessity a decidedly political one.

Theology in The Episcopal Church

To turn from the question of what the theological enterprise (ideally) is to the question of the future of theology in The Episcopal Church requires careful consideration of the *current* state of theology in The Episcopal Church, in its strengths and its weaknesses. This task is made more difficult by a level of internal theological disagreement that it would not be an overstatement to call "profound." In a report published in 2009 based on data collected from 2004 to 2008, researchers found that upwards of 80 per cent of bishops, priests, and lay deputies to the General Convention agreed that it was "highly accurate" to describe "diverse theological positions" as part of the current identity of The Episcopal Church.[11]

There is, of course, little to be surprised by or automatically to object to with regard to the presence of a diversity of theological positions given the "inclusivist impulse in the Anglican tradition, one that sought for practical and theological reasons to incorporate—that is, comprehend—within its ambit as many people from as many ecclesial camps as possible, along with their diverse theological perspectives."[12] The theological latitude granted by Anglican "comprehensiveness" is not infinite, however. The concept of *adiaphora* implicitly recognizes the existence of essential matters concerning which disagreement is not appropriate.[13] The reason that Richard Baxter and his moderate Puritan colleagues were ultimately unable to remain in the Church of England was not because Anglicanism disagreed with his plea for "Unity in things necessary, and Liberty in things unnecessary, and Charity in all," but rather that the aphorism provides no shared grounds for determining which doctrinal questions constitute "things necessary."[14]

No particular clarity as to the precise contours of the appropriate scope for theological disagreement has graced the Anglican

---

11. David T. Gortner et al., "Around One Table: Exploring Episcopal Identity, Expanded Version" (College for Bishops / CREDO Institute, Inc., 2009), 75, https://www.episcopalchurch.org/wp-content/uploads/2020/08/aot_report.pdf.

12. Scott MacDougall, *The Shape of Anglican Theology: Faith Seeking Wisdom*, Brill Research Perspectives in Humanities and Social Sciences (Leiden: Brill, 2022), 37.

13. MacDougall, *The Shape of Anglican Theology*, 74.

14. Richard Baxter and Matthew Sylvester, *Reliquiæ Baxterianæ: Or, Mr. Richard Baxter's Narrative of the Most Memorable Passages of His Life and Times* (London: Printed for T. Parkhurst, J. Robinson, J. Lawrence, and J. Dunton, 1696), 103, http://archive.org/details/reliquiaebaxteri00baxt.

tradition in the intervening centuries since Richard Hooker, Baxter, and the Elizabethan Settlement. In broader Anglicanism, perhaps the nearest thing to an articulation of the content of the category "essentials" is found in the Chicago-Lambeth Quadrilateral of the nineteenth century. In the aftermath of the American Civil War, the bishops of The Episcopal Church adopted a statement intended to promote ecumenical reunion.[15] In it the bishops declared that "in all things of human ordering or human choice, relating to modes of worship and discipline, or to traditional customs, this Church is ready in the spirit of love and humility to forego all preferences of her own" and to insist only upon "the principles of unity exemplified by the undivided Catholic Church during the first ages of its existence."[16] These were identified, in summary, as the authority of "Holy Scripture, the historic Creeds of the Church, the two dominical Sacraments, and the Historic Episcopate."[17]

These four principles, offered originally as the minimum necessary for union between The Episcopal Church and non-Anglican traditions, cannot, therefore, be taken as a description of what makes a theological project properly *Episcopal*, but they can serve as both a starting point and a measuring stick to aid in determining which theological conclusions and approaches are incompatible with the teaching of The Episcopal Church. They do not provide us with a tidy and final answer to the question of where the line between essential and non-essential teachings is to fall. If the question of what further affirmations are entailed by the affirmation that the Old and New Testaments are the "revealed Word of God" had an obvious answer, it

---

15. MacDougall, *The Shape of Anglican Theology*, 71.

16. BCP 1979, 876.

17. General Convention, "Journal of the General Convention of...The Episcopal Church, Minneapolis, 2003" (New York: General Convention, 2004), 615.

might well put an end to virtually all Christian theological disagreement, and not just the question of which disagreements concern only *adiaphora*.

One especially crucial effect that turning and re-turning to these principles might have for Episcopal and Anglican theology specifically is that of allowing it to flourish apart from any constraint to "the cultural and formal elements of Anglicanism's Englishness."[18] There is much truth to the statement that "all theology is contextual theology"—it is a project that can only be undertaken by particular people who have been brought up with particular relationships to human cultural, linguistic, political, and economic forms.[19] The legacy of British colonialism has meant that Anglicans throughout the world have inherited doctrinal expressions, forms of polity, and liturgies that were produced in contexts radically different from their own. And yet, just as the principle of worship in the vernacular has come (in time, haltingly, imperfectly, and often painfully) to outweigh the colonial momentum that kept Anglican prayer books in English alone across the globe, so also there are Anglicans who have undertaken the crucial work of inculturating theology in non-Anglo contexts. This is not to say that global Anglicanism is no longer shaped by the cultural assumptions of Englishness, but there are concrete reasons to hope that the future of theology in The Episcopal Church will be one that values our scriptural, credal, sacramental, and ecclesiological first principles more, and the cultural legacy of our English origins far less.[20]

---

18. MacDougall, *The Shape of Anglican Theology*, 72.

19. Stephen B. Bevans, *Essays in Contextual Theology* (Leiden: Brill, 2018), 30, https://doi.org/10.1163/9789004363083.

20. It is crucial that this process be led by and responsive to the voices of Anglicans from non-English and non-European contexts, and especially to those outside the formal structures of ecclesial or academic hierarchy. The temptation to assume the precise needs of others, or to project one's own theological desires onto them as a strategy for self-legitimation, must be proactively avoided. The key is that English

Put another way, my hope for theology in The Episcopal Church is that it will continue to be a site of possibility for what is sometimes termed "inclusive orthodoxy." Both words are freighted with questions of power, inclusion, and exclusion, and cannot readily be used without some degree of peril.[21] And yet, the fundamental claim that I see at the heart of inclusive orthodoxy is precisely the firm conviction that the Bible, the creeds, the sacraments, and the Church are not the legitimate and exclusive possession of those with socio-political power. Far too often, those who have been oppressed in society and in the Church on the basis of their gender, race, ethnicity, sexuality, or ability have been told by enemies and advocates alike that there is no place for them in a Church that has not rejected the inspiration of scripture, the authority of the creeds, the efficacy of the sacraments, and the legitimacy of ecclesial orders. Inclusive orthodoxy, as I understand it, or at least as I hope for it, is nothing more or less than insistence to the contrary.

Back to Baptism

One of the greatest gifts I have received in becoming an Episcopalian is the gift of recognizing the sacramental world. In the sacraments, God comes to me, offers himself to me, acts in and for me, not as a

---

cultural forms be rightly understood as genuinely optional, not that Anglicans from non-English cultures do not or should not ever appreciate practices with English origins. For an example of this tension over religious identity and cultural forms of expression in a Chinese Roman Catholic context, see Jeremy Clarke, *The Virgin Mary and Catholic Identities in Chinese History* (Baltimore: Project Muse, 2013), 6–8.

21. For an excellent reflection on the dangers in question, and on the distinction between normative and descriptive uses of the term "orthodoxy," see Ed Watson, "The Fissures of 'Inclusive Orthodoxy,'" The Center for Barth Studies, *God Here & Now* (blog), March 4, 2024, https://barthcenter.substack.com/p/the-fissures-of-inclusive-orthodoxy.

bare sign or mere embodied metaphor but by means of a true *symbol*, something that participates in and provides access to a reality beyond itself. The Episcopal Church set me on my journey to theological inquiry first and foremost by bringing me to encounter the living God and leading me to a faith in him that was unlike any I had ever known. In telling me of baptism, it told me of *who I am*. It provided me, when I was confused and seeking, with the faith that now seeks understanding. It showed me the familiar gospel of Jesus Christ in an unfamiliar way, a way that looked for the first time since childhood as if it might truly be good news. I pray that whatever our theology does, whatever it looks like in the future, it will be in service of the proclamation of that gospel to a world oppressed by the power of sin and death, and in need of the new life of freedom that is found in union with Jesus Christ.

Further Reading Recommendations

Belcher, Kimberly Hope. *Efficacious Engagement: Sacramental Participation in the Trinitarian Mystery*. Collegeville, MN: Liturgical Press, 2011.

Carter, J. Kameron. *Race: A Theological Account*. New York: Oxford University Press, 2008.

Copeland, M. Shawn. *Enfleshing Freedom: Body, Race, and Being*, 2nd Edition. Minneapolis: Fortress Press, 2023.

Larson-Miller, Lizette. *Sacramentality Renewed: Contemporary Conversations in Sacramental Theology*. Collegeville, MN: Liturgical Press, 2016.

Becoming (Still) a Theologian

James W. Farwell

I became a theologian, in significant part, because of my grandmother—how she lived and how she died. Especially, how she died. This requires some explanation.

* * *

My grandmother—we called her "Mum"—was born in Kentucky in 1899, raised on a chicken farm, and never finished high school. She lived with my mother, father, sisters, and me, in a little house built next to ours. My sisters had both moved out by the time I was eight, and my parents both worked. Mum, who worked the midnight shift as a nurse's aide tending to the sick children at the local children's hospital, during the afternoon and early evening tended to me, on the five acres where we lived south of Jacksonville, out in the Florida pinelands, among orange trees and moss-draped oaks, with the alligator who lived in the pond on the farm next door.

We played checkers. I have no recollection of how checkers became our thing. But it was our ritual. Endless time of hers over a checkerboard spent listening to her grandson share his juvenile thoughts about things. We'd play checkers on a table set up on her small front porch when it was cool enough; otherwise, inside her little house. We sat near bookshelves that had a handful of books on them. I didn't know what they were. Not at first.

Mum was always there, present, available, without drama. With a mother who (I now realize) had an undiagnosed anxiety disorder and a father who was affable and loving, a war veteran, but who lacked intellectual curiosity, my grandmother was the light, the living invitation to ponder, the rock, the steady and attentive presence. My parents loved me, to be sure. But in my grandmother's presence, I knew myself, *as* myself, *beloved*.

* * *

My parents raised me Episcopalian. They went to church frequently enough to call us churchgoers. Mum always went with us on Christmas and Easter and very occasionally at other times. I developed, during those years, an early love for the steadiness, the rhythm, the mystery, and the beauty of liturgy. I was a musician, early on—I started playing guitar when I was eight and turned out to be good at it. I think the musicality of liturgy may be what spoke to me in its practice. I began reading Scripture in church at about twelve. The parish priest started taking me with him to nursing homes on his pastoral visits to celebrate Communion. I would read the Scripture lessons and play the guitar and lead hymns. But checkers with Mum continued.

Checkers with Mum continued into my adolescence while I traced a path through the charismatic movement in some Episcopal churches in the 1970s. Those years ignited spiritual and intellectual curiosity in me, inspired my understanding that to be religious was not just to believe but to *be a disciple*. By the time I was fifteen, I was already a bit suspicious of the charismatic movement, though I continued to play for, and eventually lead, a "praise band" at my charismatic parish. But charismatics were mostly answer people, and

I was becoming a question guy. My grandmother was interested in my questions. She had, it turns out, her *own* questions and, as I got older, she started to share them with me. Over checkers, we talked about spirituality and theology, before I had any sort of a theological method to go on. At fifteen, I was immature in such matters, probably even annoying to some, and yet Mum was interested in my experience, in what I thought, in what I wondered, about God and good and evil and the proper ends of a human life.

Eventually, I came to understand that Mum, quite inexplicably for her age and formal education, was spiritually curious well beyond the range of Christian preoccupations. Those books she had on her shelf were not just the Christian Bible and the Jewish Psalms but the Bhagavad-Gita, the Upanishads, the Dhammapada, the writings of the Theosophical Society, and various Indian poets. I have no idea how she became acquainted with such texts and, if only she had lived longer, I would have developed the sense to ask. I see in retrospect, from the standpoint of my own greater maturity, that she was an intellectual explorer, inter-spiritually wise and inquiring. She was exploring the borderlands of religions, open to truth wherever it might be found. And she was interested in what an intellectually precocious adolescent boy was also exploring.

* * *

When I was sixteen, Mum was taken to the hospital suddenly with severe stomach pain. During emergency surgery, the doctors found cancer that had metastasized well beyond remedy, especially given medical knowledge in 1976. They closed her back up. Hospice care was not a significant going concern at that time, not where I lived. I sat by her bedside in the hospital and played my guitar, singing her the psalms I led in the midweek liturgies of my church. In a matter of days, she was dead. I am grateful to this day for the nurses who allowed a sixteen-year-old boy to lug his Martin guitar into the hospital room and play and sing for his dying grandmother.

* * *

Some kind of intellectual nuclear fusion occurred in me at my grandmother's death. At precisely that time, I was beginning to study theology with Fr. George Young Jr. (another significant influence) at Episcopal High School in Jacksonville. With a group of tenth graders, I was reading, among other things, Robert Capon's *The Third Peacock*.[1] My grief over my grandmother's *death*—a good woman who loved me and *saw* me in her steady, attentive presence, who welcomed my nascent contemplative temperament, who loved the earth, who faithfully cared for suffering children—absorbed in full the existential force of the question of theodicy that Capon addressed. Mum's absence was a deep loss, the manner in which she died an obscenity. I was bereft. I needed a heart-mind understanding of this.

So, this life and death we live, *her* life and death, was the prompt into theology as a discipline, and theological inquiry as consolation. My drive to understand, or at least to make some peace with Mum's death, was the spark that lit the kindling. The question of human suffering and travail has never been far from my inquiries, throughout my years reading philosophy as an undergraduate (first of the post-Heideggerian sort at Furman University and then, because I wanted to engage more deeply with the classical tradition, at The Catholic University of America), and in my graduate study of theology at The General Theological Seminary and Emory University. The profound

---

1. Robert Farrar Capon, *The Third Peacock: A Book about God and the Problem of Evil* (Garden City, NY: Image Books/Doubleday, 1972).

commitment to the critical catholic, incarnational-exemplarist tradition that I encountered in my professors at General and, in the case of Richard Norris, at Union Seminary, and the deep work on theology and suffering that was the focus of Walter Lowe, Wendy Farley, and Rebecca Chopp at Emory, coalesced also around my experience with my grandmother. Whether or not I would have become a theologian despite my grief over the loss of my grandmother is hard to say. But her death was surely the catalyst. What emerged as a *later* influence on me was the inter-spiritual energy awakened in me by Mum's own curiosity and openness to truth wherever it be found. It would be some time before that surfaced as a contributor to my theology, and even then, I did not immediately notice that it was operative. I'll come back to that.

* * *

As a relevant aside to my role as a theologian, I also sought the *priesthood* from the time I was sixteen because my grandmother died in the way that she did. Until then, I had been working already toward a career in music. I had recorded in Nashville for Old Dominion Records at fourteen and performed in many places along the East Coast. But—this desire was supplanted summarily, at my grandmother's death, by the desire to be a priest. That I wanted to be a priest because my grandmother died is not, in so many words, exactly what you tell your "Commission on Ministry" in The Episcopal Church. It was early, then, in The Episcopal Church's recovery of a sense of the importance of the whole baptismal assembly. I know now that I could have been a theologian in a Christian community without being ordained. But, as the saying goes, "God writes straight with crooked lines."

Perhaps my instincts were not entirely wrong. Priests, as I had experienced them, were the theologians of their communities. Priests held open the space in which people came together to hold their travail around signs of consolation and hope in God and speak of it, wrestle with it. The space that priests held open for us to come with our sorrow and mourning and gratitude and joy was centered on *liturgy*, and liturgy had captivated me from the very beginning. By instinct, I knew, early on, that liturgical and sacramental practice had something to do with *becoming*, becoming who we are, without suppressing our griefs, full of hope that God might make the remembrance of suffering the site of divine visitation. Thus, liturgy was a *safe space* for that becoming—ordered and rhythmic and predictable, as ritual is, shaped by Scripture, communicated in material signs, forth-telling God's judgment as mercy and God's mercy as the invitation to flourish. Of course, that is language I have developed over time and would not have used when I was sixteen, setting my hope on being a priest. In fact, I credit my friend and colleague Robert Heaney with helping me to see, just lately, that a question underneath all my writing has always been: given that we are ritualizing creatures, and that ritual is a performance of identity, *who is it that we are to become?*

So, becoming a priest and becoming a theologian were melded for me, for better or for worse, and the initial impetus for that becoming was the death of my grandmother. If my life as a theologian, in the parish and in the academy, can be conceived as a river, it flows from the confluence of two feeder streams: the love of my grandmother—her care for human beings, her attentive modeling of a life of (inter) spiritual inquiry, her unfair death—and the health-making, orienteering power of liturgical practice that offered a structured path for becoming alive in the midst of our travail.

God, I think, wastes nothing of our lives in calling us to our place in the world. Or, more elegantly, in Simon Tugwell's account of divine providence: "God's providence means that wherever we have got to, whatever we have done, that is precisely where the road to heaven begins. However many cues we have missed, however many wrong turnings we have taken, however unnecessarily we have complicated our journey, the road still beckons, and the Lord still 'waits to be gracious' to us."[2]

* * *

As I swim this river of my experience, my understanding of the theological enterprise is that it is testimony, in speech and writing, to the Incarnation. In this way, I hope, I am classically Anglican in my approach. *Theos/logos*, theology, begins in the *logos tou theou*: the "Word of God" who is at once the heartbeat, the scaffolding, the motion, the true nature, and the telos of all reality. To be a theologian, as I understand it, is to bear witness to the *logos* in creation and the *logos* incarnate, to Jesus Christ in his life, death, and resurrection as the living sacrament of the world's true nature and life, whose Christ-life is our own flourishing. He is the sacrament of Life, how true life moves, how true life is oriented in its value and behavior. Although the *logos* in its nature and dynamism is the only way to *be*, at all, we have the capacity to ignore, distort, and obscure this true life such that we wreck ourselves and the world in the process. But never permanently. The *Logos-in-the-Spirit* continues God's work. We must open our hands and set down our idols to participate in that very *logos* that gives us life, that *logos* in which paradoxically we *already* live and move and have our being, something from which we strain and tear ourselves when we live without gratitude, trust, and love, which are among the virtues of the *logos*-nature of existence itself.

As I view it, the Christian theologian works from those bodies of literature, testimony, and experience that bear witness to the Incarnate

---

2. Simon Tugwell, *Prayer: Living with God* (Springfield, IL: Templegate, 1975), n.p.

logos: the book of Scripture, the Tradition with all its wisdom and its follies, the wordless book of Nature. But to the extent that the incarnate *logos* of God has (re)gathered all our finite existence into the divine life,[3] then experience in *all* its dimensions is a source of theology. Human experience in its full expanse is "read" in the light of Scripture and Tradition to be sure; but to the extent that Scripture and tradition testify to the incarnate *logos* in whom all creation lives, then it is in all of creation and all of experience in which we also encounter God and must witness to that encounter. There is no place in which the *logos* of God in motion through the Spirit is not present and working, even under the signs of absence and in the places of death or suffering. There is no place in which creation is not participating in the sacrificial heartbeat of God's life, by grace. The Christian tradition testifies to this, but the Christian tradition has *no monopoly on this*.

My own incarnational emphasis has led me as a theologian, more often than not, to be concerned with the material practices of faith, principally liturgical and sacramental practices. Engaging with the whole body, taking up all the concerns and joys that come with living a life, the liturgical assembly *enters in* to the paschal life of Christ the incarnate *logos*, to participate in this between-time before all creation is consummated in his crucified and risen life. In liturgy, we enact the very ends of that creation: praise, gratitude, reconciliation with the source of all life. We practice who God is inviting us to be. We practice attention to God. We practice care for the world in our intercessions; peacemaking with one another; we receive in the broken bread the risen life of the Crucified One who, as Augustine said, is already our very own identity. Here, I take it, Augustine is acknowledging what I have pointed to

---

3. This is variously expressed with nuances by Irenaeus, Clement of Alexandria, Maximus the Confessor, and many others; e.g., Athanasius, *On the Incarnation*, sect. 54.3.; Gregory of Nyssa's *Great Catechism*, sect 37.

above: there is only one Life, the *logos*, who lived and died and rose for us and in whom our own life is found. Liturgy, then—its ritual structure in performance, its diverse imagery like the Bible itself, its sounds and its silences—is the practice of life in the *logos tou theou*, in the sense of participation in that life and in the sense of (re)formation into that Life. Liturgy is its own end, because it is the practice of the very life we seek in Christ. Liturgy is, then, for me—I would argue for all theologians, though that argument exceeds the bounds of this chapter—the primary site and source for theological reflection on *who God is calling us to become*, and how in the suffering that arises in the course of that becoming, God accompanies us and brings us to ourselves. All this we celebrate and practice in liturgy. And all theology, as a Zen teacher once said of the teaching of Dōgen, is "writing down practice." That is certainly true for me as a liturgical and sacramental theologian.

How has this worked its way out in the themes and topics that have preoccupied me? While I have taught, spoken, and written on a variety of topics, including some general accounts of liturgical life,[4] with an eye to meaning and leadership, the red thread in my work has been the way suffering and its remedy and the shape of a flourishing human life in general are *performed* in and by Christ and in our liturgical celebration. To put it another way, I have been concerned with what my doctoral mentor Don Saliers calls "humanity at full stretch" before God as liturgy both shapes and expresses it.[5]

My early journal articles and professional addresses were mostly concerned with suffering and the way in which Christians participate

---

4. James W. Farwell, *The Liturgy Explained* (New York: Morehouse, 2013), and *Ritual Excellence: Best Practices for Leading and Planning Liturgy* (New York: Seabury, 2023).

5. Don E. Saliers, "Toward a Spirituality of Inclusiveness," in *Human Disability in the Service of God: Reassessing Religious Practice*, eds. Nancy L. Eiesland and Don E. Saliers (Nashville: Abingdon, 1998), 19–32.

in the Life of Christ, both wounded and risen. My first book—*This is the Night: Suffering, Salvation, and the Liturgies of Holy Week*[6]—a modest revision of my dissertation some twenty years ago—interpreted the Proper Liturgies of the Prayer Book, and especially the liturgies of the Sacred Triduum, as a performance of resistance to the modern inclination to sideline suffering and silence it. I have taught many courses and given many addresses over the years that focus on theology, liturgy, and prayer in relation to suffering, trauma, and human flourishing. Recent writings focus on anaphoral attention to the whole life of Christ, and not just to his death, so that our remembrance resources a hope reflecting not just suffering but the shape of a flourishing life.[7] To locate this concern in the schematics of the theological discipline, it is perhaps most accurate to say that I have been preoccupied with *practiced* soteriology and, in a related sense, theological anthropology. As a teacher, which has been for me as important to my theological vocation as writing, it is soteriology and suffering within liturgical and sacramental *ascesis* that have preoccupied my work in several academic communities as well.

A few years ago, though, I realized something else operating in my work of which I was only dimly aware but, upon its discovery, had led those who know me well to say "of course": an inter-spiritual openness bequeathed to me, I think, by my grandmother. My own journey had led me to engage in certain forms of Zen Buddhist practice from the mid-1990s, initially as part of a doctoral seminar with John Fenton at Emory University, interrogating manifestations of non-duality in Christian and non-Christian practices, their convergences and

---

6. James W. Farwell, *This is the Night: Suffering, Salvation, and the Liturgies of Holy Week* (New York: T&T Clark, 2005).

7. E.g., James W. Farwell, "Salvation, the Life of Jesus, and the Eucharistic Prayer: An Anglican Reflection and Proposal," *Liturgy*, 31.3 (April 2016): 19–27.

divergences. I tell a brief version of that story elsewhere.⁸ But over time it became clear to me that my early writings on suffering and liturgy, and especially my interpretation of the Triduum, were shaped in significant part by the sensitivity to the damage that dualisms and binaries can do to our ability to proclaim the gospel of one who was and is in his risen manifestation marked by the scars of his suffering, known in bread broken. I did not explicitly acknowledge in that book on the Triduum the influence of Buddhist non-dualism on my interpretation of the Triduum liturgies as interrelated non-dualistically, in which God offers salvation and wholeness not just after but even in the midst of brokenness, suffering, and trauma. But in retrospect, papers I had delivered at a regional academic conference in 1998 and at the Parliament of the World's Religions in 1999, comparing possible Buddhist and Christian constructive responses to suffering in modernity, apparently stayed with me to the degree that I moved beyond a comparative religious approach and into a comparative *theological* approach without realizing it. Beginning with an AAR/Luce Fellowship year in Comparative Theology, several years after the publication of *This Is the Night*, I have become more consciously engaged with the impact of my practice and study in the Dōgen Zen tradition on my being and becoming (continuously) a Christian. Thus it is the interface between liturgical/sacramental theology and comparative theology—what has been called the liturgical turn in comparative theology⁹—to which I now devote my attention. My work

---

8. James W. Farwell, "On Whether Christians Should Participate in Buddhist Practice: A Critical Autobiographical Reflection," *Journal of Interreligious Studies and Intercultural Theology* I:2 (2017): 243–56.

9. James W. Farwell, "Not-Two with Christ: Toward a Comparative Theological Account of the Eucharist with the Help of Dōgen." Paper for Session on "The Liturgical Turn in Comparative Theology," American Academy of Religion, Annual Meeting (Nov 2015).

in the last few years on inter-religious monastic dialog, on Barth and Dōgen (the founder of Soto Zen Buddhism), and on the Eucharistic Fraction, all fall into this category.[10] I am currently moving toward the book-length articulation of a Christian comparative sacramental theology in the light of Dōgen's nondualism.

* * *

I don't know that I have a single overarching vision for the future of theology in The Episcopal Church, but I certainly have hopes. One of these hopes is for theologians, whatever their focus, to increase their role in resourcing our communities of practice. On the heels of the liturgical movement and the adoption of the 1979 Prayer Book, whose sacramental ecclesiology assumes and encourages continuing Christian formation, there was great expectation for a deepening in our adult catechesis, including but not limited to the restoration of the catechumenate for those coming to faith in their adulthood. Some parishes have fulfilled that expectation of a deep dive into formation, but too many have not. In my travels around The Episcopal Church, I am disappointed by the number of parishes in which little or no formal adult education is happening at all. I would like us theologians to help expand the capacity for theological

---

10. James W. Farwell, "Taking the Liturgical Turn in Comparative Theology: Monastic Interreligious Dialogue as a Supporting Case," in *Interreligious Relations and the Negotiation of Religious Boundaries: Explorations in Interrituality*, ed. Marianne Moyaert (Cham, Switzerland: Palgrave, 2019), 159–72; "Barth's Theology of Religion and Dōgen's Nondualism," in *Karl Barth and Comparative Theology*, eds. Martha Moore-Keish and Christian Collins Winn (New York: Fordham University Press, 2019), 67–84; "Broken Whole: Christian Reflections on the Eucharistic Action in a Comparative-Interreligious Light," in *The Wiley Blackwell Companion to Liturgical Theology*, eds. Porter C. Taylor and Khalia J. Williams (Sussex: Wiley-Blackwell, 2025), 228–41.

discernment and reflection on life and vocation in all the people of God, not just in those engaged in theological work at a professional level. Coupled with an expanding crisis of attention to the humanities throughout our educational systems, our seminaries must now often tend not only to advanced formation of its students for theological leadership, but to basic Christian catechesis. Theologians alone cannot walk into this multi-factor landscape and set it right, but they can play a significant role in resourcing the problem. The institutions in which our theologians teach must find ways to encourage and underwrite the contributions of our theologians not only to our scholarly guilds and teaching but to the deep formation of our congregations.

A second hope I have for the future of theology in The Episcopal Church will perhaps come as no surprise to the reader at this point. It is a two-sided hope. I would like to see theologians help the church to wrestle with what it means to be Christian in a world of religious "manyness," where interaction with other religious traditions can lead to the deepening of spiritual life, and which, for some of our members, leads to dual practice. And I would like to see theologians ourselves become more literate in the cognate disciplines that would help us think about this phenomenon.

North America has always had its share of religions other than Christianity. But we have come a very long way since 1893, when the first Parliament of the World's Religions in Chicago offered many Americans their first encounter with South and East Asian religious practitioners outside of the immigrant communities that have been so important to this nation's development. It is a data-driven observation that we are the most religiously pluralistic nation on the planet.[11] One might say: very well, leave to those commu-

---

11. For exploration of American religious diversity, see https://pluralism.org

nities their own theological and philosophical challenges. But it is not so simple. Our neighbors, our children's teachers, and our co-workers are of different faiths, and we have more awareness and appreciation of religious differences as a result. But there is more: in our churches today sit many Christians whose spiritual lives have been deepened by the practice and study of other spiritual traditions. Some now even consider themselves to be members of more than one tradition. The phenomenon is sufficiently emergent that the attention of the World Council of Churches has been drawn to study and comment on it.[12]

Exemplary cases of inter-religious learning, multiple religious practice, or multiple religious belonging among Episcopalians would take pages to cite. There is the vestry member who meditates with the Zen community every Wednesday and learns from the dharma talk. There is the lector who reads Pema Chödrön and tries to practice what she teaches in living with a psychological disability. There is the woman who comes to Christianity through Pure Land Buddhism, a tradition that, upon a conversation with her, clearly continues to live in her understanding of Christ's intercession for the world. There is the man raised in a Muslim-Christian household who regularly attends church, who contributes generously to the annual stewardship campaign, but has not been and will likely not be baptized. There is the priest who practices the remembrance of God once a month with a Sufi order. I am not addressing conversion from one tradition to another here. That does occur. The more interesting and more common reality is the formation of inter-religious identity in persons who continue to practice faithfully in their "home" tradition. (The

---

12. See Peniel Jesudason, Rufus Rajkumar, and Joseph Prabhakar Dayam, ed., *Many Yet One?: Multiple Religious Belonging* (Geneva: World Council of Churches, 2016).

complexity of what is home and away in religious practice and affiliation is a related topic all its own.)[13]

The phenomenon of dual practice or even dual-belonging and hybrid inter-religious identity is a particularly challenging issue for the Abrahamic communities whose commitment to the worship of one God has often been expressed in theologies in which the religious other is seen not simply as different, but deficient. The Episcopal Church has a canonical position on religious manyness,[14] but—offering at best a nuanced position of "inclusivism" regarding plurality—it offers little wisdom for the situation of religious hybridity I reference in the cases above. The Episcopal Church had its own brief and unhappy moment, in 2009, with two cases of Christian dual-practice or dual-belonging—one of a candidate for bishop who had a dual practice in a Buddhist community, and the other an outstanding scholar-priest who understood herself as both Christian and Muslim—that showed, in the public responses around the church, an unfortunate, almost complete lack of literacy in "religion" and religions or in theological history or sources that might illumine the possibility of nuanced engagements across religious "borders." Notwithstanding the merits and particulars of these two cases or a final judgment on their cogency—the lack of depth in the public responses was embarrassing. As a church priding itself on openness to deep inquiry and hard questions, we can do better, and it will take theologians, among others, to help us do so.

---

13. E.g. Mark Heim, "Home in Three Dimensions: Personal Location in Comparative and Transreligious Theologies," *Toronto Journal of Theology* 39:1 (June 2023): 41–49.

14. See Lucinda Allen Mosher, *Toward our Mutual Flourishing: The Episcopal Church, Interreligious Relations, and Theologies of Religious Manyness* (New York: Peter Lang, 2012).

In a pluralistic context, where no one is "just one thing" and where we all live in the flux and flow of cultural forces and resources—religion being one of them—I would hope to see theologians help us think through the ways in which our own Christian faith might be strengthened, stretched, and even deepened by the faith resources and practices of our "others." Among other growing edges, this will require theologians to stretch beyond their usual sources and connect with the field of religious studies. Many contemporary theories of religion take better account of the internal complexity, the porosity of boundaries, and the mutual influences of the religious traditions of our world than we theologians have previously done. If the *logos* of God, manifested in Christ, is at work in the heartbeat of the whole world, including its religious traditions ... if the Spirit of God blows as the breath of every living being on the planet ... then surely theologians can help us answer the question, as it has been put by the Hindu theologian Anant Rambachan: "What is the meaning of my neighbor's faith for my own?"

As for myself, as a Christian who has long practiced and studied in the Dōgen Zen tradition—becoming Christian Buddhist-ly, one might say—and as the grandson of a woman who flourished by walking the borderlands of religious inquiry without ever fearing that it drew her from the One whose love gives rise to all things, Rambachan's question is the one I will continue to ask.

Further Reading Recommendations

Farwell, James W. *This Is the Night: Suffering, Salvation, and the Liturgies of Holy Week.* London: T&T Clark/Bloomsbury, 2004.

Mosher, Lucinda Allen. *Toward Our Mutual Flourishing: The Episcopal Church, Interreligious Relations, and Theologies of Religious Manyness.* New York: Peter Lang, 2012.

Rajkumar, P. J. R. and J. P. Dayam, eds. *Many Yet One? Multiple Religious Belonging.* Geneva: World Council of Churches, 2016.

Williams, Rowan. *Discovering Christianity: A Guide for the Curious.* London: SPCK, 2025.

The Future of the *Via Media* in The Episcopal Church

Sameer Yadav

Given the existential crises facing The Episcopal Church (hereafter, TEC), the question of its theological future is bound up with the question of whether the church itself has a long-term future. By many accounts, its days are numbered.[1] Though no one can know for sure how TEC will fare under the accidents and contingencies it now faces *in via*, the rapid decline in its membership, destabilization in its conventional sources of social reproduction, and its embattled fronts in American culture wars alongside the rest of the mainline all spell trouble for its continued existence.[2] When confronting matters of institutional life and death, we don't ordinarily consult theologians for help, and for the most part, that is probably as it ought to be. However, TEC has been and remains an important context of theological reflection for American Christians.

---

1. See, for example, political scientist Ryan Burge's analyses of the demographic data, leading him to conclude that "The end is coming fairly rapidly for the TEC as it exists today": https://religioninpublic.blog/2022/07/19/covid-19-only-accelerated-the-decline-of-the-episcopal-church/. Even if not dead by 2040, as Burge had previously suggested, estimates about how the church might look if it were to survive until 2050 nevertheless remain rather grim: https://livingchurch.org/covenant/the-episcopal-church-in-2050/.

2. John Marcum, "W(h)ither the Mainline? Trends and Prospects," *Review of Religious Research* 59/2 (June 2017): 119–134.

Theologians invested in that context must be part of discerning the way forward for the work of Christian sense-making that occupies the present challenges of TEC.

My credentials for taking up this task nevertheless seem rather dubious. While I come to this volume as a professional Christian theologian and confirmed Episcopalian, one would be hard-pressed to regard me as an *Episcopal theologian*. For one thing, although a confirmed Episcopalian, I am currently a committed member of a Baptist congregation. Nor have I been much of an ecclesial theologian. My research and writing have focused on theologies of divine presence and absence in conversation with early Christian mystical traditions, as well as historical and contemporary intersections of Christianity with race and racism in the United States and their implications for Christian theologies of liberation. Reflection on questions of interdisciplinary theological method and the ethics of Christian belief and practice have been important dimensions of my thinking on these topics. Still, none of this work has been carried out with any explicit or self-conscious relationship to TEC. If I purport to have any wisdom to offer for its theological future, I had therefore better explain myself.

I will endeavor to do that in two ways below. First, I offer an autobiographical narrative of the idiosyncratic path by which my vocation as a professional theologian has come to intersect with my Episcopal formation. In the second half of the essay, I'll turn to reflect on an Episcopal *via media* ("middle way") in theology. Recalling my own narrative of struggle to make a home in structurally unstable spaces between various oppositions and tensions, I will suggest an understanding of a theological *via media* not as a principled "balance between extremes" but rather as an openness to seeking out God's life with us at the interstices, between opposing forces of social, political, and religious disintegration, fragmentation, and dispossession. The future of theology in TEC ought to include unflinching attention to these "in between" spaces in the precarious conditions that currently beset its own institutional life.

I

By the time my wife and I decided to be confirmed in TEC, I had already begun my career as a professional theologian, having started a three-year teaching postdoctorate at the John Wesley Honors College of Indiana Wesleyan University in Marion, Indiana. Prior to our years at the JWHC, I had been something of an aimless ecclesial drifter. I was raised in a Hindu household in rural Idaho. While an excellent premise for a sitcom, growing up there was an experience of profound cultural disorientation, tinged with routine but stark encounters with bigotry and alienation from secure belonging. As a second-generation Indian American, I could never quite manage to fit inside my home or outside of it. Aside from a weekly gathering for puja with a small enclave of Indian families in Boise, the most determinate form of community that eventually laid claim to my life came just as I was entering college at Boise State University. A group of evangelical friends succeeded in converting me and my identical twin brother to Christianity. Both my intellectual awakening as a philosophy major and my newfound religious identity catalyzed a strong desire for philosophical and theological knowledge-seeking.

My conservative and non-denominational Bible Church nurtured my evident religious questing by funneling me into a fundamentalist seminary. I had only the faintest idea of what seminaries were (indeed, I scarcely knew what Christian denominations were!). Gradually, I came to observe a widening chasm between what I was getting in my classes and what I was getting from my library studies, where

I would regularly hide out to chase down the mainstream scholarly literature on various matters related to the Bible, theology, ethics, and philosophy of religion. When I approached my professors to help me name and span this divide, I was met with a range of muted to open hostilities that surprised and confused me. Eventually the chasm swallowed me whole. After finishing an M.Div. ahead of schedule and starting a Th.M. in Hebrew Bible, I was treated punitively for balking at doctrines of male headship, dispensationalism, and biblical inerrancy in my written work. They kicked me out in the last year of my program.

This unwanted lesson in sectarian gatekeeping also left me feeling painted into a vocational corner. I knew by this time that I had no interest in being a pastor but wished to make an academic career, figuring out the nature and limits of Christian sense-making. But I was stuck in a theological and institutional backwater with no clear path out. During my asylum in the seminary library, I came to appreciate the theological provocations of Stanley Hauerwas, so I found his Duke address and wrote him a letter detailing my story, appending some of my writing. To my surprise, he wrote back. Stanley began advising me on how to move forward in an academic career, and I managed to get into Yale Divinity School for an S.T.M. degree. There, my spouse and I became part of a Presbyterian Church in America (PCA) congregation, experiencing our first more liturgically-developed worship service. When we relocated to Durham, North Carolina, for me to begin my doctoral program in theology and ethics at Duke, we joined another Presbyterian congregation, but this time one belonging to the mainline PCUSA, and a bit more liturgically relaxed.

At the time, the joke about Duke's "neo-traditional" bent in theology was that everyone who came in went out at least one level higher in liturgical church affiliation (e.g., non-denominational evangelicals or Baptists came out Presbyterians, Presbyterians came out Episcopalians, Episcopalians came out Roman Catholics). But when we arrived at JWHC for my postdoc, our Episcopalian upgrade was more pragmatic than principled. Our choices were to either join a congregation of the Wesleyan Church, which belonged to an evangelical pietist and holiness tradition, or Gethsemane Episcopal, a small church with more Anglo-Catholic sensibility. Having acquired significant allergies toward evangelical pietist sensibilities and (I'll admit it) a cultivated taste for liturgical ecclesiologies imparted during grad school, our choice was clear.

In retrospect it is hard to say what it was that so attracted us to Gethsemane that we determined within mere weeks of attendance to become confirmed Episcopalians. We had a kind and thoughtful priest, Fr. Jim Warnock, and a caring congregation who loved us and our children well. We were relieved to find in the Book of Common Prayer (1979) a beautiful liturgy that held us up and drew us into a structured relationship with one another and God that we did not have to generate from ourselves and for ourselves. Making the Eucharistic celebration rather than the sermon the high point of the service oriented us toward a shared belonging grounded in the universality ("catholicity") of Christ's invitation to table fellowship rather than in our response to a minister's theological reflection or hot take. Like many others with religious trauma from white evangelical spaces like those from which I had come (with yet more to come, it turned out), I was attracted by the way an Episcopal identity attempted—at least in theory—to draw apparently opposing forces into a coherent union: a theologically traditional ("Protestant, yet Catholic") imagination with strongly egalitarian commitments to social justice and an ecumenical spirit of welcome both distinctively Christian and open to all.

All of these priorities resonated with my theological formation at Yale and Duke. That formation gave me a deep appreciation for the range and flexibility of intellectual and practical resources for constructive theological understanding afforded by mainstream Protestant, Catholic, and Orthodox Christian traditions—I had especially come to love the sensibilities of the so-called Christian mystics across these traditions (with a particular affinity for Gregory of Nyssa). But I had also come to see the many ways in which the white, colonial, heterosexist, ethno-nationalist, and capitalist curdling of these theological traditions have been (and continue to be) enacted in socially and politically disastrous ways. Indeed, some such ways precisely accounted for the forms of dislocation my family experienced growing up in rural Idaho. Episcopal commitments, it seemed to me, were well-positioned to embrace these tensions and discern how to chew the meat and spit out the bones (or whatever vegan equivalent you please). I began to feel a gravitational pull between my theological vocation and the church that made me curious about a scholar-priest vocation. Fr. Warnock encouraged me to begin a discernment process for pursuing holy orders.

If I were to conclude my narrative here, with my theological formation merging apparently seamlessly with my Episcopal self-identification, it would belie the reticence about my Episcopal credentials with which I began. But things changed dramatically in the decade to follow. My postdoc was ending, and I secured my first tenure-track job at a small Protestant evangelical Christian liberal arts college in Santa Barbara, California. I decided to pause my discernment process so that we could first settle into our new life in the college community, learn more about our new diocese, and get to know my new rector at All Saints-by-the-Sea, the Rev. Aimee Eyer-Delevett. The bigger obstacle, as it happened, was the college itself. Initially, the institution seemed to me to project a more "moderate" brand of evangelicalism that might afford the academic freedom to develop my scholarly interests in race, liberation theology, and mystical theology, illuminated in conversation with analytic philosophy and the social sciences. I collaborated with humanities and sociology colleagues to revitalize an ethnic studies minor and found many institutional spaces for meaningfully integrating my research and teaching.

To my dismay, a few (white) senior colleagues soon began to suspect that my teaching and scholarship were insufficiently "evangelical." Among their chief concerns were my commitments to liberationist and antiracist theologies, the fact that the rector of my church was a gay woman in a same-sex marriage, and my openness to readings of Scripture that rejected divine and human violence and retributive punishment. None of these things was especially unique to me—all three "concerns" equally well applied to a tenured (white) New Testament colleague, for example. Nevertheless, department gatekeepers initiated a concerted effort to have me fired. They pulled administration and board members into a campaign of scrutinizing my "orthodoxy." The relentless inquests and sanctions focused on me and my tenure candidacy over several years resulted in many executive sessions of the full faculty to assess and respond to institutional targeting and violation of my academic freedom. Despite attempted interventions from faculty members, cautions to administration about the violations of our Faculty Handbook from our Faculty Council, and a strong recommendation for tenure from the Personnel Committee, I was fired. Several other faculty and staff departures followed in protest, and the life of the college community was significantly destabilized.

A stressful job search and painful relocation away from family and friends followed my evangelical excommunication, but I was fortunate to join Baylor University's Department of Religion, where I've been for just eight months as of this writing. Given the current political climate—both nationally and especially *in Texas*, where we moved during a particularly apocalyptic election year—I have been enormously grateful to have found at Baylor a micro-climate with a significant measure of personal and academic freedom to work on liberation theologies and critical theories of race and religion. But in our search for healing from our past traumas of failed assimilation and exclusion, my family has found itself continuing its sojourn *outside* TEC, even as our previous Episcopalian spiritual formation remains inside us. This is mostly due to the same kinds of accidents of social and historical contingency that led us to TEC in the first place. We took in the landscape of churches in Waco, Texas, much as we had in Marion, Indiana, and stumbled upon a local congregation—this time Baptist—that embodies the very values we currently find ourselves needing in order to go on as Christians: deep gentleness and a refuge for those with religious trauma, a cultivated posture of unassuming welcome, and non-performative egalitarian love, especially for queer folks in our community.

II

Much of the way I was trained to think as a theologian at Duke was in terms of careful attention to the particular forms of communal life within which our theological reasoning is embedded. Theological traditions were imagined not in purely intellectual terms but as attempts to make certain material forms of Christian life intelligible, including practices of worship, citizenship, and all manner of human and divine communion. To be a Christian was to inhabit some such tradition. To think as a Christian theologian was to be a worker in traditions—critically excavating, articulating, revising, and commending the tradition to which one belongs.[3] Even those Christianities that disavow "tradition" or identify themselves in terms

---

3. Especially influential for this paradigm was Alasdair MacIntyre's *Three Rival Versions of Moral Enquiry: Encyclopedia, Genealogy, and Tradition* (Notre Dame: University of Notre Dame Press, 1994).

of decisive breaks with past Christian forms are, in fact, simply perpetuating unacknowledged (albeit haphazard) traditions, converting into another established tradition, or attempting radical revision to inaugurate new traditions.

The danger of theologians proceeding in ignorance of the traditioned forms of life that make their theological thinking intelligible is that we will generate *pseudo*-theologies: ways of thinking that might seem coherent on their surface but which fail to meaningfully connect to the forms of life that Christians actually inhabit or could inhabit. Theology in this mode reproduces a peculiarly modern incoherence—one that wrenches theological ideas from their lived contexts of Christian sense-making to serve the interests of autonomous individuals, who mistakenly see themselves as authors of their own stories.[4] The result is to hide from oneself the ways that one's apparently autonomous meaning-making is in fact a social practice cultivated by the violent and avaricious tradition of the nation-state to serve its interests in a market economy. Consenting to such Christian self-making by scavenging decontextualized fragments of theological language from the past cannot genuinely help Christians to go on responsibly—to understand what it is to think, speak, or act as Christians in the contexts they occupy.[5]

This way of imagining the enterprise of Christian theology is what first drew me to the *via media* of Episcopal theology.[6] Here was

---

4. MacIntyre diagnoses the intractability of modern moral reasoning as rooted in the fragmentation of moral discourses and their abstraction from a shared framework of social practice. See Alasdair MacIntyre, *After Virtue: A Study in Moral Theory*, 3rd edition (Notre Dame: University of Notre Dame Press, 2007).

5. See Stanley Hauerwas, "The Church as God's New Language," *The Hauerwas Reader*, edited by John Berkman and Michael Cartwright (Durham, NC: Duke University Press, 2001), 142–62.

6. See Lee Gibbs, "Richard Hooker's *Via Media* Doctrine of Scripture and Tradition," *Harvard Theological Review* 95/2 (April 2004): 227–35.

a way of articulating a theological tradition that aimed at reconciling opposing forms of Christian life, one that not only takes on the Anglican pursuit of a theology that is "Protestant yet Catholic," but also the many other oppositions that have shaped Christian life in the United States since the colonial era in which TEC has developed, finding theological resources internal to its tradition to confront and revise its collusions with oppressive ideologies. To do theology in an Episcopal tradition was to imagine Christianity as a *reconciling* form of life, one that seeks to welcome all the traditioned ways that place Christians at odds with one another, including those matters of cultural and political enmity that mark American Christianity. Such a theology would look more closely at the diverse dialects and social practices of Christian language to find a way between them—to discover together a latent *catholicity* or universal form of belonging in Christ. Our fracture as individuals and as Christians has become vulnerable to all the ways that language and life can become bent toward the greed and violence that Christ has overcome.

To be church is to manifest that overcoming in an alternative form of shared life which can be negotiated theologically by working with the fragments of Christian tradition which we continue to live out inadequately, in reproductions of mutual enmity that undermine the catholicity at its center, which is Jesus. The Book of Common Prayer and Articles of Religion were, of course, not ultimately achievements of that kind of catholicity but penultimate and imperfect achievements in forging a mutually negotiated tradition of Catholic and Protestant communion. To belong to such a tradition includes taking up its stories and practices to produce a Christian commons— the embodied advancement of a Christian tradition constituted by ongoing and mutually negotiated mediation between rival traditions and their established forms of identity and belonging, an ecclesial tradition of the *via media*. TEC thus represented an ecclesial vision that initially seemed especially congenial to an understanding of my academic vocation along the lines of this neo-traditionalist "Duke project" in theology.

Theological work in that paradigm ordinarily consisted largely in the retrieval and reconstruction of the discursive fragments of Christian tradition forged in various lived performances of Christianity, now shattered and corrupted by (e.g., colonial, Enlightenment, neoliberal) modernity. The point of such retrievals was not nostalgia—we might well find Christian discursive logics and practices corrupted in their own ways—but working out a faithful Christian form of life, one constituted by divine gifts of welcome, peacemaking, forgiveness, and sharing a human wholeness received in Christ's body and blood given to us. The discourses and practices of this way of life are projected, symbolized, and enacted through the distinctive cultural production of Christian traditions, which is to say their *liturgies*.[7] But to perform this theological task, it was important not to simply reassume the ersatz position of the modern autonomous or sovereign individual, falsely supposing we can stand outside the particular Christian cultural logic that formed us to adjudicate between traditions "from above." Avoiding that mistake required a self-understanding of one's own received tradition from which we, as exponents of our communities, were discerning how to go on with our ways of life. In sum: unities of Christian cultural logic good, fragmentations of cultural logic bad; identification with a tradition good, failures to so identify bad.

My academic formation at Duke accordingly invited me to narrate my attractions to an Episcopal identity as a paradigm shift in traditioned identity and belonging, a migration from one Christian cultural logic to another. What rendered my various "conversions"

---

7. See *The Blackwell Companion to Christian Ethics*, 2nd edition, edited by Stanley Hauerwas and Samuel Wells (Malden, MA: Wiley-Blackwell, 2011).

rational was having found that my received "grammar" (the underlying structures of meaning in the forms of language and its performance) that enabled me to make sense of the world and my place in it (e.g., as a second-generation Indian American Hindu, then an American evangelical, etc.), could gain greater coherence through my identification and work within the Episcopal tradition that I encountered, not merely intellectually, as in my Anglican social ethics course at Duke, but materially, in an Anglo-Catholic country church in Indiana. I could argue theologically, using insights from my immersion in this tradition, that its approach to healing divisions in American Christian identity—starting with my own—made superior Christian sense. The only trouble with this way of interpreting my narrative above is that it is false.

The social position from which I have engaged in projects of sense-making has never been one that comfortably fit the paradigm of the Duke project. My sense of "progress" in the unfolding of my theological understanding has not been marked by any significant movement (decisive or gradual) from greater fragmentation to greater unity. Nor have any of my deep investments in various communities and institutions resulted in corresponding consolidation in a traditioned belonging or identity. Far from being able to understand myself as belonging to any one particular tradition (Christian or otherwise), my experience of practically every community to which I've ever belonged is one of failed assimilation, never managing to quite find a secure place either as insider or outsider. This has usually meant being positioned as marginal relative to the dominant discourses and practices, even while something of whatever it means to belong to each of these traditions has also managed to lodge itself deep inside my sensibilities, yet only as an idiosyncratic assemblage of fragments (second-gen Hindu, non-denominational evangelical, political leftist, Episcopalian, etc.). As my life has unfolded, I have not experienced the shifting accretions and reordering in this assemblage as any kind of progress toward greater unity or coherence. Nor have I experienced these shifts as particularly entropic, introducing an increase of chaos and decoherence into my practices of sense-making. Others in my communities have always been more perplexed and troubled by my evident hybridity than I have. What my awareness and working with fragments has meant, however, is that yielding myself to any form of cultural or intellectual assimilation to any given tradition's singular inner-logic or itinerary of disputes inevitably seems like a self-betrayal to me, even when they are espoused as open-ended and susceptible to revision, surprise, or loss. Simply as unified trajectories of belief and practice, over-identification with them inevitably yields a deep sense of alienation. It is the assimilation itself to which I exhibit an allergy, not the goodness or badness of the joining. At least one part of me, even if only a toe, must remain outside the door, a perpetual foreigner wherever I attempt to make a home, materially or intellectually.

While this way of reading my orientation to the work of theology will surely lead to recommendations for a good therapist (I'll take them!), another kind of explanation is available. The position relative to theological traditions that I'm describing here is one that Sang Hyun Lee has identified with a particularly Asian American cultural experience of "liminality."[8] Spaces of liminality are middle spaces, characterized by destabilizing forms of marginalization that perpetually place us on a threshold of multiple ambiguities between more settled forms of life. There are lots of factors that might converge to produce such an existence, many of which for us have to do with the conditions under which Asian immigrants have come to

---

8. Sang Hyun Lee, *From a Liminal Place* (Minneapolis: Fortress Press, 2010). See also Daniel Lee's development of the way liminality might be operationalized in Asian American Theology in *Doing Asian American Theology: A Contextual Framework for Faith and Practice* (Downers Grove, IL: InterVarsity Press, 2022).

live in a white supremacist society. But the tensions, oppositions, conflicts that pressure life lived at these thresholds are also what lead Asian Americans to construct various kinds of hybrid identities and a more fluid existence, one capable of creating attenuated belongings. Liminality, Lee suggested, might be a productive way to think not merely about the social psychology of Asian American experiences, but about an approach to Christian theology oriented around navigating both the injustices and the creative potential that we might find not simply *within* traditions (whether by living and thinking more faithfully into them, or problematizing and revising them) nor *above them* (by supposing we can occupy some fundamentally autonomous or sovereign role of adjudication), but instead in our negotiations *between* them. This would be to recognize Christian identities as fluid, contested, and hybridized between a host of other fragments of belief and practice—social, political, and religious—rather than being mere exponents or novel continuations of any one identifiable or stable tradition.

This represents a rather different way of imagining the *via media*. Its principal advantage over the picture projected by the Duke school is that it is more true to our actual experiences and social constitution. Fragmented and attenuated belongings are neither exclusively modern nor exclusively the preserve of Asian Americans (whose experiences of it are nevertheless distinctive). What it can uniquely reveal to us, however, is something fundamental about our human condition that much of the infrastructure of our current political culture hides from us; namely, that there is something irreducible and uncodifiable about human social identities which resists any total or complete identification with any one form of life we might manage to construct.[9] It

---

9. Vincent Lloyd offers a powerful account of this sort of anthropology in *Black Natural Law* (New York: Oxford University Press, 2016).

follows that neither we nor those we recognize as our moral, political, and religious enemies are in fact mere exponents or representatives of any one coherent cultural logic or system of meaning-making. Nor could our material lives, whether individually or collectively, ever be exhausted by any one dominant expression of such a logic or system. We can therefore never suppose that if we only manage to cultivate sufficient internal resources within our own established beliefs and practices, we can, without violence to others or our own humanity, either absorb or else reject every lived social alternative to the form of life envisioned by our most cherished commitments.

Rather than pathologizing "fragmentation" as a modern disease standing in need of a return to tradition, we should recognize a kind of liminality as our default human relationship to the many social structures and institutions that shape our group identities. All of our belongings struggle between various opposing forces, with tensions and alienations across so many competing cultural claims on our lives: we are all fragmented selves muddling through our middle spaces, our movements toward shared belonging simultaneously bringing radical encounters with dispossession. It is on this conflicted terrain that we construct new and more or less joyful and satisfying ways of going on with one another, but not in any way that manages to incorporate all of our fragments, resolve our tensions, and present ourselves to ourselves and one another whole.[10]

It is only when we zoom out from the ordinary drama and difficulty of those spaces to observe their effects at a distance that we can

---

10. Willie Jennings draws extensively on the metaphor of "fragments" and the notion of "working with fragments" in *After Whiteness: An Education in Belonging* (Grand Rapids: Eerdmans, 2020). However, even as his deployment of fragmentation is intentionally turned against the MacIntyrean picture, Jennings seems to regard fragmented selves as finding wholeness in an elusive form of Christian communion with one another (48), a different locus of coherence.

codify larger-scale patterns into social categorizations (e.g., "white Christian nationalism," "woke religious culture," etc.). Such categorizations can be more or less useful for analyzing social structures and our positions relative to them. However, even when responsibly derived from careful cultural and social-scientific analysis, our categorizations also often become a kind of predictive model for sizing up our opponents by identifying them with the most relevant social categories in much the same way that I found Duke theology to utilize "traditions"—as a handy heuristic constraining what dispositions, affects, behaviors, beliefs, and group affinities we should expect from them. But making such categorization the main object of our theological reflections about Christian belonging misses something crucial about the fragmentary nature of identity in a way analogous to a focus on identity conferred by tradition. Namely, it hides the complexity of the liminal selves whose various coordinated agencies are producers as well as products of those categories, what John Thatamanil calls a more fundamental "relational pluralism."[11]

It is, of course, one thing to commend an Episcopal theology of the *via media*, a theology of the church attuned to the role it currently plays and ought to play in configuring the middle spaces that currently pressure those moving through its own institutional life, and quite another to say how. That is not a question I am well-positioned to answer. My movement outside the orbits of TEC and into a more diasporic kind of kinship with its church life has been driven as much or more by factors outside that life as inside it. But as TEC confronts its existential crisis, its interests in bearing witness to Christ's catholicity and welcome will not be best served by searching for proposed resolutions, strategic compromises, and rebranding to

---

11. See John J. Thatamanil, *Circling the Elephant: A Comparative Theology of Religious Diversity* (New York: Oxford University Press, 2020), 70–107.

minimize ideological conflict and maximize group identification with the form of belonging it proposes to offer—whether in a project of neo-traditional retrieval or one of multiculturalist progress. It will instead require it to become a place capable of discerning local contingencies of middle space, seeking to negotiate the particular forms of dispossession and belonging that confront its congregants, and discerning together around a Eucharistic common table novel, fluid, and hybridized forms of life that enable them to go on together without any expectation or demand of a full assimilation.

Further Reading Recommendations

Jennings, Willie James. *After Whiteness: An Education in Belonging.* Grand Rapids: Eerdmans, 2020.

Lee, Sang Hyun. *From a Liminal Place: An Asian American Theology.* Minneapolis: Fortress Press, 2010.

MacIntyre, Alasdair. *After Virtue: A Study in Moral Theory.* 3rd Edition. Notre Dame: University of Notre Dame Press, 2007.

Thatamanil, John J. *Circling the Elephant: A Comparative Theology of Religious Diversity.* New York: Fordham University Press, 2020.

Afterword

Matthew Ichihashi Potts

When I was studying for my Ph.D., one of my classmates gathered all the students of theology at Harvard to host a conference for doctoral students of theology in the region. The aim was to gather with some of those we hoped would be our colleagues as theologians in the future, and to consider together what role theologians might play in the church and for the world. The Episcopal Cathedral of St. Paul in Boston hosted the weekend event, and my classmates and I arrived early on a Saturday morning to set things up in the basement. We pulled long tables out of the corners and set out a simple breakfast of pastries, fruit, and yogurt in the basement. We brewed coffee in large urns and unstacked chairs and tables. We tested projectors and printed nametags and generally rushed around. As the opening of the conference approached, a man came down the stairwell. He carried a plastic grocery bag, and his shoes and clothing were frayed. He told me that he had recently arrived in Boston, didn't have any place to stay, and had heard the Cathedral offered a free meal. He was hungry, he said, and was looking for something to eat.

I knew that the Cathedral did serve a weekly meal, but on Mondays, not on Saturdays. I apologized and informed the man that he had the right information, but the wrong day. Though we were expecting our colleagues any minute, I walked upstairs with him and out onto Tremont Street, across from the Boston Common. I found a tourist map and used my phone to get directions to a shelter, which

I sketched out on the map, and then I told the man that he might be able to find some help there. I apologized for the mix-up in the schedule and wished him well, then invited him back for the Monday lunch. He thanked me, and I shook his hand before he walked off. I remember coming back down the stairs into the basement of the Cathedral with a sense of self-satisfaction. This is the role of theologians in the church and for the world, I said to myself. Already, by placing our scholarly conversations here where the world's needs were pressing, we were making theology matter. Just as I was finishing that thought, I rounded the corner to arrive at almost exactly the spot where the man had stood at the bottom of the stairs. Spread before me were all those long tables I had helped cover with muffins and donuts and yogurt and fresh fruit. Large carafes of coffee steamed next to tall pitchers of milk and cream. All this food was on view to our guest while he stood there telling me he was looking for something to eat. All of it was arrayed behind me as I walked him away, up the stairs and outside the cathedral, and then offered him exactly the help he didn't ask for and didn't need, and all of it somewhere else. To be clear: I would have gladly shared some of this food with him had the thought occurred to me. I just didn't think of it. This was not a failure of will or of intention; it was a failure of mind, a failure of thought.

Theology often takes itself as its own audience. Theologians usually write for other theologians. This is understandable and necessary; like any guild, theology should and does assess its own standards of excellence. But this can also cause problems, as it did in the above example, since we sometimes find ourselves talking past those who come to us seeking aid. I am a theologian; I publish monographs and journal articles meant to be read by others like me. But I'm also a pastor and a preacher at a university church, as well as a teacher of students from all fields of study. Many—sometimes most—of the people in my pews or in my classrooms are non-religious. What does theology have to say, if anything, to these people, especially those uninterested in its academic forms, or worse, allergic to them altogether? What do those outside the guild—or indeed outside Christianity—want or need to hear, and how should those of us within the theological guild try to reach them?

The truth is, I don't recognize a clear or rigid boundary between activities like writing an article and writing a sermon, or between teaching Julian of Norwich to seminarians and teaching James Baldwin to undergraduates (and vice versa). Academic theology is distinguished by a certain style and form and audience, but it isn't automatically more substantively "theological" than, say, a Sunday sermon or a lecture on *If Beale Street Could Talk*. One genre is not more theological than the other just because it's structured like a disputation or has lots of footnotes. And I believe theology—in whatever form or genre it happens to take—is made poorer when it aims to instruct its audience in belief.

This might be surprising: isn't theology primarily about doctrine, about what we should believe? It is, sometimes, but I'm not sure that's the best way to approach it. Theology is faith seeking understanding, as several of the above contributors have reminded us, but the faith is the agent of the seeking, not the object of it. To put it in more practical terms: skeptical Harvard students do not want me to tell them what to believe. Neither do the thoughtful members of my congregation. There is no better way for me to doom a sermon or deflate a lecture than to offer it as a credo, a list of beliefs for the taking, however elegantly they hang together. People don't want to be told what to believe; they want to know why it matters. They want to hear the stakes and hear them clearly stated. And when you do articulate those stakes—in a classroom or from a pulpit—people pay attention. They care. When the stakes are made clear, they will care what it means, whether they decide to believe or not. I'm content with this. Beliefs are unstable things, shifting and messy and always in process. Like every author in this book and indeed any Christian I imagine, my beliefs have changed over time, and I expect they will continue to do so. I can't say what I will believe in ten years, but I can say why these ideas matter today, why one should care about them, and the work they do in the world. And since care is the basic work of the ministry, I take it as a reasonable goal for my theology, and I invite the Holy Spirit to escort all my skeptical listeners to faith, in their own time.

Making people care about theology can be difficult, but not because the stakes are too obscure. On the contrary they are usually quite clear. They are difficult for us to talk about because they are often deeply unflattering to the Christian Church and its intellectual tradition. To take an example, one which inspired my most recent book (as well as my most popular class, not to mention many of the outreach efforts of my church): our culture could not have embraced mass incarceration at the scale and with the cruelty that American culture so manifestly has without a robust background theology of redemptive punishment, one ready to be operationalized by structures of sinful power and renamed as criminal justice.[1] This is not news to my students or to my congregants. The secular and nonreligious students with whom I engage know all this already, if only implicitly. So do the Christians. And the skeptics among them aren't suspicious of us Christians because we believe in God. It's mostly because of all the harm that we have too often justified with our beliefs. If people in my classrooms or in my pews don't want to be told what to believe, it's not because the object of our belief is supernatural. It's because the outcomes of our beliefs have so often been hurtful. We've lost our credibility. And the only way to rebuild one's credibility is to confess.

---

1. For more details, see Matthew Ichihashi Potts, *Forgiveness: An Alternative Account* (New Haven and London: Yale University Press, 2022).

So this is where I begin all my theology, whether preached from a pulpit, published in a journal, or chattered among students in a dining hall. The way we reach those beyond the boundaries of theology, whether that theology is formal and scholastic or informal and casual, is by speaking honestly about the harm we know it has caused. But in speaking honestly about that harm, we also convey theology's great power. We give a sense of how it—and we—might be transformed and turned toward redemption. If bad theology can do great wrong, then better theology can also help make things right. In other words, an effective theology, one which reaches beyond its own limits and invites others in—whether that theology is academic, pastoral, or colloquial—begins with repentance. We make ourselves credible when we are honest about our wrongs and invite others into conversations about making things right. This is because repentance is primarily about telling the truth. What I am suggesting is that the task of theology is to tell the truth, as fully and as honestly as it can, in full trust that the truth will set us free. None of this should surprise us, since repentance establishes the Christian good news and was the first teaching of Jesus in his ministry.

Repentance is hard and sometimes costly. I don't mean to end this volume on a grim note. I don't think I have done so. It is an impoverished Christianity, a toothless theology, that recoils from repentance or resists the responsibilities of redemption. Though costly at times, repentance really is good news. When we reveal the power of our ideas to shape the world for ill, we also spur theological imaginations to reshape our world for good. We have a compelling story to tell, one that nearly anyone will listen to and one that is certainly worth the risk. Because we already know how a story that begins in true repentance ends. Repentance does more than expand theology's credibility and extend its reach. More than anything, it promises resurrection.

Index

Abraham, William J., xvi
Adams, Douglas, 118-119, 129
Adams, Marilyn McCord, xiv
Allen, Diogenes, xiv
Alston, William P., xiv
Althaus-Reid, Marcella, 173
Andrewes, Lancelot, xxviii
Anselm, xxvi, xxix
Anzaldúa, Gloria, 179
Appiah, Kwame A., 164
Aquinas, Thomas, xxix, 5, 38, 59
Athanasius, 11, 21, 41, 51, 212
Augustine, xx, xxix, 17-18, 21, 24, 27, 31-32, 40-41, 43, 45, 51, 60, 71, 74-75, 126, 133, 212
Avis, Paul, 138

Baldwin, James, 243
Baldwin, Jennifer, 163
Balthasar, Hans Urs von, xxii, xxxii, 4, 124
Barth, Karl, xxix-xxx, 24, 36, 39-40, 53, 67, 73-74, 80, 85-86, 88-90, 96-97, 117, 124, 135, 181, 216
Battle, Michael, 167
Baxter, Richard, 199-200
Bellinger, Charles K., 165
Berling, Judith A., 141
Bevans, Stephen B., 201
Birkholz, Mark W., 47
Blakemore, Erin, 180
Bonaventure, 4
Bonhoeffer, Dietrich, 146, 181
Booty, John, xxviii
Brewer, Christopher R., xxv, xxxiv

Bromiley, G. W., 39, 67
Brown, David, xxv, xxxiii-xxxiv
Brown, Michael, 147
Brown, Peter, 71
Brunner, Emil, 93
Buechner, Frederick, 130
Bultmann, Rudolf, 56
Bunyan, John, 133
Burdett, Michael, 148
Burge, Ryan, 223
Burkhardt, Abel, 53
Burns, Stephen, xviii, xxv, xxxiv, 150, 160
Butler, Joseph, xxviii

Calvin, John, xxvii, 40
Cannon, Katie, 140, 156
Capon, Robert, 208
Carey, George, xxv
Carnes, Natalie, 76
Chapman, Mark, xviii
Charry, Ellen T., xxix
Chávez, César, 172
Cheng, Patrick S., xxxi-xxxii, 179
Chopp, Rebecca, 140, 209
Chuck D, 126-127
Clark Jr., Elisha S., 157
Clarke, Jeremy, 202
Clement of Alexandria, 212
Coakley, Sarah, xxxiii-xxxv, 33, 66, 140
Coffin, William Sloan, 176
Coltrane, John, 168
Cone, James, 129, 147, 156, 178
Cones, Bryan, xviii

Copeland, Shawn, 140, 203
Curry, Michael, 112

Daniel, Clifton, xxv
Daniel, Jenny Te Paa, 141, 179
Day, Dorothy, 176
Dayam, J. P., 221
Dōgen, 213, 215-216, 220
Douglas, Ian T., 143
Douglas, Kelly Brown, xxxi, 140, 145, 147, 151, 161, 169, 179
Dozier, Verna, 179

Ehrman, Bart D., 49
Endo, Shusako, 118
Eyer-Delevett, Aimee, 228

Falwell, Jerry, xxiii
Farley, Wendy, 209
Farrer, Austin, xxv, xxvii-xxviii
Farwell, James W., 213-216, 220
Fenton, John, 214
Fine, Joseph, 56
Flavor Flav, 126
Forbes, Esther, 53
Ford, David F., xxx, 132
Frei, Hans, 1, 54, 133, 135

Geldhof, Joris, 193
Gibbs, Lee, 231
Gibson, James, 77
Gold, Solveig Lucia, 96-97
Gonzalez, Juan, 180
Gore, Charles, xxviii, 3, 67
Gortner, David T., 199
Green, Garrett, xxxi
Green, Joel B., 164
Gregory of Nyssa, xxix, 22, 32, 71, 212, 228

Griffiss, James, 134
Griffiths, John, 44
Griswold, Frank, xvi, xxi
Gritsch, Eric W., 94
Grünewald, Matthias, 87
Gutierrez, Gustavo, 172

Hall, Amy Laura, 85
Hardy, Daniel W., xxv, xxx
Harnack, Adolf von, 90
Harris, Barbara C., 161
Harvey, Van, 54
Hauerwas, Stanley, xxi, xxiv-xxv, 89, 226, 231, 233
Heaney, Robert, 210
Hefling, Charles, xviii
Heim, Mark, 219
Henry, Carl, 135
Heschel, Abraham Joshua, 176
Heyward, Carter, xxxi, 179
Hilary of Poitiers, 42
Holloway, Karla F. C., 159
Holmes, David L., xviii
Holtzen, Thomas L., 43-44, 46-47
Hooker, Richard, xxviii-xxix, 3, 45-46, 66, 200, 231
hooks, bell, 154
Huerta, Dolores, 172
Hunsinger, George, xxx, 135

Imperatori-Lee, Natalia, 180, 186
Ineson, Emma, 155
Irenaeus, 39-42, 51, 212
Itcho, Hanabusa, 161

Jennings, Willie James, 85, 239
Jenson, Robert, 63, 89, 94
Jesudason, Peniel, 218
John of Damascus, 8, 22

Johnson, Elizabeth A., 149
Johnson, Maxwell E., 193
Jones, Serene, 139-140, 148, 151, 181
Joyce, Kelli, xxxiv
Julian of Norwich, xxix, 30, 243
Justin Martyr, 40, 61

Kemper, Jackson, 37
Kemper, Lewis A., 37
Kermode, Frank, 63
Kerr, Fergus, xxiv
Kierkegaard, Søren, 24
King Jr., Martin Luther, 146-147, 160, 162
King, Maxine, 74
Kingsley, Charles, 92-93
Knight, Jonathan, xxviii
Kwok, Pui-lan, xxix, 140-143, 151, 179, 186

Lakeland, Paul, 181
Lamott, Anne, 118
Lawson, James, 175
Lee, Daniel, 235
Lee, Sang Hyun, 235, 239
Leech, Kenneth, 178-179, 186
Lewis, C. S., 24, 41, 51
Lichtenberger, Scott Arthur C., xix
Liszt, Franz, 167
Lloyd, Vincent, 236
Loades, Ann, xxv, xxvii, xxxiii, 140, 150
Lorde, Audre, 168
Lowe, Walter, 209
Lubac, Henri de, xxxii
Luther, Martin, xxix, 94

MacDougall, Scott, xv, xviii, 16, 111, 138, 199

MacIntyre, Alasdair, 159, 230-231, 239
MacSwain, Robert, xxiv, xxvii-xxviii, xxxiv
Maparyan, Layli Phillips, 162
Marcum, John, 223
Marshall, Paul V., 193
Martin, Trayvon, 147
Marx, Karl, 133
Maurice, F. D., xxviii, 144
Maximus the Confessor, xxix, 4, 22, 212
McClintock Fulkerson, Mary, 155
McDougall, Joy Ann, xxxi
McIntosh, Mark, xvi, xx, xxxi, 4, 16, 134
Merton, Thomas, 176
Midgley, Mary, 196
Milbank, John, xxxiii, 178
Mitchell, Joni, 167
Moltmann, Jürgen, 137, 142, 146
Mombo, Esther, xviii, 179
Monro, Anita, 160
Moringiello, Scott D., 39
Morris, Thomas V., xxiv
Mosher, Lucinda Allen, 219-220
Moyse, Ashley, 148
Muers, Rachel, xxx
Mumme, Jonathan, 47
Murray, Pauli, 161, 165, 179

Neusner, Jacob, 63
Newman, John Henry, xxviii, 44, 46
Niebuhr, Reinhold, 56
Norris, Richard, 209
Nouwen, Henri, 130

O'Dell, Scott, 54
O'Donovan, Oliver, xxxiii

O'Murchu, Diarmuid, 159
Origen, xxix, 71

Pannenberg, Wolfhart, 137
Pauw, Amy Plantinga, 140
Peare, Catherine Owens, 54
Pickstock, Catherine, xxxiii
Pike, James A., xix
Pittenger, W. Norman, xix
Placher, William C., xxxi, 135, 139
Ponticus, Evagrius, 20
Preller, Victor, xxiv
Public Enemy, 126-129
Pusey, Edward Bouverie, xxviii

Radner, Ephraim, xx
Rahner, Karl, xxxii, 135
Rajkumar, Rufus, 218
Ramsey, Boniface, 43, 51
Reichel, Hanna, 76
Rieger, Joerg, 183, 186
Rotelle, John E., 41

Saliers, Don E., 213
Salvatierra, Alexia, 174-175
Sanders, Sid, xxiii
Schleiermacher, Friedrich, 89, 181
Scudder, Vida, 179
Serina, Richard J., 47
Shakespeare, William, 29
Shattuck Jr., Gardiner H., xviii
Sherman, Jacob, 123
Shoop, Marcia W. Mount, 155
Slocum, Robert Boak, xviii-xix, xxxiv
Smith, Elwyn, 54-56, 58
Sonderegger, Katherine, xxxi, 33, 73
Spellers, Stephanie, 185
Stephen, St., 62
Stout, Jeffrey, xxiv

Strayhorn, Billy, 167
Stringfellow, William, 79-80, 82, 179
Stump, Eleonore, xxiv
Sumner, George R., xx
Swartzentruber, Orley, xxiv
Sykes, Stephen, xxv, xxviii
Sylvester, Matthew, 199

Tanner, Kathryn, xxi, xxxi, 16, 66, 134-135, 139-140, 148, 195
Tennyson, Aflred, 50
Teresa of Ávila, xxix, 32
Thatamanil, John J., 238-239
Thomas, Frank A., 154
Thomas, Owen C., xxviii
Thurman, Howard, 147
Thurneysen, Eduard, 90
Tillich, Paul, xxx, 24, 56, 183
Toliver, S. R., 159
Tolkien, J.R.R., 118
Tolstoy, Leo, 25
Tonstad, Linn Marie, 195
Torbeck, Jacob W., xxii
Torrance, Iain, 148
Torrance, T. F., 39, 67
Troeltsch, Ernst, 137
Tugwell, Simon, 210-211
Turner, Frank, 133
Tutu, Desmond, 167, 176

van Buren, Paul, 60
van Erp, Stephan, 111
Vannier, Marie-Anne, 18
Vogel, Arthur A., xxx

Ward, Graham, xxxiii
Warnock, Jim, 227
Washington, James M., 165

Watson, Ed, 202
Watson, Natalie K., 150
Webster, John, xxxiii, 148
Weems, Renita J., 158
Werpehowski, William, 138
Williams, Rowan, xxviii, xxxiii, 16, 33, 80, 123, 132, 134-135, 221
Willimon, William H., 80
Wilson, Wylin D., 157
Winner, Lauren, 75

Wohlleben, Peter, 166
Wondra, Ellen K., xxviii
Wrencher, Brandon, 174-175
Wyman, Jason, 182

Young Jr., George, 208

Zahl, Simeon, 148
Zimmermann, Jens, 148
Zink, Jesse, xx

www.ingramcontent.com/pod-product-compliance
Lightning Source LLC
Chambersburg PA
CBHW050211240426
43671CB00013B/2289